the official
theory test
for drivers of large vehicles

Approved by
Plain
English
Campaign

London: TSO

Written and compiled by the Publications Unit of the Driving Standards Agency (DSA).

Questions and answers are compiled by the Question Development Team of the DSA.

Published with the permission of the Driving Standards Agency on behalf of the Controller of Her Majesty's Stationery Office.

First published 1996
Sixth edition 2003

ISBN 0115523464

A CIP catalogue record for this book is available from the British Library.

Other titles in the Driving Skills series
The Official Theory Test for Car Drivers
The Official Theory Test for Motorcyclists
Motorcycle Riding – the essential skills
Official Motorcycling – CBT, theory and practical test
Driving - the essential skills
The Official DSA Guide for Driving Instructors
Driving Buses and Coaches – the official DSA syllabus
Driving Goods Vehicles – the official DSA syllabus
The Official Guide to Tractor and Specialist Vehicle Driving Tests
The Official Driving Test
The Official Theory Test CD-ROM – for car drivers and motorcyclists
The Official Theory Test CD-ROM – for drivers of large vehicles
The Official Goods Vehicle Driving Video
The Official Guide to Accompanying Learner Drivers

Acknowledgements

The Driving Standards Agency would like to thank their staff and the following organisations for their contribution to the production of this publication:
Transport Research Laboratory
Department for Transport
Driver & Vehicle Testing Agency, Northern Ireland
Every effort has been made to ensure that the information contained in this publication is accurate at the time of going to press. The Stationery Office cannot be held responsible for any inaccuracies.

Information in this book is for guidance only.

All metric and imperial conversions in this book are approximate.

Information

Theory and Practical Tests
DSA Bookings and Enquiries: 0870 01 01 372
DVTA (Northern Ireland) Booking and Enquiries: 0845 600 6700

Faxes: 0870 01 04 372
Minicom: 0870 01 06 372
Welsh speakers: 0870 01 00 372

Postal applications for theory tests to:
Driving Standards Agency or Driver and Vehicle Testing Agency
PO Box 148
Salford M5 3SY

Driving Standards Agency
(Headquarters)
Stanley House
Talbot Street
Nottingham NG1 5GU

Tel: 0115 901 2500
Fax: 0115 901 2510

Driver & Vehicle Testing Agency
(Headquarters)
Balmoral Road
Belfast BT12 6QL

Tel: 02890 681831
Fax: 02890 665520

Driver Vehicle Licensing Agency
(GB Licence Enquiries)

Tel: 0870 240 0009
Fax: 01792 783071
Minicom: 01792 782787

Driver and Vehicle Licensing Northern Ireland
Customer Services
Tel: 02870 341469
02890 250 500 (24 hours)
Minicom: 02870 341 380

Website addresses
DSA: www.driving-tests.co.uk
DVTA: www.doeni.gov.uk/dvta

The Driving Standards Agency (DSA) is an executive agency of the Department for Transport. You'll see its logo at test centres.

DSA aims to promote road safety through the advancement of driving standards, by

- establishing and developing high standards and best practice in driving and riding on the road; before people start to drive, as they learn, and after they pass their test
- ensuring high standards of instruction for different types of driver and rider
- conducting the statutory theory and practical tests efficiently, fairly and consistently across the country
- providing a centre of excellence for driver training and driving standards
- developing a range of publications and other publicity material designed to promote safe driving for life.

DVTA

The Driver & Vehicle Testing Agency (DVTA) is an executive agency within the Department of the Environment for Northern Ireland. Its primary aim is to promote and improve road safety through the advancement of driving standards and implementation of the Government's policies for improving the mechanical standards of vehicles.

DSA Website

www.driving-tests.co.uk

DVTA Website

www.doeni.gov.uk/dvta

Contents

A special message from the Chief Driving Examiner

As the driver of a large goods vehicle (LGV) or passenger carrying vehicle (PCV) you must have a high degree of vehicle handling skill to be considered 'professional' in the true sense of the word. You must also have knowledge and a clear understanding of the principles of safe driving and how to apply them. Whether you're responsible for the safe transportation of goods or passengers, the need for comprehensive knowledge is recognised by the requirement for a separate theory test.

Passing the theory test is an important step to becoming a professional driver. The knowledge you've learnt should be put into practice on the road. When you drive a large vehicle you should demonstrate your ability to drive safely and set a good example to others. Your attitude and approach should be courteous and considerate. The safety of the goods or passengers you carry could depend on it.

This book will help you to prepare for the multiple choice part of the theory test. It contains the questions, set out in an easy-to-read style. It also includes explanations as to why the answers are correct along with advice about good driving practice.

You'll never know all the answers, throughout your driving career there will always be more to learn. Remember, the passengers or goods you carry are your responsibility. By being reliable, efficient and safe you'll be on your way to becoming a good professional driver.

Robin Cummins

The Chief Driving Examiner
Driving Standards Agency

The theory test

Large vehicles include

- large goods vehicles (LGVs) and

- passenger carrying vehicles (PCVs)

This part of the book explains how you get started and general information about the theory test.

It has advice on

- Getting started

  your licence and starting to drive on the road

- The theory test

  why is there a theory test?

- Preparing for your theory test

  details of books and other training materials

- Booking your theory test

  various ways of booking your test

- Provision for special needs

  how we provide for those with reading and hearing difficulties, physical disabilities and languages other than English

- Taking your theory test

  arriving at the test centre, and information about the multiple choice and hazard perception parts of the test

- After your test

  the next stage

- Questions and answers

  how to use the question and answer part of the book.

Getting started

Applying for your licence

To obtain your provisional licence you should apply to the Driver and Vehicle Licensing Agency (DVLA), or, in Northern Ireland, Driver and Vehicle Licensing Northern Ireland (DVLNI). Application forms (D1) and information leaflets (D100) are available from post offices.

To drive a large vehicle you must

- have a full car driving licence

- hold a provisional licence for the category of vehicle you want to drive

- meet the eyesight and medical requirements

- normally be over 21 years of age.

In Northern Ireland you must also complete a criminal records check if you want to drive a PCV.

You can get full details from the DVLA enquiry line on 0870 240 0009 (in Northern Ireland the DVLNI enquiry line is 02870 341469)

Medical requirements

You'll be responsible for goods or passengers, so it's vital that you meet exacting medical standards. The medical requirements apply to both LGV and PCV licences.

You can't hold an LGV or a PCV licence unless your eyesight meets the high standard required.

You must be fit and free from any condition that affects your ability to retain control of a large vehicle. If you're disabled, you may drive a vehicle that has been specially adapted for you.

You must have a medical, carried out by a doctor. The doctor has to complete a medical report form, D4 (DLM1 in Northern Ireland) and then this has to be sent in with your licence application.

On the road

When you receive your provisional licence you should check all details are correct. You can then drive on the road as long as you

- drive under the supervision of a person who holds a current licence for the category of vehicle being driven (minimum licence requirements apply, check these with your trainer)

- display L-plates (or D-plates if you prefer when driving in Wales) at the front and back of the vehicle

- display LGV or PCV plates to the front and back of the vehicle when driving in Northern Ireland.

To help you choose an LGV instructor, DSA has a Register of LGV Instructors. To be placed on this list, instructors have to pass rigorous tests of their driving and instructional ability. You can obtain details from 0115 901 2625. There is no comparable register in Northern Ireland or for PCVs.

The theory test

To become a professional driver you must have a thorough knowledge of the regulations that apply to your work. When you combine this with a high level of driving skill, it should help you to carry out your work safely.

If you're driving an LGV you have to make sure that your goods arrive at their destination safely. This will involve not only the safety of your load, but also your attitude to others on the road.

If you're driving a PCV you're providing a service to your customers. These passengers have been entrusted to your care. You should be aware of the responsibility this carries.

From the start, you must be aware of the differences between driving smaller vehicles and driving large buses or lorries.

You must have a sound knowledge of *The Highway Code,* including the meaning of traffic signs and road markings. You must be particularly aware of those signs that show a restriction for lorries or buses.

Your knowledge of the above information is tested in the first part of the theory test, as a series of multiple choice questions. More information about this part of the test is given on page 10 and the questions are given in the main part of the book, beginning on page 16.

There is now a second part of the theory test called the hazard perception part, more information about this is given on page 12.

Frequently asked questions

Can I take the practical test first?

No. You have to pass your theory test before you can book a practical test.

Does everyone have to take a theory test?

Normally, if you upgrade your licence within the same category you won't have to sit the test. For example, if you upgrade from a rigid-bodied to an articulated lorry you won't have to take another theory test.

However, if you have sub-category C1 and D1 entitlement on your licence from when you passed your car test, and you want to upgrade to a C or D licence, you'll have to obtain the correct provisional entitlement and pass a theory test.

If you have a full category C licence and wish to take a practical test for category D you will have to pass the appropriate theory test first, and vice versa.

Preparing for your theory test

Although you have to pass your theory test before you can take your practical test, it's recommended that you start studying for your theory test, but don't actually take it until you have some practical experience of driving larger vehicles.

To prepare for the multiple choice part of the theory test, we strongly recommend that you study the books from which the questions are taken as well as the questions themselves. These books are:

The Highway Code – this is essential reading for all drivers. Even if you studied it when you took your car test, it's worth getting an up-to-date copy to ensure that you have the most recent advice on road safety and the laws which apply to all road users.

Know Your Traffic Signs – this contains most of the signs and road markings that you are likely to come across.

Driving – the essential skills – although this is mainly for car drivers, it includes much general information about driving.

Driving Goods Vehicles and *Driving Buses and Coaches* – these books cover all aspects of driving the specified vehicle, in particular the regulations and the way in which driving these larger vehicles differ from driving smaller vehicles. They also contain the appropriate practical test syllabus.

These books will help you to answer the questions correctly and will also help you when studying for your practical test. The information in them will be relevant throughout your driving life so make sure you always have an up-to-date copy that you can refer to.

Other study aids

The Official Theory Test CD-ROM for Drivers of Large Vehicles – this is an alternative way of preparing for the multiple choice part of the theory test. You can randomly test yourself against the complete range of theory test questions.

RoadSense – the official guide to hazard perception for all drivers. We recommend that you prepare for the hazard perception part of the theory test by studying and working through *RoadSense*, preferably with your trainer.

The Official Goods Vehicle Driving Video – this should help clarify different aspects of driving goods vehicles.

All the training materials listed are available by mail order from 0870 241 4523. The books, together with relevant books from other publishers, are also available from good bookshops.

Frequently asked questions

Why do the questions keep changing?

To make sure that all candidates are being tested fairly, questions and video clips are under continuous review. Some of the questions may be changed as a result of customer feedback. They may also be changed to reflect revised legislation, and the publications listed above are updated to reflect such changes.

> It's important that you study,
> not just to pass the test,
> but to become a safer driver.

Booking your theory test

The easiest ways to book your test are online or by telephone, but it can also be booked by post.

Online or by telephone

If you book by either of these methods, you'll be given the date and time of your test immediately.

You can book your theory test online at
www.driving-tests.co.uk or
www.dsa.gov.uk.

To book by telephone, call 0870 0101 372 (0845 600 6700 for Northern Ireland) between 8 am and 6 pm Monday to Friday.

If you're deaf and use a minicom machine, call 0870 0106 372 and if you are a Welsh speaker, call 0870 0100 372.

You will need your

- DVLA or DVLNI driving licence number
- credit or debit card details. Please note that the person who books the test must be the card holder. We accept Visa, Access, Switch, Delta, Solo and Electron.

You'll be given a booking number and sent an appointment letter that you should receive within eight days.

By post

If you prefer to book by post, you'll need to fill in an application form. These are available from theory test centres or driving test centres, or your trainer may have one.

You should normally receive an appointment letter within ten days of posting your application form.

Frequently asked questions

Where can I take the test?

There are over 150 theory test centres throughout England, Scotland and Wales, and six in Northern Ireland. Most people have a test centre within 20 miles of their home, but this will vary depending on the density of population in your area.

You can find a list of test centres on page 434.

When are test centres open?

Test centres are usually open on weekdays, some evenings and Saturdays.

What if I don't receive an acknowledgement?

If you don't receive an acknowledgement within the time specified above, please telephone the booking office to check that an appointment has been made.

We can't take responsibility for postal delays. If you miss your test appointment you will lose your fee.

How do I cancel or postpone my test?

To cancel or postpone your theory test appointment you should contact the booking office at least **three clear working days** before your test date, otherwise you'll lose your fee.

Only in exceptional circumstances, such as documented ill-health or family bereavement, can this rule be waived.

Provision for special needs

Every effort is made to ensure that the theory test can be taken by all candidates.

It's important that you state your needs when you book your test so that the necessary arrangements can be made.

Reading difficulties

There's an English language voiceover, on a headset, to help you if you have reading difficulties or dyslexia.

You can ask for up to twice the normal time to take the multiple choice part of the test.

You will be asked to provide a letter from an appropriate person (such as a teacher, psychologist or doctor, or possibly an independent person who knows about your reading ability). Please check with the Special Needs section (on the normal booking number, see page 7) if you're unsure about who to ask.

We can't guarantee to return any original documents, so please send copies only.

Hearing difficulties

The introduction to both the multiple choice and hazard perception parts of the test can be delivered in British Sign Language (BSL) by an on-screen signer if you're deaf or have other hearing difficulties.

A BSL interpreter or lip speaker can be provided if requested at the time of booking.

Physical disabilities

If you have a physical disability which would make it difficult for you to use a mouse button to respond to the clips in the hazard perception part of the test, we may be able to make special arrangements for you to use a different method if you let us know when you book your test.

If you need wheelchair access and your nearest test centre doesn't provide this, then we may be able to arrange for you to take your test at another location (for example a library or another test centre).

Languages other than English

In Wales, and at theory test centres on the Welsh borders, you can take your theory test with Welsh text on screen.

To take your test in any other language, you may bring a translator with you to certain theory test centres. The translator must be approved by DSA and you must make arrangements when you book your test. You have to arrange and pay for the services of the translator yourself.

Tests with translators can be taken at the following test centres: Aldershot, Birkenhead, Birmingham, Cardiff, Derby, Edinburgh, Glasgow, Ipswich, Leeds, Milton Keynes, Palmers Green and Preston.

Taking your theory test

Arriving at the test centre

You must make sure that when you arrive at the test centre you have all the relevant documents with you, or you won't be able to take your test and you'll lose your fee.

You'll need

- your signed photocard licence and paper counterpart, or
- your signed driving licence and photo identity (if you don't have a photocard licence). The type of photo identity which is acceptable can be found on page 433).

All documents must be original. We can't accept photocopies.

The test centre staff will check your documents and make sure that you take the right category of test.

Make sure that you arrive in plenty of time so you aren't rushed. If you arrive after the session has started you may not be allowed to take the test.

> **Remember**
> - **No photo**
> - **No licence**
>
> **NO TEST**

You'll then be ready to start your test. It's a computer-based test and is made up of a multiple choice part and a hazard perception part.

Multiple choice questions

You'll begin by taking the multiple choice part of the theory test. This consists of 35 multiple choice questions and you select your answers for this part of the test by simply touching the screen. This 'touch screen' has been carefully designed to make it easy to use.

Before you start this part of your test you'll be given the opportunity to work through a practice session for up to 15 minutes to get used to the system. Staff at the test centre will be available to help you if you have any difficulties.

The questions will cover a variety of topics relating to road safety. Only one question will appear on the screen at a time. Most questions will ask you to mark one correct answer from four possible answers given. Some questions may ask for two or more correct answers from a selection, but this is shown clearly on the screen. If you try to move on without marking the correct number of answers you'll be reminded that more answers are needed.

To answer, you need to touch the box alongside the answer or answers you think are correct. If you change your mind and don't want that answer to be selected, touch it again. You can then choose another answer.

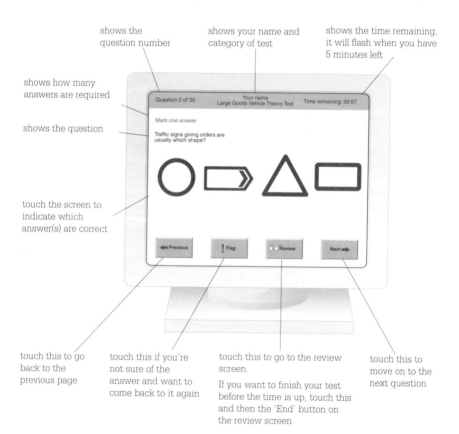

shows the question number

shows your name and category of test

shows the time remaining, it will flash when you have 5 minutes left

shows how many answers are required

shows the question

touch the screen to indicate which answer(s) are correct

Question 2 of 35   Your name
Large Goods Vehicle Theory Test   Time remaining: 39:57

Mark one answer

Traffic signs giving orders are usually which shape?

Previous   Flag   Review   Next

touch this to go back to the previous page

touch this if you're not sure of the answer and want to come back to it again

touch this to go to the review screen.

If you want to finish your test before the time is up, touch this and then the 'End' button on the review screen

touch this to move on to the next question

Take your time and read the questions carefully. You're given 40 minutes for this part of the test, so relax and don't rush. Some questions will take longer to answer than others, but there are no trick questions. The time remaining is displayed on screen. Extra time can be provided if you have special needs and you let us know when you book your test. You'll be able to move backwards and forwards through the questions and you can also 'flag' questions that you'd like to look at again. It's easy to change your answer if you want to.

Try to answer all the questions. If you're well prepared you shouldn't find them difficult.

Before you finish, if you have time, you can use the 'review' feature to check your answers before you end this part of the test. If you want to finish your test before the full time, press the 'review' button and then the 'end' button on the review screen.

When you press the review button you will see the following screen.

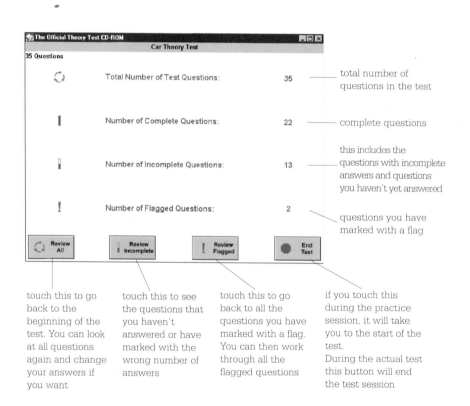

Total Number of Test Questions:	35	total number of questions in the test
Number of Complete Questions:	22	complete questions
Number of Incomplete Questions:	13	this includes the questions with incomplete answers and questions you haven't yet answered
Number of Flagged Questions:	2	questions you have marked with a flag

Review All — touch this to go back to the beginning of the test. You can look at all questions again and change your answers if you want

Review Incomplete — touch this to see the questions that you haven't answered or have marked with the wrong number of answers

Review Flagged — touch this to go back to all the questions you have marked with a flag. You can then work through all the flagged questions

End Test — if you touch this during the practice session, it will take you to the start of the test. During the actual test this button will end the test session

Hazard perception

After you've finished the multiple choice part, you may have a break of up to three minutes if you wish, before you start the hazard perception (HP) part of the test. This part of the test will consist of a series of film clips, shown from a driver's point of view.

Before you start this part of the test you'll be shown a short tutorial video that explains how the test works and gives you a chance to see a sample film clip. This will help you to understand what you need to do. You can run this video a second time if you want to.

During the HP part of the test you'll be shown 14 film clips. Each clip contains one or more developing hazards. You should respond by pressing the mouse button **as soon as you see** a hazard developing that may result in you, the driver, having to take some action, such as changing speed or direction. The earlier you notice a developing hazard and make a response, the higher your score. There are 15 scoreable hazards in total.

Your response will not cause the scene in the video to alter in any way. However, a red flag will appear on the bottom of the screen to show that your response has been noted.

Before each clip starts, there will be a 10-second pause to allow you to familiarise yourself with the new road situation.

The HP part of the test lasts about 20 minutes. For this part of the test there is no extra time available, and you can't repeat any of the clips – you don't get a second chance to notice a hazard when you're driving on the road.

Trial questions

We're constantly checking the questions and clips to help us decide whether to use them in future tests. After each part of the test you may be given the option of doing an additional trial question or clip. You don't have to do these if you don't want to, and if you answer them they won't count towards your final score.

Customer satisfaction survey

We want to ensure our customers are completely satisfied with the service they receive. At the end of your test you'll be shown some questions designed to give us information about you and how happy you are with the service you received from us.

Your answers will be treated in the strictest confidence. They are not part of the test and they won't be used in determining your final score or for marketing purposes. You'll be asked if you want to complete the survey, there's no obligation to do so.

The result

You should receive your result at the test centre within 30 minutes of completing the test.

You'll be given a score for each part of the test (the multiple choice part and the HP part). You'll need to pass both parts to pass the theory test. If you fail one of the parts you'll have to take the whole test again.

Frequently asked questions

What's the pass mark?

To pass the multiple choice part of the theory test you must answer at least 30 questions correctly.

To pass the HP part you must reach the required pass mark. This part of the test was introduced in November 2002 and initially the pass mark was set at 44 out of a total of 75 marks. This will eventually rise to 50. The increase in pass mark and the timing of the increase are being kept under review in the light of actual operational experience.

If I don't pass, when can I take the test again?

If you fail your test, you've shown that you're not fully prepared. You'll have to wait at least three clear working days before you take the theory test again.

Good preparation will save you time and money.

After your theory test

When you pass your theory test you'll be given a certificate. Keep this carefully, you'll need it when you go for your practical test.

This certificate has a life of two years from the date of your test. This means that you have to take and pass the practical test for the category of vehicle you wish to drive within this two year period. If you don't, you'll have to take and pass the theory test again before you can book your practical test.

Driving is a life skill

Your driving tests are just the beginning

Certificate Number: 0000000045180170
Expiry Date: 12 January 2002

DSA
SAFE DRIVING FOR LIFE

Driving Theory Test Certificate

This certificate is to confirm that

MR THOMAS PETER B NEWHOLM

Driver Licence Number: NEWHO70808/TP9UV

has been examined and has PASSED the Driving Theory Test prescribed under section 89 of the Road Traffic Act 1988 in respect of the B - Car category on 13 January 2000 at the 6316 Theory Test Centre.

Chief Executive
Driving Standards Agency

DETR
ENVIRONMENT
TRANSPORT
REGIONS

An executive agency of the
Department of the Environment,
Transport and the Regions

Awarded for excellence

The questions and answers

How to use this part of the book

The following part of the book contains all the questions that could be used in the multiple choice part of the theory test.

For easy reference, and to help you to study, the questions have been divided into topics and put into sections. Although this isn't how you'll find them in your test, it's helpful if you want to refer to particular subjects.

The questions are in the left-hand column with a choice of answers beneath. On the right-hand side of the page you'll find the correct answers and a brief explanation of why they are correct. There will also be some advice on correct driving procedures.

Don't just learn the answers. It's important that you know why the answers are correct. This will help you with your practical skills and prepare you to become a safe and confident driver.

Taking exams or tests is rarely a pleasant experience, but you can make your test less stressful by being confident that you have the knowledge to answer the questions correctly.

Make studying more enjoyable by involving friends and relations. Take part in a question-and-answer game. Test those 'experienced' drivers who've had their licence a while: they might learn something too!

Most of the questions refer to drivers of all large vehicles, however there are some that are only relevant to a specific group of vehicles.

Questions specifically for PCV drivers are marked with a bus symbol.

Questions specifically for LGV drivers are marked with a lorry symbol.

Some of the questions in this book will not be used in Northern Ireland theory tests. These questions are marked as follows:

NI EXEMPT

Weights and dimensions

This section looks at rules on vehicle weights and dimensions.

The questions will ask you about

- **Vehicle size**

  the dimensions of your vehicle

- **Stowage and loading**

  the importance of a secure load

- **Vehicle markings**

  the requirement for clear markings showing vehicle size and dimensions

- **Speed limiters**

  rules concerning speed limiters.

Q. 1.1

Mark one answer

This sign means no entry for goods vehicles

- under 7.5 tonnes maximum authorised mass
- over 7.5 tonnes maximum authorised mass
- over 7.5 metres overall height
- under 7.5 metres overall height

Answer

☑ **over 7.5 tonnes maximum authorised mass**

It's essential that all limits are complied with to avoid breaking the law and facing possible prosecution. Weight restrictions normally apply to the plated weight of a vehicle, often referred to as the maximum authorised mass (MAM).

Q. 1.2

Mark one answer

Your lorry is over 7.5 tonnes maximum authorised mass. This sign means you may use

- either the left-hand or middle lane
- only the left-hand lane
- only the middle lane
- any of the lanes

Answer

☑ **only the left-hand lane**

Lanes at roadworks often carry weight restrictions to keep larger vehicles in the left-hand lane. The width of the lanes through the roadworks are very often narrow and therefore not wide enough for large vehicles to pass each other safely.

Always look for restriction signs at roadworks. They are usually placed well in advance to give you time to move safely into the correct lane in good time.

questions

answers

Q. 1.3

Mark one answer

You are driving a lorry with a maximum authorised mass of 7 tonnes. What is the maximum speed limit on a single carriageway?

- [ ] 30 mph
- [ ] 40 mph
- [ ] 50 mph
- [ ] 60 mph

Answer

☑ **50 mph**

Vehicles up to 7.5 tonnes MAM are allowed to travel at speeds of up to 50 mph on single carriageway roads. You should always be aware of the speed limit for the type of vehicle you are driving.

Q. 1.4

Mark one answer

What is the national speed limit on a single carriageway road for a rigid lorry weighing more than 7.5 tonnes maximum authorised mass?

- [ ] 30 mph
- [ ] 40 mph
- [ ] 50 mph
- [ ] 60 mph

Answer

☑ **40 mph**

Vehicles exceeding 7.5 tonnes MAM are restricted to a maximum of 40 mph on single carriageway roads.

Q. 1.5

Mark one answer

Which of these lorries may normally use the right-hand lane of a three-lane motorway?

☐ Under 7.5 tonnes

☐ Over 7.5 tonnes

☐ Under 7.5 tonnes

☐ Over 7.5 tonnes

Answer

☑ **Under 7.5 tonnes**

Vehicles under 7.5 tonnes MAM may normally use the right-hand lane on a motorway, providing they are not pulling a trailer. Be careful that you don't pull out into the path of faster traffic and make other drivers brake sharply to avoid a collision.

Q. 1.6

Mark one answer

You are driving a lorry over 7.5 tonnes maximum authorised mass. On a three-lane motorway you can only use the right-hand lane

☐ to overtake slower lorries

☐ when the left-hand lane is closed

☐ if you do not go faster than 60 mph

☐ if you are not towing a trailer

Answer

☑ **when the left-hand lane is closed**

Use of the right-hand lane on motorways with three or more lanes is not normally permissible for vehicles over 7.5 tonnes MAM, except in special circumstances such as the left-hand lane being closed.

Q. 1.7

Mark three answers

When driving a low loader you should be aware of grounding on

☐ level crossings

☐ traffic calming humps

☐ yellow rumble strips

☐ hatched road markings

☐ hump-back bridges

Answers

☑ **level crossings**

☑ **traffic calming humps**

☑ **hump-back bridges**

Traffic calming measures are becoming more common. You should know the size of your vehicle and plan well ahead.

Look out for signs informing you of hazards that will affect your vehicle. Change your route if necessary rather than take risks.

questions

answers

Q. 1.8

Mark one answer

You are driving a low loader. You see this sign. Your main concern is

- the ground clearance
- the weight limit
- the height limit
- the load

Answer

☑ **the ground clearance**

As the driver of a low loader you have a special responsibility to be aware of the dimensions, including ground clearance, of your vehicle. When planning your route you will have to consider the following

- weight
- length
- height
- ground clearance.

Q. 1.9 🚚

Mark one answer

You are driving a vehicle that is over 17 metres (55 feet) long. What should you do at a level crossing?

- Cross over using your horn and hazard warning lights
- Stop before the crossing and phone the signal operator
- Increase your speed to clear the crossing quickly
- Stop before the crossing and look both ways before going on

Answer

☑ **Stop before the crossing and phone the signal operator**

If your vehicle is over 17 metres (55 feet) long and you wish to cross a level crossing, you must stop before the level crossing and telephone the signal operator.

Q. 1.10

Mark one answer

What types of fastenings or restraints should you use when carrying a heavy load of steel?

- ☐ Chains
- ☐ Straps
- ☐ Ropes
- ☐ Sheeting

Answer

☑ **Chains**

YOU are responsible for the safety of the load you're carrying. At no time should the load endanger other road users. It's therefore vital that you ensure your load is secure and safely distributed on your vehicle. The method to ensure this will differ according to

- bulk
- weight
- the type of vehicle you're driving (flat bed, curtain side, etc.)
- the nature of the load.

Q. 1.11

Mark one answer

You are driving a lorry carrying a load which is 4.5 metres (14 feet 9 inches) wide. What is your maximum allowed speed on a motorway?

- ☐ 10 mph
- ☐ 20 mph
- ☐ 30 mph
- ☐ 40 mph

Answer

☑ **30 mph**

Speed limits imposed on vehicles carrying abnormal loads can be frustrating for other drivers, but don't be tempted to exceed the speed limit. Remember, the more weight you are carrying, the longer it will take you to stop safely.

Q. 1.12

Mark one answer

What is the maximum speed limit on a dual carriageway for a lorry carrying a load which is 4.5 metres (14 feet 9 inches) wide?

- ☐ 15 mph
- ☐ 25 mph
- ☐ 35 mph
- ☐ 45 mph

Answer

☑ **25 mph**

Crossing traffic can be a danger on dual carriageways. Don't exceed the speed limits imposed on your loaded vehicle. The distance you need to stop will increase significantly with each extra mile per hour.

questions   answers

Q. 1.13

Mark one answer

Markings are required on the rear of lorries over 7.5 tonnes maximum authorised mass. What colour are these?

- Red/white
- Red/yellow
- Black/yellow
- Black/white

Answer

☑ **Red/yellow**

All vehicles over 7.5 tonnes must have markings on the rear of the vehicle. These are to inform other road users of the different characteristics of your vehicle. These markings are rectangular and coloured red and yellow. They should be kept clean so that they can be seen clearly at all times, especially at night and in poor visibility.

Q. 1.14

Mark one answer

When this vehicle turns, the overhang of the top deck will swing through

- a greater arc than the cab
- a lower arc than the cab
- a smaller arc than the cab
- the same arc as the cab

Answer

☑ **a greater arc than the cab**

As the top deck is longer than the cab and trailer, it will take up more room as the vehicle turns. You must make sure before turning that you've allowed for the wider swing of the deck. Even though your cab is well clear, the overhanging deck could hit telegraph poles or traffic signs as you go round the corner.

Q. 1.15

Mark one answer

You are the driver of an articulated car transporter. When turning corners, you should be aware that the overhang of the top deck swings through a

- smaller arc than the cab
- shorter arc than the cab
- lower arc than the cab
- greater arc than the cab

Answer

☑ **greater arc than the cab**

The longer top deck needs a wider turning circle than the cab below it. To avoid hitting lamp posts or telegraph poles etc., you must be careful to allow for this overhang when turning.

Q. 1.16

Mark one answer

The driver of a car transporter must be most aware of the trailer front-overhang when

- overtaking
- turning
- loading
- braking

Answer

☑ **turning**

The long overhang at the front of a car transporter can cause problems where street furniture, such as lamp posts and traffic signs, is sited close to junctions. Particular problems may be encountered when there are 'Keep left' bollards in the middle of the road you are turning right into. Plan your route carefully to avoid such hazards.

Q. 1.17

Mark one answer

You are scheduled to make a delivery. You arrive at your destination during the morning rush hour. The road is edged with double red lines. You should

- unload only within a 'white box' area
- unload only within a 'red box' area
- delay your delivery until after the rush hour
- limit your stop to a maximum of 30 minutes

Answer

☑ **unload only within a 'white box' area**

White boxes allow you to unload at any time, but during the day the length of stay is restricted. You should check nearby signs for specific times. At other times, when it's not so busy, there may not be any restrictions on parking.

questions   answers

Q. 1.18

Mark one answer

You are driving a lorry with a maximum authorised mass of more than 7.5 tonnes. What is the national speed limit on a dual carriageway?

- 40 mph
- 50 mph
- 60 mph
- 70 mph

Answer

☑ **50 mph**

Be considerate to other road users who may be travelling faster than you are. Don't hog the middle or outside lane unnecessarily. Make effective use of your mirrors well before signalling your intention to change lanes.

Q. 1.19

Mark one answer

You are driving a petrol tanker. 'Roll-over' is least likely to occur on vehicles fitted with

- tandem axles with double wheels
- tandem axles with air suspension
- tri-axles with single wheels
- tri-axles with double wheels

Answer

☑ **tri-axles with single wheels**

The type of suspension fitted to a vehicle will influence its resistance to 'roll-over'. Modern tri-axle semi-trailers fitted with single wheels on each side extend the tracking width available, compared to twin-wheeled units, and are more stable.

Q. 1.20

Mark one answer

You are driving a petrol tanker. The change from 'rear wheel lift' to 'roll-over' occurs

- only at roundabouts
- with very little warning
- with plenty of warning
- only when fully loaded

Answer

☑ **with very little warning**

The transition from 'rear wheel lift' to 'roll-over' is more rapid on vehicles equipped with air suspension systems. Make sure you take advantage of any extra training that may be available to drivers of this type of vehicle.

questions   answers

Q. 1.21

Mark one answer

You are the driver of a refrigerated vehicle loaded with hanging meat carcasses. You should be especially careful when turning corners because of the

- wave effect
- camber effect
- gravity effect
- pendulum effect

Answer

☑ **pendulum effect**

As you turn a corner, the hanging meat carcasses will all swing to one side of your vehicle adding extra pulling forces towards the outside of the curve. The faster you turn a corner, the greater this force will be. Even after taking the corner the carcasses will continue to swing back and forth, like pendulums, making the vehicle unstable. Keeping your speed down while cornering will help prevent your vehicle from being in danger of turning over.

Q. 1.22

Mark one answer

At overnight stops many drivers park with their rear doors close to another lorry. This is to

- keep the load safe
- ensure a clear path
- keep 'same company' lorries together
- stop the theft of their fuel

Answer

☑ **keep the load safe**

Load security is extremely important. Make sure you park legally and, preferably, in a well lit area. Some lorry parks are patrolled regularly by the police or security services.

Q. 1.23

Mark one answer

You are driving an articulated lorry on a narrow road. There is a left bend ahead. Why may you need to move out before going through the bend?

- To leave more room for braking
- To prevent anyone from overtaking
- To make room for the trailer cutting in
- To make sure oncoming drivers see you

Answer

☑ **To make room for the trailer cutting in**

You should always be aware of the amount of room your trailer needs when going through bends and corners. If you need to go onto the other side of the road, make sure there is no oncoming traffic before you negotiate the bend.

questions   answers

Q. 1.24

Mark one answer

Which of these should be fitted to a lorry with a maximum authorised mass of more than 7500 kg?

■ ◆

■ *(arc marking)*

■ *(striped chevron marking)*

■ *(black chevron marking)*

Answer

☑

Motor vehicles over 7500 kg maximum authorised mass (MAM) and trailers over 3500 kg MAM should have these markings fitted to the rear of the vehicle.

Q. 1.25

Mark one answer

How far can a load overhang at the rear before you must use triangular projection markers?

■ 1 metre (3 feet 3 inches)

■ 1.5 metres (5 feet 0 inches)

■ 2 metres (6 feet 6 inches)

■ 2.9 metres (9 feet 6 inches)

Answer

☑ **2 metres (6 feet 6 inches)**

It's not only important that you're aware of the length of your vehicle, but other road users should also be informed. This is to enable them to understand the reason why you might take up certain positions before turning. Marker boards must be fitted if the load on your vehicle overhangs by more than 2 metres (6 feet 6 inches).

Q. 1.26

Mark one answer

You are driving a lorry with a high load. Telephone companies on the route must be told if the height is more than

■ 4.00 metres (13 feet)

■ 4.30 metres (14 feet 2 inches)

■ 5.00 metres (16 feet 6 inches)

■ 5.25 metres (17 feet 6 inches)

Answer

☑ **5.25 metres (17 feet 6 inches)**

You should tell telephone companies of your intended route when planning the movement of loads over 5.25 metres (17 feet 6 inches) high. You should tell them in plenty of time prior to making the journey.

Q. 1.27

Mark one answer

How wide can a load be before you must have side markers?

- 2.0 metres (6 feet 6 inches)
- 2.9 metres (9 feet 5 inches)
- 3.5 metres (11 feet 5 inches)
- 4.3 metres (14 feet 2 inches)

Answer

☑ **2.9 metres (9 feet 5 inches)**

Side markers must be displayed if your load is over 2.9 metres (9 feet 5 inches) wide. Make sure that they're clearly visible, at both the front and rear, and that they indicate the actual width projection.

Q. 1.28

Mark one answer

You must drive your lorry at lower speed limits when its load is wider than

- 2.7 metres (9 feet)
- 3.4 metres (11 feet)
- 4.0 metres (13 feet)
- 4.3 metres (14 feet 1 inch)

Answer

☑ **4.3 metres (14 feet 1 inch)**

The following speed limits apply to wide loads that are 4.3 metres (14 feet 1 inches) to 5 metres (16 feet 6 inches) in width

- 30 mph on motorways
- 25 mph on dual carriageways
- 20 mph on all other roads.

Q. 1.29

Mark three answers

You are driving a lorry with a wide load. The width of the load is between 3.5 metres (11 feet 5 inches) and 4.3 metres (14 feet 1 inch). Which three of the following apply?

- Side markers must be shown
- The police must be notified
- An attendant must be carried
- Reduced speed limits apply
- Department of Transport approval must be obtained

Answers

☑ **Side markers must be shown**

☑ **The police must be notified**

☑ **An attendant must be carried**

Side markers must comply with regulations so that they show clearly on both sides of the projection to the front and rear. All marker boards must be independently lit at night.

questions

answers

Q. 1.30

Mark one answer

Triangular projection markers are required when your load is wider than 2.9 metres (9 feet 5 inches). What colour are these?

- Black/yellow
- Red/yellow
- Black/white
- Red/white

Answer

☑ **Red/white**

The marker boards should be red and white. To ensure that they can be seen clearly by other road users they must be kept clean and independently lit at night and in poor visibility.

Q. 1.31

Mark one answer

How should you secure an ISO steel cargo container onto your vehicle or trailer?

- Using battens and chocks
- Using straps
- Using twist locks
- Using ropes

Answer

☑ **Using twist locks**

If you're carrying a steel ISO (International Standards Organisation) cargo container, ropes or straps won't be strong enough to take the strain. This type of load requires a special type of restraint using twist locks.

Q. 1.32

Mark one answer

What does this sign mean?

- No entry for two-axled trailers
- No entry for vehicles with two-speed axles
- Maximum gross weight of 2 tonnes
- Axle weight limit of 2 tonnes

Answer

☑ **Axle weight limit of 2 tonnes**

Always look out for road signs, but be especially aware of those that refer to large or heavy vehicles. Get into the habit of checking for signs at junctions. There might be an indication on the junction layout sign. Before you turn, ensure that the road you're using doesn't have any restrictions for the vehicle you're driving.

questions

answers

Q. 1.33

Mark one answer

What does this sign mean?

- ▇ Slippery road
- ▇ Double bend
- ▇ Overhead electrified cable
- ▇ Cable laying ahead

Answer

☑ **Overhead electrified cable**

Look out for restrictions that you may not have seen on a map. These may be temporary or permanent. It is essential to know how high your vehicle is before setting off.

The height of your vehicle, and load when applicable, should be clearly marked, usually in the cab, and visible from the driving position.

Q. 1.34

Mark one answer

This sign means

- ▇ no vehicles over 14 feet 6 inches wide
- ▇ no vehicles over 14 feet 6 inches high
- ▇ road humps 14 feet 6 inches apart
- ▇ weight limit of 14.6 tonnes

Answer

☑ **no vehicles over 14 feet 6 inches high**

Always be aware of the height of the vehicle you're driving, particularly if you drive different vehicles.

Special maps are published that show weight and height limits on roads in the UK.

questions answers

Q. 1.35

Mark one answer

This sign warns of

- low bridge ahead
- accident ahead
- tunnel ahead
- accident blackspot ahead

Answer

✓ **tunnel ahead**

There may also be additional signs showing height and width restrictions. If you're driving a high vehicle, make sure that there's enough headroom available for you to proceed through the tunnel.

Q. 1.36

Mark one answer

This sign means

400 yds

- length of tunnel
- length of low bridge
- distance to tunnel
- distance to low bridge

Answer

✓ **distance to tunnel**

In addition to height restrictions the tunnel may have restrictions with regard to the available width of headroom for high vehicles. The advance warning gives you the opportunity to find another route if your vehicle is too high or wide to proceed through the tunnel.

questions

answers

Q. 1.37

Mark three answers

You are driving a vehicle higher than 3.0 metres (10 feet). Extra care must be taken when driving

- ☐ through arched bridges
- ☐ through road tunnels
- ☐ near airports
- ☐ near overhead cables
- ☐ up steep hills
- ☐ over narrow bridges

Answers

- ☑ **through arched bridges**
- ☑ **through road tunnels**
- ☑ **near overhead cables**

You must take care when approaching any hazard where height is limited. Know the height of your vehicle, and don't take any risks. Stop if you're in any doubt, and if you're not sure that it's safe, take another route.

Q. 1.38

Mark one answer

What is the minimum height of an unmarked bridge?

- ☐ 4.5 metres (15 feet)
- ☐ 4.7 metres (15 feet 6 inches)
- ☐ 4.8 metres (16 feet)
- ☐ 5.0 metres (16 feet 6 inches)

Answer

 ☑ **5.0 metres (16 feet 6 inches)**

If a minimum height isn't shown on the bridge the headroom (in the UK) will be at least 5 metres (16 feet 6 inches).

Q. 1.39

Mark one answer

Your vehicle collides with a bridge. You must report it to

- ☐ the police
- ☐ the local authority
- ☐ your local garage
- ☐ the fire brigade

Answer

- ☑ **the police**

Hitting a bridge with your vehicle can obviously have serious consequences for road and rail traffic. You must report the incident to the police within 24 hours.

If the bridge is a railway bridge, immediately call the railway authority as well as the police to report the incident. In Northern Ireland you must report it to NIR and the police.

questions

answers

Q. 1.40

Mark three answers

Your vehicle has collided with a railway bridge. You must telephone the railway authority to inform them of the

- [ ] damage caused
- [ ] type of bridge
- [ ] vehicle height
- [ ] bridge number
- [ ] vehicle number
- [ ] bridge location

Answers

- [✓] **damage caused**
- [✓] **bridge number**
- [✓] **bridge location**

It's vital that the railway authority are given this information promptly, so that they can take action to prevent railway passengers being put at risk.

Q. 1.41

Mark one answer

Bells hanging across the road warn of

- [ ] a weight restriction
- [ ] trams crossing ahead
- [ ] overhead electric cables
- [ ] a railway level crossing

Answer

- [✓] **overhead electric cables**

If your vehicle exceeds the safe travelling height beneath electrified overhead cables, bells suspended over the road will give you an audible warning. If your vehicle disturbs the bells you must stop immediately and seek advice.

Q. 1.42

Mark one answer

What does this sign mean?

▢ The width of the road is
6 feet 6 inches (2 metres)

▢ No vehicles over 6 feet 6 inches
(2 metres) wide

▢ No vehicles over 6 feet 6 inches
(2 metres) high

▢ Trailer length must not exceed
6 feet 6 inches (2 metres)

Answer

☑ **No vehicles over 6 feet 6 inches
(2 metres) wide**

You must always be aware of the size of
your vehicle. Look out for road signs that
show a width restriction. There should be
an indication of this at the entrance to the
road.

Don't get into a situation where you have to
reverse out of a narrow road because you
haven't seen a sign.

Q. 1.43

Mark one answer

This sign on a motorway means

▢ 11 tonnes weight limit

▢ stop, all lanes ahead closed

▢ leave the motorway at the next exit

▢ lane ahead closed

Answer

☑ **lane ahead closed**

Warning lights show when there are
dangers ahead, such as

• lane closures

• accidents

• fog

• icy roads.

questions   answers

Q. 1.44

Mark one answer

You are driving on a motorway. You see this sign. It means end of

- ▪ restriction
- ▪ crawler lane
- ▪ weight limit
- ▪ hard shoulder

Answer

☑ **restriction**

Look out for variable-message warning signs advising you of

- lane closures
- speed limits
- hazards.

Q. 1.45

Mark one answer

You are driving a long vehicle. Your main concern at this hazard is your vehicle's

- ▪ height
- ▪ width
- ▪ weight
- ▪ length

Answer

☑ **length**

Always be alert for situations where the size of your vehicle can get you into difficulties. You should know the weight, width, length, height and ground clearance of your vehicle. If in doubt, don't attempt to go where you may have to reverse an unreasonable distance.

Q. 1.46

Mark three answers

In which of the following places might vehicles over a certain length be restricted?

- On ferries
- At freight terminals
- In road tunnels
- On dual carriageways
- On motorways
- On level crossings

Answers

- ✓ **On ferries**
- ✓ **In road tunnels**
- ✓ **On level crossings**

Look out for restrictions for long vehicles. There are few, compared to width or height restrictions, but they're found where turning facilities are restricted or there's a risk of grounding.

Q. 1.47

Mark one answer

Thick black smoke is coming from the exhaust of your vehicle. You should

- continue on to the nearest garage
- return to your depot and report the problem
- stop in a safe place and get help
- drive slowly with your hazard warning lights on

Answer

- ✓ **stop in a safe place and get help**

Causing excessive smoke is an offence and could contribute to causing an accident. Mechanical defects could become dangerous if ignored. You could also end up creating traffic chaos if your vehicle breaks down in a difficult location.

Q. 1.48

Mark one answer

At this roundabout you intend to take the fourth exit. On this road there is a limit on

- height
- weight
- width
- length

Answer

- ✓ **height**

Be alert for signs giving you advance warning of height restrictions. As a professional driver you should always know the height of your vehicle or load. If you aren't sure of the safe height, STOP and check. Don't take chances.

questions answers

Q. 1.49

Mark one answer

When using passing places on narrow roads you will MOST need to be aware of your vehicle's

- length
- roof height
- ground clearance
- weight

Answer

☑ **length**

On single track roads, if your vehicle is too long to get completely into a passing place you may need to wait opposite it to allow a following or approaching road user to pass. When you use this type of road you need to plan and look well ahead so as to avoid meeting another road user at an inappropriate place.

Q. 1.50

Mark one answer

When driving in traffic on a motorway you see a lorry too close behind. You should

- increase your distance from the vehicle in front
- touch the brake pedal sharply to show your brake lights
- briskly accelerate away from the vehicle behind
- switch your rear fog lamps on and off

Answer

 increase your distance from the vehicle in front

The faster the traffic is moving, the greater the distance which needs to be kept between vehicles to maintain safety margins. If you find another vehicle driving too close behind you, gradually reduce your speed to increase your distance from the vehicle in front. You'll then be able to brake more gently when you need to, reducing the likelihood of the vehicle behind running into the back of your vehicle

Q. 1.51

Mark one answer

You are driving on a motorway. Your stopping distance can increase by up to ten times if the road surface is

- bumpy
- icy
- worn
- wet

Answer

☑ **icy**

Winter weather conditions affect all types of roads. Don't be misled by other drivers who are driving too fast. All but the gentlest braking will lock your wheels on ice. If your front wheels lock, you can't steer. If you can't steer, you can't keep out of trouble.

questions answers

Q. 1.52

Mark one answer

You are driving on the motorway in icy conditions. Your stopping distance can increase by up to

■ 2 times

■ 4 times

■ 10 times

■ 20 times

Answer

 10 times

Adequate separation distances are vital when driving on icy roads. You can never have too much safe space around your vehicle in these conditions. Motorways that appear wet may in fact be frozen.

Remember, all braking should be carried out gently to reduce the risk of losing control.

Q. 1.53

Mark one answer

When towing a trailer the maximum speed allowed on a motorway is

■ 40 mph

■ 50 mph

■ 60 mph

■ 70 mph

Answer

 60 mph

On motorways with more than two lanes, caravans or trailers must not be towed in the outside lane unless other lanes are closed.

Q. 1.54

Mark one answer

Certain types of crossings are shared by pedestrians and cyclists. Which one of these may a cyclist ride across at?

■ Puffin

■ Zebra

■ Pelican

■ Toucan

Answer

 Toucan

Where a cycle track meets a busy road you may also find a toucan crossing. They're similar to other types of crossing, but have no flashing amber signal.

questions   answers

Q. 1.55

Mark one answer

You are about to overtake a motorcyclist. They look over their right shoulder. It is most likely that

- the rider intends moving to the right
- something has fallen from the machine
- the drive chain is slack
- the rear tyre is flat

Answer

 the rider intends moving to the right

Anticipating the rider's next action in good time could prevent a serious accident, the assessment you make is part of the forward planning of your overtaking manoeuvre.

Q. 1.56

Mark one answer

Having just overtaken a motorcyclist on a motorway you MUST always check the

- speedometer
- left mirror
- right mirror
- road ahead

Answer

 left mirror

When overtaking with a long vehicle it is very important to be aware of the position of the road user you are overtaking. You must carefully check the nearside mirror to ensure that you have passed safely before returning to the left.

Motorcyclists require special attention as they are more vulnerable and may be affected by buffeting from your vehicle.

Q. 1.57

Mark one answer

'Red Routes' tell you that

- special waiting restrictions apply
- part-time traffic lights operate
- drivers have to pay a toll
- night-time and weekend weight limits apply

Answer

☑ **special waiting restrictions apply**

The main types of 'Red Route' controls are

- double red lines
- single red lines
- parking boxes
- loading boxes (red and white).

Red loading boxes allow up to 20 minutes for loading outside of rush hours. White loading boxes allow up to 20 minutes for loading at any time during the day.

questions   answers

Q. 1.58

Mark one answer

You are driving behind a moped. You want to turn left at a junction just ahead. You should

- ☐ stay behind until the moped has passed the junction
- ☐ overtake the moped before the junction
- ☐ pull alongside the moped and stay level until just before the junction
- ☐ sound your horn as a warning and pull in front of the moped

Answer

☑ **stay behind until the moped has passed the junction**

Planning your driving will ensure that you anticipate where the moped rider will be in relation to the junction as you arrive to turn left. Overtaking prior to making a left turn is selfish and could result in an avoidable accident, particularly when driving a long vehicle.

Q. 1.59

Mark one answer

Why should you allow EXTRA room to motorcyclists who are riding through road works?

- ☐ There may be a reduced speed limit
- ☐ There may be temporary traffic lights
- ☐ They may swerve to avoid potholes
- ☐ The traffic may be in single file

Answer

☑ **They may swerve to avoid potholes**

Motorcyclists ride through narrow gaps in traffic and generally don't take up as much room as a car. However, other factors, including road surface, can affect their stability. It is wise to give them an extra safety margin when possible.

Q. 1.60

Mark one answer

At roadworks motorcyclists might swerve to avoid potholes. You should

- ☐ give them extra room
- ☐ keep alongside them
- ☐ try to pass them
- ☐ stay close behind them

Answer

☑ **give them extra room**

Always try to anticipate the other road user's next move. Good forward planning by you can help to keep other road users out of trouble. Information to help you do this is available if you look for it. Keep your eyes moving and watch for clues, for example a motorcyclist taking a 'lifesaver' look over their shoulder could show they are going to change direction.

questions

answers

Q. 1.61

Mark one answer

Another vehicle has overtaken you and has pulled in too close in front. You should

- slow down
- drive on close behind
- overtake the vehicle
- flash your headlights

Answer

☑ **slow down**

Always maintain a safe following distance from the vehicle in front. If another vehicle pulls into the gap you have left slow down to re-establish a safe following distance.

Following too close is dangerous and places you and other road users in unnecessary danger; your view of the road ahead will be seriously reduced, and you won't be able to see or plan effectively.

Q. 1.62

Mark one answer

A large vehicle is most stable when driven in a straight line under

- harsh acceleration
- gentle braking
- gentle acceleration
- harsh braking

Answer

☑ **gentle acceleration**

A vehicle is most stable when travelling in a straight line under gentle acceleration. Sudden acceleration, steering or braking can cause severe loss of control. Your driving should be as smooth as possible.

Q. 1.63

Mark one answer

You should be careful NOT to allow your vehicle to spill diesel fuel onto the road. It can be a serious risk ESPECIALLY to

- motorcycles
- empty tankers
- towed vehicles
- fire engines

Answer

☑ **motorcycles**

Those on two wheels don't have the same stability as other vehicles. Where the road surface has been made slippery, for example by spilt diesel fuel, motorcyclists are particularly vulnerable to skidding.

Q. 1.64

Mark one answer

You are driving in a town. Ahead is a stationary bus showing this sign. You should

▢ accelerate quickly

▢ stop behind the bus and wait until it moves off

▢ drive past slowly

▢ drive normally, the driver will look after the children

Answer

☑ **drive past slowly**

You must be very careful when approaching any hazard where children are concerned, and even more so when the view is restricted. Children getting off the bus will be hidden from your view, and they may not be able to see you. Even if they can see you, they may still suddenly run across the road. It's vitally important that you drive slowly in this situation. Look under the bus, if you can, for signs of feet heading towards the road. Consider sounding the horn, if necessary, to help make the children aware that you're there.

Always be ready to stop.

Q. 1.65

Mark two answers

You are driving a vehicle with excessive exhaust smoke. Which of the following is correct?

▢ You risk being reported

▢ You risk reducing your vision ahead

▢ You could cause the brakes to fade

▢ You are breaking the law

Answers

☑ **You risk being reported**

☑ **You are breaking the law**

Apart from the fact that excessive smoke causes pollution, it can also make it more difficult for those following you to see properly. If you become aware of excessive smoke you should take steps to have the problem attended to as soon as possible.

Q. 1.66

Mark one answer

You have been convicted of a drink-drive offence whilst driving your car, and banned from driving. This ban will affect

▢ all your driving entitlements

▢ only your car entitlement

▢ only your lorry entitlement

▢ only your bus entitlement

Answer

☑ **all your driving entitlements**

The dangers of drink-driving are well publicised. Anyone convicted of this serious offence will lose their entitlement to drive any motor vehicle on the road.

questions   answers

Q. 1.67

Mark three answers

You are following this scooter on a poor road surface. You should

- [ ] overtake without any delay
- [ ] stay close behind until you can pass
- [ ] make sure you stay well back
- [ ] look out as they may wobble
- [ ] sound your horn as you get close
- [ ] be aware they may suddenly swerve

Answers

- ☑ **make sure you stay well back**
- ☑ **look out as they may wobble**
- ☑ **be aware they may suddenly swerve**

On a poor road surface, the rider may need to move out to avoid potholes. You may not get much warning. Look out for signs that the rider may be about to move out – a look to the right or 'lifesaver' check may indicate this. You should also keep a watch on the road surface yourself, to try and predict what path the rider may take. While such road conditions persist, you should stay well back, allowing the rider plenty of room.

Q. 1.68

Mark one answer

You should be extra careful when following riders of scooters as they may suddenly

- [ ] look down
- [ ] give signals
- [ ] swerve
- [ ] accelerate

Answer

- ☑ **swerve**

Scooter riders may suddenly change direction to avoid potholes or raised covers on the road. They can also be blown off course in windy conditions, especially when passing junctions or gaps in buildings, where they may be exposed to sudden gusts.

questions   answers

Q. 1.69

Mark one answer

You are following a scooter. The rider has left it too late to avoid potholes in the road. You should be aware that the rider may suddenly

■ accelerate

■ slow down

■ overtake

■ turn left

Answer

 slow down

A rider on two wheels may need to slow down quickly to avoid a pothole. Wherever the road surface is poor, you should always be prepared for those on two wheels to make sudden movements, and stay well back to allow for this.

Q. 1.70

Mark one answer

You are driving on a motorway. There has been an accident on the other side of the carriageway. You should take extra care as traffic in your lane may

■ leave at the next exit

■ slow down to have a look

■ pull out to overtake

■ stop on the hard shoulder

Answer

 slow down to have a look

Many people cannot resist the temptation to slow down to look at an accident, even if it is on the other side of the carriageway. Further collisions can sometimes occur as a direct result of this. Keeping a safe following distance and planning well ahead should enable you to keep out of trouble in situations like this.

Q. 1.71

Mark one answer

You are driving on a motorway. There has been an accident on the opposite carriageway. What should you do?

■ Concentrate on your driving

■ Slow down to look across

■ Switch on your hazard lights

■ Stop on the hard shoulder

Answer

 Concentrate on your driving

Drivers slowing down to watch what's happening on the other carriageway can often cause further accidents by not concentrating on their driving. Don't allow yourself to be distracted – concentrate on what's happening on your own side of the motorway.

questions   answers

Q. 1.72

Mark one answer

You are driving on a motorway. There has been an accident on the opposite carriageway. Busy traffic ahead is slowing to look. You should

- ■ concentrate on the road ahead
- ■ slow down to take a look
- ■ pull up on the hard shoulder
- ■ overtake using the hard shoulder

Answer

☑ **concentrate on the road ahead**

'Rubber-necking' drivers at accident scenes can often end up having collisions themselves, when they allow their vehicle to wander or fail to notice that the driver ahead has slowed right down or stopped. You need to keep your concentration in a situation like this and ignore what's happening on the other carriageway.

Q. 1.73

Mark one answer

On a motorway the colour of reflective studs on the right-hand edge of the carriageway is

- ■ amber
- ■ green
- ■ red
- ■ blue

Answer

☑ **amber**

Reflective studs on motorways and dual carriageways are provided to help drivers in bad visibility. Reflective studs are coloured

- red on the left-hand edge of the carriageway
- white to indicate lane markings
- green at slip roads and lay-bys
- amber on the right-hand edge of the carriageways marking the central reservation.

Q. 1.74

Mark one answer

You are driving on a three lane motorway. There are red reflective studs on your left and white reflective studs on your right. Which lane are you in?

- ■ Hard shoulder
- ■ Middle lane
- ■ Right-hand lane
- ■ Left-hand lane

Answer

☑ **Left-hand lane**

White reflective studs separate each of the lanes. Red studs mark the left-hand edge of the carriageway where the hard shoulder begins.

Q. 1.75

Mark one answer

On a motorway, green-yellow fluorescent studs

- mark the lanes in a contraflow system
- separate the slip road from the motorway
- mark access points for emergency services
- separate the edge of the hard shoulder from the grass verge

Answer

✓ **mark the lanes in a contraflow system**

Roadworks can involve complex lane layouts. To make it easier for you as a driver, reflective green-yellow fluorescent studs are used to separate the lanes in a contraflow traffic system.

Always look well ahead for traffic signs giving you advance information which may relate to the size or type of vehicle you are driving.

Q. 1.76

Mark one answer

Whilst driving at night you see a pedestrian wearing reflective clothing and carrying a red light. This means you are approaching

- men at work
- an organised walk
- an accident blackspot
- slow moving vehicles

Answer

✓ **an organised walk**

Pedestrians who are part of an organised walk using the road at night should wear bright or reflective clothing. The walker in front should display a white light while the one at the back should display a red one. As a driver, though, you need to be aware that they may not always do this. Be particularly careful, slow down and give the walkers plenty of room.

Q. 1.77

Mark one answer

Diamond shaped signs give instructions to drivers of

- lorries
- trams
- buses
- tractors

Answer

✓ **trams**

You need to show caution when driving in areas where trams operate. You may not hear their approach and they cannot change direction to avoid you. There may also be crossing points where you will need to give way to them, or areas specifically reserved for trams which you are not allowed to enter.

questions

answers

Q. 1.78

Mark one answer

This sign means

▢ tramway speed limit

▢ distance to level crossing

▢ maximum passenger capacity

▢ goods vehicle weight limit

Answer

☑ **tramway speed limit**

Tramways are becoming increasingly common in large towns and cities, as the move to more environmentally-friendly transport continues. They may either cross the road you're driving on, or share it with you. Always be aware of their virtually silent approach, and look out for places where you may be required to give way to them.

Q. 1.79

Mark one answer

What does this sign mean?

▢ Warning of lorry crossing a one-way road

▢ No entry for vehicles over 32 feet 6 inches (10 metres) long

▢ No entry for vehicles over 32.6 tonnes

▢ Warning of lorry straight ahead

Answer

☑ **No entry for vehicles over 32 feet 6 inches (10 metres) long**

You need to know the length of your vehicle as well as the height and width. Places where the length of your vehicle will be relevant are

- road tunnels
- level crossings
- ferries
- bridges.

Q. 1.80

Mark one answer

What does this sign mean?

- Humpback bridge
- Risk of grounding
- Uneven road
- Road liable to subsidence

Answer

 Risk of grounding

If you see this sign, you must be alert to the danger of grounding. This can happen where there's a pronounced bump in the road, such as at a level crossing or a humpback bridge.

Q. 1.81

Mark one answer

As you approach this sign your main concern should be your vehicles

- height
- width
- weight
- length

Answer

 length

At humpback bridges there is a risk of long vehicles grounding. If you're not sure whether the floor of your vehicle will clear the bridge find another route.

questions   answers

Q. 1.82

Mark one answer

You are driving a long vehicle on a two lane road. You want to turn left into a narrow road. What should you do?

- [ ] Keep well to the left on the approach
- [ ] Move out to the right immediately before turning.
- [ ] Keep to the left and turn later than normal
- [ ] Straddle the lanes to make more room for the turn

Answer

- ☑ **Straddle the lanes to make more room for the turn**

As the driver of a long vehicle you will often need to straddle lanes to turn into narrow roads. You need to watch out for smaller vehicles, especially motorcycles and cycles, trying to squeeze past on your inside.

Q. 1.83

Mark one answer

You are driving a long vehicle. You want to turn right. There is a painted mini-roundabout. What should you do?

- [ ] Make sure none of your wheels touch the roundabout
- [ ] Avoid going over the roundabout if possible
- [ ] Go ahead, and turn right at the next junction
- [ ] Carefully mount the left-hand kerb to make more room

Answer

- ☑ **Avoid going over the roundabout if possible**

When turning at a small roundabout, it is unlikely that you will be able to avoid going over the marked area. You should, however, avoid going over the roundabout where possible.

Q. 1.84

Mark three answers

When planning your route which of the following should be taken into consideration?

- [ ] Any weight restrictions
- [ ] Any height restrictions
- [ ] Any speed restrictions
- [ ] Any parking restrictions
- [ ] Any width restrictions

Answers

- ☑ **Any weight restrictions**
- ☑ **Any height restrictions**
- ☑ **Any width restrictions**

You should plan your route very carefully to avoid vehicle restrictions which may prevent your access. Width, height, and weight restrictions are particularly important.

Q. 1.85

Mark one answer

Your vehicle is more than 3 metres (9 feet 10 inches) high. Where is this information usually displayed?

■ On the tax disc

■ On the weight plate

■ In the driver's cab

■ In the engine bay

Answer

☑ **In the driver's cab**

This information is usually displayed in the cab. It is a legal requirement that it can be read by the driver, when in the driving position.

It is important to know the height of your vehicle so that you can avoid low bridges or obstacles such as overhead electrical cables.

Q. 1.86

Mark one answer

The height of your vehicle is 4.2 metres (14 feet). What action should you take on the approach to this bridge?

■ Keep to the centre of the arch and give way to oncoming traffic

■ Drive through slowly, keeping to the left of the marked limits

■ Keep to the centre of the arch and take priority over oncoming traffic

■ Drive through quickly, keeping to the left of the marked limits

Answer

☑ **Keep to the centre of the arch and give way to oncoming traffic**

The headroom under bridges in the UK is at least 5 metres (16 feet 6 inches) unless marked otherwise. But remember, this might mean the maximum height at only the highest point of an arch.

If your vehicle hits a bridge, you must report the incident to the police. If a railway bridge is involved, you must also report it to the railway authorities.

WEIGHTS AND DIMENSIONS

questions   answers

Q. 1.87

Mark one answer

Unless otherwise shown, the headroom under bridges in the UK is at least

- 4.0 metres (13 feet)
- 4.1 metres (13 feet 4 inches)
- 5.0 metres (16 feet 6 inches)
- 5.5 metres (18 feet)

Answer

☑ **5.0 metres (16 feet 6 inches)**

Every year there are about 800 accidents where vehicles hit railway or motorway bridges. Most involve buses, coaches and lorries. Don't let one of them be yours. Not only can it cause major disruption, but if you're carrying passengers it could injure or kill them. There are also the costs involved in making the bridge safe, realigning railway tracks and ensuring the safety of rail passengers.

Q. 1.88

Mark one answer

In which one of these places may you park large vehicles at night without lights on?

- In an off-road parking area
- On a road with a 20 mph speed limit
- At least 10 metres (32 feet) away from any junction
- In most lay-bys

Answer

☑ **In an off-road parking area**

Off-road lorry and coach parks are often well lit and patrolled by police or security firms. Never leave your vehicle unlit on a public road or in a lay-by after dark.

Q. 1.89

Mark one answer

The repair of a Speed Limiter must be carried out at

- an authorised Speed Limiter centre
- any Vehicle Inspectorate site
- your nearest Service Centre
- the depot by a mechanic

Answer

☑ **an authorised Speed Limiter centre**

Repair of speed limiters can only be entrusted to authorised Speed Limiter centres. They will ensure that all connections are sealed and that the system is tamper-proof.

questions   answers

Q. 1.90
Mark one answer

You are driving a vehicle fitted with a speed limiter. You should allow for its effects when

- ☐ cornering
- ☐ braking
- ☐ overtaking
- ☐ changing gear

Answer

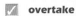 **overtaking**

Forward planning is important whenever you consider overtaking another road user. You should carefully assess the speed of the vehicle you intend to overtake. Remember that your vehicle's speed is limited and this could considerably increase the distance and time needed to complete overtaking safely.

Q. 1.91
Mark one answer

You must be aware of the effect a speed limiter has on your vehicle, especially when you intend to

- ☐ brake
- ☐ change gear
- ☐ overtake
- ☐ reverse

Answer

☑ **overtake**

Plan well ahead before overtaking. Your vehicle's speed limiter may cause you difficulties if you attempt to pass another vehicle when climbing a hill.

Q. 1.92
Mark one answer

You are driving on a motorway in a vehicle fitted with a speed limiter. You should be aware of

- ☐ the lower running costs
- ☐ the smoother ride
- ☐ the limited power available when overtaking
- ☐ the increased fuel consumption

Answer

☑ **the limited power available when overtaking**

When driving on a motorway, the speed difference between two large vehicles can be extremely small. If you wish to overtake, plan well ahead to avoid causing a long tailback of frustrated drivers.

questions

answers

Q. 1.93

Mark one answer

Maximum authorised mass refers to the weight of

- [ ] your vehicle with passengers but no luggage
- [ ] your vehicle without passengers or luggage
- [ ] your vehicle with luggage but no passengers
- [ ] Your vehicle with both luggage and passengers

Answer

- [x] **Your vehicle with both luggage and passengers**

Weight limits are imposed on roads and bridges for two reasons, the structure may not be capable of carrying heavier loads and to divert larger vehicles to more suitable routes.

You're responsible for knowing the weight of your vehicle. Be aware of and understand the limits relating to any vehicle you drive. The unladen weight can be found on the side of your vehicle.

Q. 1.94

Mark one answer

Fifteen passengers on your vehicle would increase the weight by about

- [ ] 0.5 tonnes
- [ ] 1 tonne
- [ ] 2.5 tonnes
- [ ] 3 tonnes

Answer

- [x] **1 tonne**

You must be aware of the maximum authorised mass (MAM), which refers to the weight of your vehicle with both passengers and luggage. Fifteen passengers would add approximately one tonne to the weight of your vehicle. You should also allow for any luggage that they may be carrying.

Q. 1.95

Mark one answer

As a guide, how many passengers equal about one tonne?

- [ ] 15
- [ ] 20
- [ ] 25
- [ ] 30

Answer

- [x] **15**

Your bus will move away more slowly and handle differently when fully laden with passengers and their luggage. You'll have to make allowances for this, especially when moving off uphill.

questions   answers

Q. 1.96

Mark one answer

Certain weight limit signs do not apply to buses. How would the driver know?

- By a plate fitted beneath the weight limit sign
- By the colour of the weight limit sign
- By a plate attached to the vehicle
- By a certificate carried by the driver

Answer

✓ **By a plate fitted beneath the weight limit sign**

Some weight restrictions apply to large goods vehicles (LGVs) only and not to passenger carrying vehicles (PCVs). Look out for a plate beneath a restriction sign that indicates this.

Road signs show weight restrictions in various ways, and you should make yourself familiar with all of them, so that you're in no doubt about their meaning and relevance.

Q. 1.97

Mark one answer

A passenger comments on exhaust smoke in the vehicle. You should

- report it as soon as you return to the depot
- stop and have the fault put right
- avoid heavy revving of the engine when stationary
- have the emissions checked at the next vehicle inspection test

Answer

✓ **stop and have the fault put right**

If exhaust fumes are getting into the vehicle this could cause a danger to your passengers. Stop and have the fault put right before continuing.

questions   answers

Q. 1.98

Mark one answer

You are driving a bus on a local service. You can use this lane

- between 4 pm and 6.30 pm only
- before 4 pm and after 6.30 pm only
- at any time of the day
- any time except Saturdays

Answer

☑ **at any time of the day**

As a local service bus driver you may use the bus lane at any time. The restrictions apply to other road users to keep it clear for you at peak times. Don't be tempted to speed when driving up the inside of slow-moving or stationary traffic. Be alert for pedestrians who may be trying to cross the road.

Q. 1.99

Mark one answer

The national speed limit for buses and coaches on a dual carriageway is

- 55 mph
- 60 mph
- 65 mph
- 70 mph

Answer

☑ **60 mph**

Don't be tempted to drive on the limiter when using dual carriageway roads. The speed limit for passenger carrying vehicles is 60 mph. Be considerate to faster moving traffic by not using the middle or outside lanes unnecessarily.

Q. 1.100

Mark one answer

The D1 category licence allows you to drive buses with a maximum of

- 16 passenger seats
- 24 passenger seats
- 32 passenger seats
- 48 passenger seats

Answer

☑ **16 passenger seats**

The D1 category allows any bus with 9 to 16 passenger seats to be driven for hire or reward.

Q. 1.101

Mark one answer

A driver should know the vehicle's unladen weight. Where can this information be found?

- ▪ On the dashboard of the vehicle
- ▪ On the driver's duty roster
- ▪ On the side of the vehicle
- ▪ On the depot noticeboard

Answer

✅ **On the side of the vehicle**

As a driver of a passenger carrying vehicle (PCV) you'll need to know about the vehicles

- weight (for restrictions)
- height (for clearances)
- width (for restrictions)
- length and ground clearance (for humpback bridges, grass verges, kerbs etc).

Q. 1.102

Mark one answer

What category of licence is required to drive an articulated bus?

- ▪ D
- ▪ D + E
- ▪ D1
- ▪ D1 + E

Answer

✅ **D**

A full category D licence entitles you to drive all buses and coaches including the increasingly common articulated type.

A full category D licence on its own does not cover you to drive buses or coaches drawing detachable trailers of more than 750 kg; for this you will need a D+E licence.

Q. 1.103

Mark one answer

The front of your bus overhangs well past the front wheels. Why should you allow for this when cornering?

- ▪ The steering will become much heavier
- ▪ Your speed will become more difficult to control
- ▪ You might hit a post or fence
- ▪ You will need to brake much sooner

Answer

✅ **You might hit a post or fence**

The front of a bus or coach often extends well beyond the front wheels. Make allowances for this when turning. Try to avoid overhanging the pavement where possible but if you have to do this look out for fences, posts, traffic signs etc. Be especially careful where pedestrians are present, for example in bus stations.

questions answers

Q. 1.104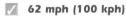

Mark one answer

Your bus has a speed limiter fitted. What other related item must it have?

- [ ] An audible warning device for the driver
- [ ] A plate in the cab showing the limited speed
- [ ] A warning sign on the back of the bus
- [ ] A manual over-ride switch for emergencies

Answer

☑ **A plate in the cab showing the limited speed**

You need to know if your bus is fitted with a speed limiter. A quick look inside the cab should tell you this. A plate must be fitted in an obvious position with the speed setting printed on it.

Q. 1.105

Mark one answer

You are the driver of a 1996 bus, which must be fitted with a speed limiter. At what speed is the limiter set?

- [ ] 60 mph (96 kph)
- [ ] 62 mph (100 kph)
- [ ] 70 mph (112 kph)
- [ ] 75 mph (120 kph)

Answer

☑ **62 mph (100 kph)**

A speed limiter is designed to prevent the vehicle from exceeding a set limit.

Q. 1.106

Mark one answer

When a speed limiter is fitted to a bus, where must the setting be displayed clearly?

- [ ] In the driver's cab
- [ ] On the nearside of the vehicle
- [ ] On the rear of the vehicle
- [ ] On the driver's side at the front of the vehicle

Answer

☑ **In the driver's cab**

If there's a speed limiter fitted to the vehicle, there should be a notice clearly displayed in the driver's cab, showing the speed at which it's set.

Q. 1.107

Mark one answer

Speed Limiters are fitted to most modern buses and coaches. They normally work by

- [ ] applying the service brake
- [ ] applying the secondary brake
- [ ] reducing fuel supplied to the engine
- [ ] changing to a lower or higher gear

Answer

- [x] **reducing fuel supplied to the engine**

Most speed limiters work by taking a speed signal from the tachograph and transmitting it to the engine management system. This reduces the fuel supply to the engine, and allows the speed of the vehicle to be controlled to specific limits.

The speed at which a limiter is set must be shown on a plate clearly displayed in the cab. You should be aware of the effect a speed limiter will have on your vehicle, especially when overtaking.

Drivers' hours and rest periods

This section looks at drivers' hours and rest periods.

The questions will ask you about

- **Driving limits**

  the EC driving limits and UK domestic hours rules

- **Keeping records**

  the records you must keep, and how long to keep them

- **Tachograph rules**

  the rules concerning the use of tachographs in the UK and abroad

- **Tiredness**

  the reasons for not driving when tired

- **Vehicle security**

  your responsibility for your vehicle and load.

questions   answers

Q. 2.1 🚚

Mark three answers

Goods vehicle drivers' hours of work are controlled for three reasons. They are

- ■ vehicle sympathy
- ■ fair competition
- ■ fair road use
- ■ vehicle security
- ■ road safety
- ■ working conditions

Answers

- ☑ **fair competition**
- ☑ **road safety**
- ☑ **working conditions**

Working conditions are governed by EC regulations. These set the maximum driving time and the minimum requirements for rest and break periods.

Q. 2.2 🚚

Mark two answers

Goods vehicle drivers' hours are controlled in the interests of

- ■ fuel economy
- ■ road safety
- ■ traffic calming
- ■ fair competition

Answers

- ☑ **road safety**
- ☑ **fair competition**

Drivers who break the rules are subject to heavy fines and could lose their licence to drive lorries.

Q. 2.3 🚚

Mark one answer

Under the rules for domestic drivers' hours you must

- ■ keep a written record of hours worked
- ■ only record any driving off public roads
- ■ keep a written record of driving time only
- ■ always use a vehicle fitted with a tachograph

Answer

- ☑ **keep a written record of hours worked**

Domestic rules apply to certain journeys within Great Britain which are not subject to EC rules. Under domestic rules you must keep written records of your hours of duty when driving goods vehicles.

questions   answers

Q. 2.4

Mark two answers

What types of vehicle must be fitted with a tachograph when operating in the UK under EC rules?

- Light goods vehicles drawing a trailer exceeding 3.5 tonnes maximum authorised mass
- Only vehicles between 3.5 and 7.5 tonnes maximum authorised mass
- Vehicles over 3.5 tonnes maximum authorised mass
- Vehicles over 7.5 tonnes maximum authorised mass only used for driving instruction
- Vehicles manufactured before 1947

Answers

- ✓ **Light goods vehicles drawing a trailer exceeding 3.5 tonnes maximum authorised mass**
- ✓ **Vehicles over 3.5 tonnes maximum authorised mass**

EC rules on drivers' hours and tachographs apply to drivers of most goods vehicles where the maximum authorised mass (MAM) limit (including any trailer) exceeds 3.5 tonnes. Domestic rules govern the remainder, with some exceptions. You must be aware of which set of rules applies to the vehicle you're driving. You'll be responsible if the information isn't recorded in the proper way.

Q. 2.5

Mark one answer

You must have enough tachograph charts with you for your journey. You will need at least one for every

- 10 hours
- 24 hours
- 36 hours
- 48 hours

Answer

- ✓ **24 hours**

Your employer should supply you with enough tachograph charts for the entire journey. You'll need at least one for every 24 hours.

Q. 2.6

Mark one answer

One tachograph chart covers a period of

- 24 hours
- 48 hours
- 5 days
- 7 days

Answer

- ✓ **24 hours**

Your tachograph is a legal document; it is a record of your work covering a rolling 24-hour period. Drivers who break the rules are subject to heavy fines and could lose their vocational licence entitlement. Altering your tachograph chart with intent to deceive is against the law and could lead to a prison sentence. Similar penalties exist for those who permit such offences.

questions   answers

Q. 2.7

Mark one answer

Your tachograph chart becomes dirty or damaged. What should you do?

- Continue with the same chart and enter the details in writing

- Use a spare chart and destroy the damaged chart

- Use a spare chart and attach it to the damaged one

- Continue to use the chart

Answer

☑ **Use a spare chart and attach it to the damaged one**

If your current tachograph chart becomes damaged you should start another and then attach it to the damaged one. Your records must be clear and up to date at all times. It's sensible to carry more tachograph charts than you think you'll need for your journey. Then you'll be able to use a spare if one becomes dirty or damaged.

Q. 2.8

Mark one answer

During your break your vehicle will be moved by another person. What should you do with the tachograph chart?

- Leave the chart in the vehicle and record the changes on the back

- Put in a new chart on your return to the vehicle

- Switch to rest mode to record the break

- Remove the chart and make a manual record of the break period

Answer

☑ **Remove the chart and make a manual record of the break period**

If your vehicle is likely to be used by another person while you're away from it, you should take your tachograph chart with you. Your break from driving should be entered on the reverse of the chart.

Q. 2.9

Mark one answer

You have been driving a lorry without a break for four and a half hours. Under EC rules a break must be taken. How long must it be?

- 30 minutes

- 35 minutes

- 40 minutes

- 45 minutes

Answer

☑ **45 minutes**

If you're driving under EC rules you must not drive continuously for more than four and a half hours without taking a break. If you've driven continually for four and a half hours you must take a break of at least 45 minutes.

Include your stops in the timetable when planning your journey.

questions

answers

Q. 2.10

Mark three answers

You are driving a lorry at night. What can you do to help you keep alert?

- Eat a heavy meal before setting off
- Keep plenty of cool fresh air moving through the cab
- Keep the cab warm and comfortable
- Take proper rest periods at correct intervals
- Drive faster to get to your destination sooner
- Walk around in fresh air at a rest stop

Answers

✓ **Keep plenty of cool fresh air moving through the cab**

✓ **Take proper rest periods at correct intervals**

✓ **Walk around in fresh air at a rest stop**

Driving at night can make you feel tired more quickly. If you're starting your shift at the end of the day, make sure that you have enough rest before you start work. You must be able to stay alert for the duration of your shift.

Make sure that you have good ventilation in the cab. Ensuring that there's enough fresh air will help you to stay alert. Stale, warm air can dull your senses and cause drowsiness.

Q. 2.11

Mark one answer

You are driving a lorry on a motorway and you are getting drowsy. There are no service areas or exits for some distance. What should you do?

- Stop on the hard shoulder and rest
- Open the window and turn the heating down
- Slow down and use the hazard warning lights
- Increase your speed to get to the next service area sooner

Answer

✓ **Open the window and turn the heating down**

During very cold weather it's tempting to have the heating in the cab turned on full. Try to be aware of the effect this can have on your reactions and anticipation. It may dull them by making you feel drowsy and tired.

questions   answers

Q. 2.12

Mark one answer

You are driving a lorry. During the journey you are feeling ill and unable to concentrate. What should you do?

- [ ] Stop in a safe place and seek help
- [ ] Continue your journey and keep your windows open
- [ ] Increase your speed to finish your work earlier
- [ ] Keep stopping at regular intervals for rest

Answer

- [x] **Stop in a safe place and seek help**

If you become unwell it will affect your concentration. You must be fully alert and ready for any hazards that might occur while you drive. Stop in a safe place and seek assistance. You may have to call out a relief driver to complete the journey for you.

Q. 2.13

Mark two answers

Which two of the following would NOT be helpful when trying to keep your load from being stolen?

- [ ] Giving a lift to a stranger
- [ ] Making sure all doors and windows are locked
- [ ] Discussing your load with members of the public
- [ ] Having a kingpin or drawbar lock fitted
- [ ] Parking in secure well-lit places when possible

Answers

- [x] **Giving a lift to a stranger**
- [x] **Discussing your load with members of the public**

Be careful of giving lifts to strangers. Some employers actively discourage this for very good reasons. Allowing strangers in your cab or letting slip information about your load could put the security of your vehicle and load at risk and may put you in danger.

Q. 2.14

Mark one answer

When leaving your vehicle for an overnight stop, it is good practice to park with the

- [ ] rear doors close up to another vehicle
- [ ] rear doors well away from another vehicle
- [ ] front doors well away from another vehicle
- [ ] front doors close up to another vehicle

Answer

- [x] **rear doors close up to another vehicle**

Being responsible for the safety of your vehicle is very important. It is your responsibility.

questions   answers

Q. 2.15

Mark two answers

How can you reduce the risk of your lorry or trailer being stolen?

- Fit an alarm and immobiliser
- Fit a king pin lock to your trailer
- Use the same route and rest periods
- Park in quiet areas away from other vehicles

Answers

- ☑ **Fit an alarm and immobiliser**
- ☑ **Fit a king pin lock to your trailer**

Planning and taking sensible precautions can help to deter the most determined thief.

Q. 2.16

Mark three answers

You are parking overnight with a high-value load and intend sleeping in the cab. You should

- lock doors but leave a window open for ventilation
- ensure doors and windows will be secure
- be in a reputable, lit lorry park
- be in a quiet, unlit, non-residential area
- stay at the same location regularly
- block access to the rear door if possible

Answers

- ☑ **ensure doors and windows will be secure**
- ☑ **be in a reputable, lit lorry park**
- ☑ **block access to the rear door if possible**

Taking a few simple precautions will help to ensure your lorry and load are safe.

Q. 2.17

Mark three answers

You are often involved in the carrying of high-value goods. What security measures can you adopt?

- Vary your routes and rest stops
- Always discuss details of your load
- Give lifts to anyone for added security
- Park overnight in well-lit areas
- Remove keys when not in attendance
- Keep your journeys to a strict routine

Answers

- ☑ **Vary your routes and rest stops**
- ☑ **Park overnight in well-lit areas**
- ☑ **Remove keys when not in attendance**

Use your common sense to plan your journeys. Avoid developing a set routine or pattern by using different routes whenever possible.

Q. 2.18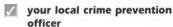

Mark one answer

It is necessary to leave your trailer unattended. It should be parked

- [ ] in a public car park
- [ ] on the public highway
- [ ] on secure premises
- [ ] in a quiet residential area

Answer

☑ **on secure premises**

Instances of theft of vehicles and trailers are unfortunately common. You are responsible for the safety and security of your vehicle and trailer. Try to avoid leaving any trailer unattended unless on approved secure premises.

Q. 2.19

Mark one answer

You are planning to carry high value goods on a regular basis. You should seek advice from

- [ ] other drivers in your area
- [ ] your local crime prevention officer
- [ ] other operators in your area
- [ ] your local road safety officer

Answer

☑ **your local crime prevention officer**

Research has shown that more than 3000 lorries with an insured value of £30 million were stolen in the UK, in one year. To prevent their lorries becoming another statistic, operators are advised to seek advice from their local crime prevention officer.

Q. 2.20

Mark one answer

Your trailer should be fitted with a kingpin or drawbar lock when

- [ ] driving on motorways
- [ ] being driven abroad
- [ ] partly loaded
- [ ] left unattended

Answer

☑ **left unattended**

Instances of theft are unfortunately common. You are responsible for your vehicle. You should ensure that a kingpin or drawbar lock is fitted to any trailer that has to be left unattended.

questions   answers

Q. 2.21

Mark one answer

A drivers week is defined as

- 0.00 hours Monday to 24.00 hours the following Sunday
- 0.00 hours Sunday to 24.00 hours the following Saturday
- any seven consecutive days
- any 56 hours driven

Answer

 0.00 hours Monday to 24.00 hours the following Sunday

A week is defined as a period between 0.00 hours on Monday to 24.00 hours the following Sunday.

Q. 2.22

Mark one answer

When driving you notice your tachograph is not working. What should you do?

- Stop immediately until it is repaired
- Report it to the nearest police station
- Telephone the vehicle inspectorate and report the fault
- Continue your journey but make manual entries on the chart

Answer

 Continue your journey but make manual entries on the chart

If you cannot return to base within a week of the tachograph becoming defective, it must be repaired during the journey. While it is broken you must keep a manual record.

Q. 2.23

Mark one answer

Only lorries above a specific maximum authorised mass need a tachograph. That weight is

- 3.5 tonnes
- 5 tonnes
- 7.5 tonnes
- 10 tonnes

Answer

✓ **3.5 tonnes**

Normally, a tachograph should be fitted and in full working order if your vehicle is over 3.5 tonnes. You should be aware of how it works and the regulations that govern its use.

questions

answers

Q. 2.24 🚛

Mark one answer

Your vehicle breaks down during a journey. You continue by driving in another vehicle with the same type of tachograph. What must you do with your tachograph chart?

☐ Leave it in the broken down vehicle

☐ Take it with you for security, but use a new chart in the new vehicle

☐ Telephone the Vehicle Inspectorate for permission to drive without a chart

☐ Take it with you, using it in the new vehicle

Answer

☑ **Take it with you, using it in the new vehicle**

When changing vehicles, you should also record the following information

- closing odometer reading
- registration number of new vehicle
- odometer start reading
- time of vehicle change.

Q. 2.25 🚛

Mark one answer

Before starting driving, which of the following should you complete on the centre field of your tachograph chart?

☐ The place from which you start your days journey

☐ Details of the goods carried

☐ The name and address of your employer

☐ The amount of daily rest taken prior to starting the shift

Answer

☑ **The place from which you start your days journey**

Before starting on your journey there are a number of items that must be recorded on your tachograph chart. One of these is where the journey begins.

Q. 2.26 🚛

Mark one answer

During your working day you are changing to another vehicle with the same type of tachograph. What should you do with your tachograph chart?

☐ Use the chart that is already in the other vehicle

☐ Take the chart with you and use it in the other vehicle

☐ Record your driving hours in a record book

☐ Install a new chart in the other vehicle

Answer

☑ **Take the chart with you and use it in the other vehicle**

If you're changing vehicles during the working day, you should take your chart with you and use it in the next vehicle. This isn't always possible, however, as charts produced by different manufacturers may not be interchangeable. In this case you should use another chart, ensuring that all the information for the day is recorded.

questions

answers

Q. 2.27

Mark one answer

A lorry driver must take care of the vehicle and load. Which of the following is NOT good practice?

- Always parking it in a quiet area out of sight
- Parking with the rear doors hard up against another vehicle
- Avoiding using the same route and stops too often
- Always asking to see the identity of any officer who may stop you

Answer

☑ **Always parking it in a quiet area out of sight**

Load security is one of the many responsibilities placed on the driver. When choosing a site to park your vehicle overnight, you should always look for a location which is legal and well lit. Many allocated lorry parks are patrolled by the police or security firms.

Q. 2.28

Mark three answers

Why are drivers' hours under close control?

- To keep to a delivery schedule
- For fuel economy
- To save wear and tear
- For fair competition
- For road safety
- For safe working conditions

Answers

☑ **For fair competition**
☑ **For road safety**
☑ **For safe working conditions**

Altering drivers' hours records with intent to deceive, or tampering with the tachograph, is against the law and could lead to a prison sentence.

Q. 2.29

Mark one answer

Who is responsible for the issue of tachograph charts to a bus/lorry driver?

- The driver's employer
- The Department of Transport
- The authorised calibration centre
- The local MOT testing station

Answer

☑ **The driver's employer**

Your employer is responsible for the issue of tachograph charts. You, the driver, must ensure that the correct information is recorded on the tachograph chart.

Q. 2.30

Mark two answers

Drivers who break EC tachograph regulations

- are allowed three warnings
- may lose their licence
- will be heavily fined
- are let off if they are not used to tachographs

Answers

- ☑ **may lose their licence**
- ☑ **will be heavily fined**

You, the driver, must take responsibility to ensure that you comply with the drivers' hours and tachograph rules.

Q. 2.31

Mark two answers

When using a tachograph which of the following apply?

- You must carry enough approved charts
- Damaged charts can be used if they are clean
- Dirty charts can be used if they are undamaged
- All charts must be clean and undamaged

Answers

- ☑ **You must carry enough approved charts**
- ☑ **All charts must be clean and undamaged**

Make sure you carry enough approved tachograph charts for your journey. Keep your spare charts in a plastic wallet to ensure they remain clean and undamaged.

Q. 2.32

Mark one answer

You are driving a vehicle requiring the use of a tachograph. You must carry charts for the current week and the last

- day of the previous week on which you drove
- seven days on which you drove
- 14 days on which you drove
- 28 days on which you drove

Answer

- ☑ **day of the previous week on which you drove**

Vehicle Inspectorate (VI) enforcement staff and the police have powers to inspect drivers' hours and other documents. In Northern Ireland the inspections are carried out by the Department of the Environment for Northern Ireland (DOENI).

The obligation to make sure that all records are completed correctly falls on you, the driver, as well as the operator. Heavy fines are imposed for the misuse or falsification of charts.

questions   answers

Q. 2.33

Mark one answer

Within how many days must drivers return completed tachograph charts to their employer?

■ 21 days

■ 25 days

■ 30 days

■ 35 days

Answer

☑ **21 days**

An enforcement officer is entitled to inspect and copy any tachograph chart. The officer can detain a vehicle for inspection and, if a false record is suspected, the chart may be taken and kept for up to six months. The officer will either issue you with a receipt or write their name and telephone number on the back of the replacement chart.

To ensure that all records are kept up to date and available for inspection by enforcement staff, you must give completed charts to your employer within 21 days.

Q. 2.34

Mark one answer

The tachograph on your vehicle becomes faulty. It can be repaired on return to base, if this is within

■ one day

■ three days

■ one week

■ two weeks

Answer

☑ **one week**

If the tachograph on your vehicle becomes faulty you should take it to an approved tachograph repairer as soon as possible. If your vehicle can't return to your base within a week of discovery of the fault, the repair must be carried out while you're away on the journey. While the tachograph is faulty or broken you must keep a manual record of your activities on a temporary chart.

Q. 2.35

Mark one answer

Tachograph records must be available for inspection. An enforcement officer keeps one of your charts. Who should sign the back of the replacement chart?

■ You, the driver

■ Your transport manager

■ The vehicle owner

■ The officer

Answer

☑ **The officer**

If an enforcement officer retains a record chart, the driver should ask the officer to sign the back of the replacement chart with their name, telephone number and the number of charts retained.

This replacement chart must be used to continue the journey. You should always carry more blank charts than you need to use.

questions answers

Q. 2.36

Mark two answers

When an enforcement officer keeps your tachograph records, the officer should sign the replacement chart with their

- name
- telephone number
- home address
- date of birth

Answers

- ☑ **name**
- ☑ **telephone number**

The enforcement officer should also record the number of charts retained. Alternatively, a receipt may be issued.

Q. 2.37

Mark one answer

You can find out when the tachograph was last recalibrated by

- a date on the tachograph chart
- contacting the vehicle's manufacturer
- checking the vehicle's service record
- a plaque on or near the tachograph

Answer

- ☑ **a plaque on or near the tachograph**

A tachograph must be checked every two years and recalibrated every six years. A plaque on or near the tachograph will say when these checks were last done.

Q. 2.38

Mark one answer

Why should you carry spare tachograph charts?

- As a defence against a speeding prosecution
- To record when you have been in a traffic delay
- For recording extra loading duties and overtime
- To replace the original chart if it gets dirty

Answer

- ☑ **To replace the original chart if it gets dirty**

Your employer should supply sufficient approved charts for your journey, plus some spares in case any get damaged, or are taken by an authorised inspecting officer.

questions

answers

Q. 2.39

Mark one answer

Under EC rules a tachograph must be re-calibrated every

■ 4 years

■ 6 years

■ 8 years

■ 10 years

Answer

 6 years

When a tachograph is installed and calibrated, an installation plaque is fixed near the tachograph. This shows the date of the most recent tachograph calibration.

Q. 2.40

Mark one answer

Under EC rules a tachograph must be checked at an approved calibration centre every

■ 2 years

■ 5 years

■ 7 years

■ 10 years

Answer

 2 years

The first inspection is due two years after the date shown on the installation plaque. Subsequent inspections are due every two years from the date shown on the two-yearly inspection plaque.

Q. 2.41

Mark one answer

Under EC rules a driver must take a break after a continuous driving period of

■ 3 hours

■ 4 hours

■ 4.5 hours

■ 5.5 hours

Answer

☑ **4.5 hours**

Whether you're driving a lorry or a bus it's essential that you don't become drowsy through driving for excessively long periods. EC rules are in place to prevent this happening. You must follow these rules, and ensure that the details of your journey are recorded.

Journey details must be available for inspection by VI or DOENI enforcement staff. For this reason you should make sure that you know the rules relating to the vehicle you're driving and the journey you're making.

questions   answers

Q. 2.42

Mark one answer

You have been driving non-stop since 5 am. The time is now 9.30 am. Under EC rules you must have a break of at least

- ■ 15 minutes
- ■ 30 minutes
- ■ 45 minutes
- ■ 60 minutes

Answer

 45 minutes

Your 45-minute break is a legal requirement under EC rules. It can be taken at the end of the driving period, or as two or three shorter breaks of at least 15 minutes during or immediately after the driving period. Remember that breaks of less than 15 minutes DO NOT count towards the 45-minute statutory break.

Q. 2.43

Mark one answer

Under EC rules you can split your daily rest into two or three periods. Each period must be at least

- ■ 15 minutes
- ■ 30 minutes
- ■ 45 minutes
- ■ 60 minutes

Answer

 60 minutes

If you split your daily rest period, you must take a total of 12 hours rest in two or three periods, the last of which must be at least eight consecutive hours. The minimum rest period must be at least one hour.

Q. 2.44

Mark one answer

Under EC rules the break needed after a maximum period of driving may be replaced by several shorter breaks taken during the driving period. Each shorter break must be at least

- ■ 15 minutes
- ■ 20 minutes
- ■ 30 minutes
- ■ 45 minutes

Answer

 15 minutes

A 45-minute continuous break can be replaced by several shorter breaks during the four and a half hours' driving period. These breaks must be at least 15 minutes.

questions answers

Q. 2.45

Mark one answer

Under EC rules you can drive for a maximum of nine hours daily. How many days of the week can this be extended to ten hours?

◼ One

◼ Two

◼ Three

◼ Four

Answer

☑ **Two**

Under EC rules your normal daily driving must not exceed nine hours. This nine-hour period must be the time between

• any two daily rest periods

• a daily rest period and a weekly rest period.

It's permitted to extend these hours to ten hours twice a week.

Q. 2.46

Mark one answer

Under EC rules what is the maximum daily driving time allowed?

◼ Nine hours extended to 11 hours on three days of the week

◼ Ten hours extended to 11 hours on two days of the week

◼ Nine hours extended to ten hours on two days of the week

◼ Ten hours extended to 11 hours on three days of the week

Answer

☑ **Nine hours extended to ten hours on two days of the week**

You are allowed to extend your daily driving time twice a week to ten hours a day. If you drive your maximum hours each day for a six-day week this brings your total driving time to the EC maximum of 56 hours.

A 'day' is generally any 24-hour period beginning with the resumption of driving or other work after the last daily or weekly rest period.

Q. 2.47

Mark one answer

Under EC rules your minimum daily rest is 11 hours. On three days of the week this may be reduced to

◼ seven hours

◼ eight hours

◼ nine hours

◼ ten hours

Answer

☑ **nine hours**

Under EC rules you must have a minimum daily rest of 11 consecutive hours. This may be reduced to nine hours on not more than three days a week, as long as the reduction is compensated by an equivalent rest before the end of the following week.

Q. 2.48

Mark one answer

Under EC rules your daily rest can be reduced to 9 hours but NOT more often than

■ 1 day per week

■ 2 days per week

■ 3 days per week

■ 4 days per week

Answer

 3 days per week

Under EC rules any reduction in your daily rest must be compensated before the end of the following week.

Q. 2.49

Mark one answer

Under EC rules your normal daily rest period should be at least

■ 8 hours

■ 11 hours

■ 13 hours

■ 14 hours

Answer

 11 hours

Under EC rules you can reduce your daily rest period to nine hours up to three times in a week.

Q. 2.50

Mark one answer

Under EC rules what is the normal weekly rest that must be taken?

■ 40 hours

■ 41 hours

■ 42 hours

■ 45 hours

Answer

✓ **45 hours**

The working week is defined as the period between 0.00 hours on Monday and 24.00 hours on the following Sunday. When taking the weekly rest period, a daily rest period must normally be extended to at least 45 consecutive hours.

questions   answers

Q. 2.51

Mark one answer

You are taking a weekly rest period away from your normal base. Under EC rules the minimum number of consecutive hours this rest period must be is

- 18 hours
- 24 hours
- 36 hours
- 45 hours

Answer

✓ **24 hours**

Under EC rules reduced rest time must be compensated by an equivalent period of rest taken before the end of the third week following the week concerned. It must be attached to a daily or weekly rest period of at least eight hours.

Q. 2.52

Mark one answer

When a vehicle has two drivers each driver should

- share the same tachograph chart
- use a separate tachograph chart for every driving period
- use their own tachograph chart
- not use the tachograph for such duties

Answer

✓ **use their own tachograph chart**

Your tachograph chart is your personal work record and, as such, should reflect the hours that you drive or carry out other work. The law requires these charts to be held on file by your employer for a period of at least one year.

Enforcement officers can require charts to be handed over for inspection.

Q. 2.53

Mark one answer

You are making a journey with a co-driver. When the other person is driving you may show some of this time as

- a daily rest period
- a weekly rest period
- a break in daily driving
- driving time

Answer

✓ **a break in daily driving**

You may only record a break when you are not engaged in any other type of work. It is permissible to take a break on a double-manned vehicle while the vehicle is driven by the other crew member. Any break must be a minimum of 15 minutes, otherwise it doesn't count.

76

Q. 2.54

Mark three answers

A tachograph will record

- load weight
- driving time
- fuel consumption
- rest periods
- engine temperature
- vehicle speed

Answers

- ☑ **driving time**
- ☑ **rest periods**
- ☑ **vehicle speed**

The tachograph is designed to be used as a tool to help you be a safe and responsible driver.

Q. 2.55

Mark one answer

The tachograph will start recording as soon as the

- engine is started
- vehicle starts moving
- ignition is switched on
- chart is inserted

Answer

- ☑ **chart is inserted**

The tachograph will record a time trace on your chart. This accurately records the movement times of your vehicle.

Q. 2.56

Mark one answer

Which one of the following symbols on your tachograph indicates your break/rest period?

Answer

☑

A tachograph is fitted with a switch that allows you to select the task that you're undertaking. Time spent on that task is then recorded onto the chart automatically. Each task has a different symbol. You should know the meaning so that your records are correct. The symbols, shown opposite, are

- driving
- doing other work
- on duty and available for work
- taking a break or rest.

questions

answers

Q. 2.57

Mark one answer

What does this tachograph chart symbol mean?

- Driver at rest
- Chart not required
- Other work
- Driving

Answer

✓ **Driving**

Each activity has a different symbol on a tachograph chart. You should know what the different symbols mean so that you can select the correct one. You'll be responsible if you fail to record all your activities correctly.

Some new tachographs don't have a 'driving' mode switch. This is because these tachographs will automatically record driving time on the chart whenever the vehicle is moved, no matter what mode the switch is turned to.

Q. 2.58

Mark two answers

You are driving a vehicle with a tachograph. What do these symbols mean?

- Driving period
- Rest period
- Driver doing other work
- On duty and available for work

Answers

✓ **Driver doing other work**

✓ **On duty and available for work**

If you're working away from the vehicle and can't leave your tachograph chart in, you should take the chart with you and make a manual entry on the reverse side, for example OW (other work) 09.15 – 10.20.

questions   answers

Q. 2.59

Mark three answers

The 'mode' switch on a tachograph is used to record

- ▪ driving
- ▪ illness
- ▪ taking a weekly rest period
- ▪ other work
- ▪ resting

Answers

- ☑ **driving**
- ☑ **other work**
- ☑ **resting**

It is important to change the mode switch to record your activities as they change during the working day. Failure to operate the mode switch could lead to a reprimand from your employer, or prosecution by the authorities.

Q. 2.60

Mark one answer

Under EC rules what is the maximum number of days that you can drive in a week?

- ▪ Four
- ▪ Five
- ▪ Six
- ▪ Seven

Answer

- ☑ **Six**

You are only allowed to drive for a maximum of six days in a working week. For example, four days at nine hours and two days at ten hours add up to 56 hours, which is your maximum allowed driving time in a week under EC rules.

Q. 2.61

Mark one answer

Under EC rules what is the maximum driving time allowed in a fortnight?

- ▪ 85 hours
- ▪ 90 hours
- ▪ 100 hours
- ▪ 105 hours

Answer

- ☑ **90 hours**

The maximum number of hours that you can drive in a fortnight is 90. These don't have to be split evenly, but the total number of hours spent driving in any one week shouldn't exceed 56.

Don't exceed your driving hours. You'll need to keep records of how many hours you drive in a day, a week and a fortnight. Learn the rules and adhere to them. Heavy fines can be imposed for failure to do so.

questions

answers

Q. 2.62

Mark one answer

At the end of your working week you have driven a total of 56 hours. What is the maximum number of hours that you can drive in the following week under EC rules?

▮ 34

▮ 36

▮ 38

▮ 40

Answer

 34

If you've driven a total of 56 hours in any one week you can only drive for 34 hours in the following week. If your hours add up to a total of 56 in any one week you must make sure that you don't exceed the permitted hours the following week. Keep your own record to make sure that you don't exceed these hours.

Q. 2.63

Mark one answer

An emergency situation has arisen. For safety reasons you will need to exceed the normal drivers' hours under EC rules. You should

▮ continue with the same tachograph chart and write an explanation on the back

▮ remove the tachograph chart and make a manual record of the rest of the journey

▮ continue; there is no need to give an explanation

▮ remove the tachograph chart and inform your employer of the reason

Answer

 continue with the same tachograph chart and write an explanation on the back

As long as road safety is not put at risk, you may depart from the drivers' hours rules just enough to ensure the safety of passengers, your vehicle, or its load. In these circumstances you should note all the reasons on the back of your tachograph chart.

Q. 2.64

Mark one answer

You start your journey on a foggy night. You are delayed because of the fog and exceed your permitted hours. This means

▮ you will not be committing an offence as the delay was due to the weather

▮ you could be committing an offence as the delay could be foreseen

▮ your excess hours can be transferred to another day

▮ your excess hours will not apply because of the weather

Answer

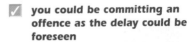 **you could be committing an offence as the delay could be foreseen**

When planning your journey you should allow for delays and unexpected hold-ups. Don't let the time pressures related to your work cause you to rush to make up time. Act responsibly at all times. As a professional driver you should set the standards for others to follow.

questions   answers

Q. 2.65

Mark one answer

In an emergency situation you need to go over your normal drivers' hours. Under EC rules you should

- [ ] take no action, the tachograph chart will record this
- [ ] note the reasons on the back of the tachograph chart
- [ ] remove the chart from the tachograph before going over the hours
- [ ] note the reasons on the front of the tachograph chart

Answer

- [x] **note the reasons on the back of the tachograph chart**

In an emergency, as long as road safety is not put at risk, a driver may depart from the drivers' hours rules just enough to get their load or passengers to a suitable stopping place.

Q. 2.66

Mark two answers

Which TWO of the following are most likely to cause tiredness?

- [ ] Making frequent and regular stops
- [ ] Driving breaks taken on board the vehicle
- [ ] Insufficient breaks from driving
- [ ] Modern vehicles with automatic gearboxes
- [ ] The cab becoming too warm.

Answers

- [x] **Insufficient breaks from driving**
- [x] **The cab becoming too warm**

Tiredness will affect your concentration. It's most important that you don't allow yourself to become weary through not taking proper breaks or rest periods. As a professional driver you have a responsibility either for goods or for passengers, as well as for overall road safety.

Try to ensure that your vehicle is well ventilated. Open a window or turn down the heating to prevent yourself becoming drowsy.

questions   answers

Q. 2.67

Mark one answer

When driving, you start to feel tired or unable to concentrate. You should

- [ ] stop as soon as it is safe to do so
- [ ] wind down a window and carry on
- [ ] switch on the radio and complete your journey
- [ ] speed up to get to your destination sooner

Answer

- [x] **stop as soon as it is safe to do so**

If you start to feel tired you should stop as soon as it's safe to do so, even if you aren't due a break.

Make sure that you get enough sleep before you're due to work, especially if you're on an early shift.

Q. 2.68

Mark one answer

You feel tired after driving for two and a half hours. What should you do?

- [ ] Slow down to a safer speed
- [ ] Reduce your planned driving time to three and a half hours
- [ ] Stop as soon as it is safe to do so
- [ ] Take a less busy route

Answer

- [x] **Stop as soon as it is safe to do so**

Most accidents happen as a result of a lapse in concentration. Don't let this happen to you. If you start to feel tired you won't perform as well as you should. Your reactions will slow down and your anticipation and judgement of hazards will become flawed. It will be better for you, and for the safety of other road users, if you stop and rest as soon as it's safe to do so.

Q. 2.69

Mark one answer

You are driving on a motorway and suddenly become tired. What should you do?

- [ ] Stop on the hard shoulder and rest
- [ ] Leave by the next exit and find a place to stop
- [ ] Stop on the next slip road and rest
- [ ] Stop on the verge of the motorway and rest

Answer

- [x] **Leave by the next exit and find a place to stop**

If you're driving for long distances on a motorway take plenty of rest stops. Many accidents have been blamed on drivers falling asleep at the wheel. If you feel yourself becoming 'mesmerised', stop at the next service area.

Q. 2.70

Mark one answer

You are feeling tired when driving on a motorway. Where can you stop?

- On the hard shoulder
- At a service station
- On a slip road
- In a deceleration lane

Answer

☑ **At a service station**

Travelling long distances on a motorway can have a 'mesmerising' effect. Any lack of concentration, however brief, could lead to an accident.

If you start to feel tired stop as soon as you can, but don't stop on the hard shoulder. Leave the motorway by the next exit and pull over in a safe place to rest. Ideally you should use a service area, where you can have a rest and refreshment before you restart your journey.

Q. 2.71

Mark one answer

You have to leave your vehicle unattended for a very short time. You should

- avoid having to stop the engine
- leave keys available in case of obstruction
- keep the engine running but lock the doors
- be aware of the risks of theft or damage

Answer

☑ **be aware of the risks of theft or damage**

Take all the precautions you can to eliminate opportunities for theft. Lock your vehicle, especially when making deliveries and leaving the vehicle unattended.

Q. 2.72

Mark one answer

The audible warning device is operating as you reverse. You should be

- relying on a clear path behind
- expecting others to be aware of your course
- taking continuous, all-round observation
- concentrating solely on your blind areas

Answer

☑ **taking continuous, all-round observation**

Don't rely on an audible warning device to claim a right of way. It is your responsibility to be cautious and take all-round observation all the time you are reversing.

questions   answers

Q. 2.73
Mark one answer

The time is 10 am. You have been driving non-stop since 6 am. Under EC rules what is the longest you may now drive without a break?

- 15 minutes
- 30 minutes
- 40 minutes
- 45 minutes

Answer
☑ **30 minutes**

The maximum driving period under EC rules is 4 hours 30 minutes, after which you must have a minimum break of 45 minutes.

Planning your route will allow you to take your statutory rest periods in a safe place, such as a service area, where you can get food, drink and a rest.

Q. 2.74
Mark one answer

Under EC rules you may drive for up to nine hours daily. On two days of the week this may be increased to a maximum of

- 9.5 hours
- 10 hours
- 11 hours
- 11.5 hours

Answer
☑ **10 hours**

Don't drive for more than the maximum hours allowed. You're permitted to extend the daily nine hours to ten hours twice a week.

Q. 2.75
Mark one answer

You are on a regular service and are not using a tachograph. What MUST you carry with you?

- Tachograph charts from the previous seven days
- Your bus driver's licence
- An extract from the duty roster and the service timetable
- Servicing and maintenance records

Answer
☑ **An extract from the duty roster and the service timetable**

Instead of using a tachograph you can carry an extract from the duty roster and a copy of the service timetable. The roster must show your name, the place where you're based and the schedule laid down in advance.

questions

answers

Q. 2.76 🚌

Mark two answers

A bus driver who is not using a tachograph on a regular service of over 50 km (31 miles) must carry which TWO of these?

- ■ A drivers' hours record book
- ■ An extract from the duty roster
- ■ A copy of the service timetable
- ■ Some small change
- ■ A detailed route map

Answers

- ☑ An extract from the duty roster
- ☑ A copy of the service timetable

Under EC rules, drivers' activities are usually recorded by means of a tachograph. If you're a bus driver on a regular service over 50 km (31 miles) you may not be required to use one, but you will be required to carry an extract from the duty roster and a copy of the route timetable.

Q. 2.77 🚌

Mark one answer

The driver of a bus with 18 seats on an excursion journey from London to Scotland should abide by which drivers' hours rules?

- ■ AETR only
- ■ Domestic
- ■ EC only
- ■ EC and AETR

Answer

- ☑ EC only

If you're driving a bus on an excursion journey (that is, not a regular journey) and your vehicle has 18 or more seats you must use EC rules and record the details on a tachograph chart.

Q. 2.78 🚌

Mark one answer

EC rules require that after driving continuously for the maximum period a bus driver must take a break. This must be at least

- ■ 15 minutes
- ■ 30 minutes
- ■ 45 minutes
- ■ 60 minutes

Answer

- ☑ 45 minutes

Always park your vehicle in a safe place off the road. Try to find somewhere you can get out of your vehicle for refreshment. This will help to ensure that you're fully refreshed.

If you're carrying passengers, they'll also be grateful for a break. Taking breaks at the correct time will ensure that your passengers are safe and comfortable.

questions   answers

Q. 2.79

Mark one answer

A driver's daily rest period may be taken in a parked vehicle if

- it is fitted with a bunk
- there is a smoke alarm fitted
- the vehicle is in an authorised coach park
- there are no passengers on the vehicle

Answer

☑ **it is fitted with a bunk**

Some vehicles are fitted with sleeping accommodation for the driver. If your vehicle is fitted with this facility you're permitted to take your daily rest period there, provided your vehicle is stationary.

Q. 2.80

Mark one answer

What should you do if asked to leave your bus by an official who is not in uniform?

- Comply with the request
- Ask to see a warrant card
- Refuse to leave the vehicle
- Invite the official aboard

Answer

☑ **Ask to see a warrant card**

If you are asked to leave your vehicle by an official who's not in uniform, ask to see their warrant card. The official is likely to be a VI or DOENI enforcement officer or a police officer, but don't presume this.

Q. 2.81

Mark one answer

When a bus is left unattended the driver MUST ensure that

- the tachograph chart is removed
- the gear lever is in reverse
- the gear lever is in first
- the parking brake is applied

Answer

☑ **the parking brake is applied**

Always ensure that your vehicle is safe when you leave it unattended. Always apply the parking brake and stop the engine.

Q. 2.82

Mark one answer

You have arrived at your destination. All your passengers want to leave the bus. Ideally their valuables should be

- ☐ placed on luggage racks
- ☐ taken with them
- ☐ placed on the seats
- ☐ left with you

Answer

☑ **taken with them**

Ideally passengers should take any personal property and valuables with them, unless they can be locked in secure luggage compartments.

Braking systems

This section looks at braking systems.

The questions will ask you about

- **Types of brake**

  the different types of braking systems used on vehicles

- **Maintenance and inspection**

  the importance of ensuring that your brakes are in good working order

- **Connection and proper use of the brakes**

  how to connect and use them

- **Tailgating**

  why following too closely is dangerous and how to avoid it

- **Freezing conditions**

  the effects of freezing weather on the braking system

- **Anti-lock brakes**

  how the system works.

Q. 3.1

Mark one answer

You have to drive on to a muddy building site. Why should you switch on your diff-lock?

- [ ] It will make your steering lighter
- [ ] It will improve your fuel consumption
- [ ] It will increase your engine power
- [ ] It will make the wheels less likely to spin

Answer

- [x] **It will make the wheels less likely to spin**

Engaging the diff-lock means that power is shared between the driven wheels. This reduces the chances of wheelspin. Remember to switch off the diff-lock as soon as you are on firm ground again, otherwise you could damage the transmission.

Q. 3.2

Mark one answer

Your lorry does not have an anti-lock braking system fitted. You may prevent the wheels from locking under heavy braking by

- [ ] pushing the brake pedal harder until you stop
- [ ] depressing the clutch pedal as you brake
- [ ] rapid pumping of the brake pedal
- [ ] changing down through the gears as you brake

Answer

- [x] **rapid pumping of the brake pedal**

Use maximum pressure to the point where the wheels are about to lock, momentarily release the brake pressure, then quickly apply it again. This technique is known as cadence braking. Only use this method when the vehicle is NOT fitted with an anti-lock braking system. It should only be used in an emergency situation to avoid skidding.

Q. 3.3

Mark three answers

Trailer swing is more likely to occur on a lorry and draw bar combination when

- [ ] braking on a bend
- [ ] oversteering at speed
- [ ] the brakes are out of adjustment
- [ ] braking lightly several times
- [ ] steering at slow speed and fully loaded
- [ ] an endurance brake (retarder) is fitted

Answers

- [x] **braking on a bend**
- [x] **oversteering at speed**
- [x] **the brakes are out of adjustment**

All braking and changes of direction should be carried out smoothly and under full control. Make sure all the brakes are properly adjusted.

questions answers

Q. 3.4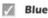

Mark one answer

Your vehicle is fitted with a 'diff-lock'. You would normally use it when

- driving on straight roads
- towing an empty trailer
- driving on muddy construction sites
- uncoupling a trailer

Answer

☑ **driving on muddy construction sites**

The differential gears in the drive axle allow the drive wheels to rotate at different speeds, which is very important to enable you to negotiate corners and bends safely. The 'diff-lock' effectively locks the driven wheels together, so that power is transmitted equally to both. This is very useful in slippery or muddy conditions where otherwise the drive wheels can spin at different speeds and result in a loss of traction.

Q. 3.5

Mark one answer

On a three-line braking system to the trailer of a lorry what colour is the auxiliary line?

- Red
- Blue
- Green
- Yellow

Answer

☑ **Blue**

If you're driving an articulated vehicle or a trailer combination it's vital that you understand the rules that apply to coupling and uncoupling the brake lines. If you're taking a test with a trailer, you'll be expected to demonstrate this during your practical test. The lines must be connected strictly in accordance with the correct procedure. Study the information in the publication *Driving Goods Vehicles – the Official DSA Syllabus* (published by The Stationery Office) to ensure that you know and understand the way this should be done.

Q. 3.6

Mark one answer

The emergency line is common to both two and three-line brake systems. What is its colour?

- Red
- Blue
- Black
- Yellow

Answer

☑ **Red**

The red emergency line is common to both two- and three-line braking systems. ALWAYS set the parking brake before disconnecting any brake lines.

Q. 3.7

Mark one answer

Air brake systems usually have two lines. What additional line is fitted on a three-line system?

- Emergency
- Service
- Electrical
- Auxiliary

Answer

☑ **Auxiliary**

The blue (auxiliary) line is not used when connecting to a two-line system. Follow the manufacturer's instructions about what to do with the third (blue) line.

Q. 3.8

Mark one answer

In frosty weather, what precaution could a lorry driver take to prevent moisture freezing in brake air storage tanks?

- Drain the tanks daily
- Cover the tanks with a blanket
- Keep the engine at high revs when starting
- Pump the brakes

Answer

☑ **Drain the tanks daily**

You should make sure that you drain the tanks daily to avoid moisture freezing in the system. Most modern vehicles have an automatic draining system, which should be checked regularly.

questions

answers

Q. 3.9

Mark one answer

What action would you take if a brake pressure warning device comes on?

- Continue to drive the vehicle
- Drain the air tanks
- Stop and get the fault put right
- Disconnect all the air lines

Answer

☑ **Stop and get the fault put right**

Air brake systems are fitted with a warning device that operates if the air pressure in the tanks drops below a safe level. This may be a warning buzzer and/or pressure gauges. You must be aware of the function of all gauges on your vehicle, and check them as you drive.

Q. 3.10

Mark one answer

To help to avoid 'brake fade' lorry drivers should ensure that

- the air tanks are drained before journeys
- the air pressure is correct
- the handbrake is applied before stopping
- the appropriate gears are engaged before downhill gradients

Answer

☑ **the appropriate gears are engaged before downhill gradients**

It's important that you engage a low gear as you approach the hill to ensure the engine is building up air and can assist with braking. If the road has a long downhill gradient this is doubly important. You should be anticipating hazards like this as you drive. Good planning and preparation will ensure that you are always in the correct gear for the situation.

Q. 3.11

Mark one answer

Exhaust brakes give greatest efficiency when used

- at high engine speed in low gears
- at low engine speed in high gears
- on stop-start town work
- on high-speed motorway runs

Answer

☑ **at high engine speed in low gears**

Because excessive braking can have serious effects on the brakes, some vehicles are fitted with exhaust brakes. These brakes alter the engine's exhaust flow, using it to assist with the braking. They're most efficient when the engine is at high speed and in a low gear, such as when descending a long hill. Using the exhaust brakes can relieve the service brakes, preventing them from becoming hot and failing through over-use.

questions answers

Q. 3.12

Mark one answer

The principal braking system on a lorry is called the

- [ ] endurance brake (retarder)
- [ ] service brake
- [ ] parking brake
- [ ] handbrake

Answer

- [x] **service brake**

The service brake is usually operated by the foot control. It is used to control the speed of the vehicle and to bring it to a halt safely. It may also incorporate an anti-lock braking system.

Q. 3.13

Mark three answers

The three main braking systems fitted to lorries are known as

- [ ] over-run
- [ ] cadence
- [ ] exhaust
- [ ] service
- [ ] secondary
- [ ] parking

Answers

- [x] **service**
- [x] **secondary**
- [x] **parking**

The service brake performs the primary function of stopping the vehicle when you depress the footbrake. The secondary brake system is for use in the event of failure of the service brake. The parking brake should normally only be used when the vehicle is stationary.

Q. 3.14

Mark one answer

What is the national speed limit for a lorry over 7.5 tonnes on a motorway?

- [ ] 50 mph (80 kph)
- [ ] 55 mph (88 kph)
- [ ] 60 mph (96 kph)
- [ ] 70 mph (112 kph)

Answer

- [x] **60 mph (96 kph)**

Be aware of, and obey, all speed limits. On a motorway a lorry that is articulated or towing a trailer, or that is over 7.5 tonnes, must not exceed 60 mph (96 kph).

questions   answers

Q. 3.15

Mark one answer

You are driving a lorry at a speed of 50 mph (80 kph) in good, dry conditions. What distance should you stay behind the vehicle in front?

- At least 20 metres (66 feet)
- At least 30 metres (98 feet)
- At least 40 metres (131 feet)
- At least 50 metres (164 feet)

Answer

✓ **At least 50 metres (164 feet)**

You should always leave a safety margin between you and the vehicle in front. This gap will give you a better view of the road ahead. It will also allow you more time to react if the traffic in front changes speed or direction.

Q. 3.16

Mark one answer

You are driving a lorry and trailer. You change to a lower gear when going too fast. This could cause the

- vehicle to jack-knife
- engine to stall
- brakes to fail
- trailer to uncouple

Answer

✓ **vehicle to jack-knife**

Jack-knifing is usually more likely to occur with an unladen vehicle, particularly when not travelling in a straight line. Severe braking or selection of a gear too low for your road speed can cause the tractor unit to be pushed by the semi-trailer pivoting around the coupling (fifth wheel).

Q. 3.17

Mark three answers

An articulated vehicle is more likely to jack-knife when

- unladen
- manoeuvring slowly
- braking sharply
- fully loaded
- on a bend
- fitted with an endurance brake (retarder)

Answers

✓ **unladen**

✓ **braking sharply**

✓ **on a bend**

A combination of sharp braking and excessive steering can cause your vehicle to become unstable. Jack-knifing is more likely to occur when the vehicle is empty.

questions   answers

Q. 3.18

Mark one answer

Your lorry is stuck in snow. You use the diff-lock to move off. When should you switch the diff-lock off?

- [ ] Only after selecting top gear
- [ ] Once the engine has warmed up
- [ ] As soon as the vehicle is moving
- [ ] As soon as the snow has cleared

Answer
☑ **As soon as the vehicle is moving**

You must always disengage the diff-lock as soon as the vehicle is moving. The differential allows the rear wheels to revolve at different speeds, which allows the vehicle to be steered. Attempting to turn with the diff-lock engaged could have disastrous consequences, as your vehicle will try to go straight on.

Q. 3.19

Mark one answer

You are driving a new articulated lorry which is fully laden. You notice the steering feels heavy. What is the most likely reason?

- [ ] The road is icy
- [ ] Faulty power steering
- [ ] A tyre on the trailer has burst
- [ ] The load on the trailer has shifted

Answer
☑ **Faulty power steering**

Any suspected failure of the power steering should be investigated as soon as possible. Many large vehicles can become undriveable if it fails completely.

Q. 3.20

Mark one answer

Your tractor unit has three air lines. You are connecting to a trailer with two air lines. What colour is the line you should NOT connect to the trailer?

- [ ] Red
- [ ] Yellow
- [ ] Black
- [ ] Blue

Answer
☑ **Blue**

When connecting three lines to a two-line trailer the third (blue) line is the one that should NOT be connected to the trailer. It is vitally important to follow the manufacturer's advice. It may be necessary to reconnect the extra line to the tractor unit.

questions   answers

Q. 3.21

Mark one answer

On an articulated lorry which has a three-line connection, the red line is the

- ☐ emergency line
- ☐ service line
- ☐ auxiliary line
- ☐ electrical line

Answer

☑ **emergency line**

The red emergency line is common to both two-line and three-line brake systems. The other colours are

- blue – auxiliary
- yellow – service.

Q. 3.22

Mark one answer

You are driving a tractor unit fitted with two air lines. You want to couple up to a trailer with three air lines. How should this be done?

- ☐ The trailer auxiliary line should be left unconnected
- ☐ The trailer service line should be left unconnected
- ☐ Only the service line should be connected
- ☐ Only the auxiliary line should be connected

Answer

☑ **The trailer auxiliary line should be left unconnected**

A two-line system consists of

- emergency – red line
- service – yellow line.

It is vitally important that you understand the rules that apply to safely connecting brake systems and mixing two- and three-line systems.

Q. 3.23

Mark one answer

The correct procedure for stopping a lorry equipped with an anti-lock braking system in an emergency is to

- ☐ apply the footbrake firmly in a pumping action until the vehicle has stopped
- ☐ apply the footbrake firmly and continuously until the vehicle has stopped
- ☐ apply the footbrake and handbrake until the vehicle has stopped
- ☐ apply the handbrake only

Answer

☑ **apply the footbrake firmly and continuously until the vehicle has stopped**

If you're driving a vehicle with anti-lock brakes and you feel the vehicle beginning to skid, you should keep your foot firmly on the brake pedal until the vehicle stops. This will allow the system to work. Although anti-lock brakes on a vehicle contribute to safe braking, it doesn't take away the need to drive with good planning and anticipation, which should greatly reduce the need to brake harshly. Reliable and efficient equipment is essential, but it's your action that can prevent an accident.

Q. 3.24

Mark one answer

You are about to drive a new vehicle. It has an air brake system which may have moisture in the reservoir. What should you do?

- Rely on the automatic drain valve to clear the system
- Find out whether you need to drain the system manually
- Nothing, it is the vehicle owner's responsibility
- Leave the engine running for a while before driving

Answer

☑ **Find out whether you need to drain the system manually**

Moisture left in the braking system can cause serious problems, especially in cold weather when it could freeze, causing the brakes to fail. Most modern vehicles have a system which drains automatically, but make sure you know which system is fitted to any vehicle that you drive.

Q. 3.25

Mark one answer

Your vehicle has anti-lock brakes. This allows you to

- follow vehicles more closely
- steer while braking
- drive faster on wet roads
- brake later than normal

Answer

☑ **steer while braking**

Although anti-lock braking gives you the ability to brake and steer, it should not be relied on to keep you out of trouble. Good forward planning and anticipation will minimise the risk of skidding more effectively than relying on your braking system.

Q. 3.26

Mark one answer

What could prevent air pressure building up in an air brake system in cold frosty weather?

- Moisture in the air may form bubbles in the brake fluid
- The air will contract, reducing the pressure
- The dampness may cause valves to rust
- Moisture drawn in with the air may freeze and cause a blockage

Answer

☑ **Moisture drawn in with the air may freeze and cause a blockage**

Large vehicles normally have braking systems that use compressed air to control the action of the brake shoes. The compressed air is built up by the vehicle's engine and stored in tanks on the chassis. This compressed air is vital to the effectiveness of the brakes. You must understand the system and know how to keep it in good condition, so that the brakes won't fail when you need them.

questions answers

Q. 3.27

Mark one answer

The brake air pressure warning light comes on whilst driving. You should

▪ stop and seek help without delay

▪ report the fault on return to your depot

▪ boost the pressure through added acceleration

▪ drain air tanks and continue normally

Answer

✅ **stop and seek help without delay**

If the warning light indicating a loss of brake pressure comes on, you must stop and get the fault put right immediately. Your safety, the safety of your load or your passengers, and that of all other road users will be at risk.

Q. 3.28

Mark one answer

When the brake air pressure warning light is operating, you should NEVER

▪ leave your vehicle

▪ release the parking brake

▪ switch your engine off

▪ engage the clutch

Answer

✅ **release the parking brake**

Even though the warning device is operating, there may be sufficient pressure to release the parking brake, but you must not do this as the service brake may be ineffective.

Q. 3.29

Mark one answer

Your vehicle is fitted with an anti-lock braking system. Its main purpose is to help you to

▪ drive at faster speeds

▪ brake much later than normal

▪ apply the brakes more quickly

▪ stop safely in an emergency

Answer

✅ **stop safely in an emergency**

Anti-lock braking systems work in a similar manner to cadence braking. Just as the wheels are about to lock, the sensor control releases the brakes and immediately applies them again.

questions answers

Q. 3.30

Mark one answer

As the driver of a vehicle fitted with an anti-lock braking system, you should check it is working before each

■ service

■ day's work

■ week's work

■ journey

Answer

☑ **journey**

Modern anti-lock braking systems rely on electrical power for their operation. The satisfactory operation of the system can be checked from the warning signal on the dashboard. The warning signal should go out by the time the vehicle has reached a speed of about 10 kph (6 mph).

Q. 3.31

Mark one answer

'Pumping' the brake pedal in a vehicle fitted with anti-lock brakes will cause

■ increased effectiveness

■ reduced effectiveness

■ reduced brake wear

■ increased brake wear

Answer

☑ **reduced effectiveness**

Always refer to the owner's handbook for details of the manufacturer's recommended method of use. Remember, anti-lock brakes will enhance your skills, NOT replace them.

Q. 3.32

Mark one answer

You are driving a vehicle fitted with anti-lock brakes. When braking in an emergency, you should

■ 'pump' the brake pedal harshly

■ apply minimum force to the brake pedal

■ use the exhaust brake (retarder) then the footbrake

■ apply firm continuous pressure to the brake pedal

Answer

☑ **apply firm continuous pressure to the brake pedal**

Always check with the vehicle manufacturer for details of their recommended method of use. Plan well ahead to avoid emergency situations developing.

questions   answers

Q. 3.33

Mark one answer

You are driving a vehicle not fitted with anti-lock brakes. How can 'wheel lock' be controlled during heavy braking?

- By using engine braking
- By cadence braking
- By braking suddenly
- By using clutch and brake together

Answer

 By cadence braking

Cadence braking is a special braking technique for slowing or stopping a vehicle without anti-lock brakes in slippery conditions. It is not a substitute for lack of proper care and anticipation.

Q. 3.34

Mark one answer

Brake fade happens when the brakes get too

- hot
- cold
- dry
- wet

Answer

✓ **hot**

Brake fade occurs when the brakes become too hot. Continuous use of the brakes can result in them becoming overheated and losing their effectiveness, especially on long downhill gradients.

Q. 3.35

Mark one answer

You have to stop quickly in an emergency. Which of the following are most likely to prevent 'wheel lock'?

- Using the parking brake
- Selecting neutral
- Cadence braking
- Changing up a gear

Answer

✓ **Cadence braking**

The principle of cadence braking is to brake using maximum pressure, to the point where the wheels are about to lock; you momentarily release the brake pressure and then quickly reapply it again. You will need to do this rapidly a number of times.

Q. 3.36

Mark one answer

What is 'brake fade'?

■ Reduction of air pressure

■ Smooth progressive braking

■ Reduction of braking effectiveness

■ Low hydraulic brake fluid level

Answer

☑ **Reduction of braking effectiveness**

Continually using the brakes could cause them to 'fade'. This will mean that they are less effective.

Make sure that you're in the correct gear before you negotiate downhill stretches of road. A low gear will assist with braking and help prevent the vehicle gaining momentum as you negotiate the hill. Look out for road signs and 'dead ground', which indicate a dip or a hill.

Q. 3.37

Mark two answers

To prevent brake fade you should

■ use the endurance brake (retarder)

■ apply the parking brake

■ select a lower gear

■ repeatedly pump the brake pedal

■ select neutral for a short distance

Answers

 use the endurance brake (retarder)

 select a lower gear

Brake fade occurs due to the brakes overheating. Good forward planning and correct use of the gears to descend long hills, combined with proper use of the endurance brake (retarder), can help eliminate brake fade.

Q. 3.38

Mark one answer

'Brake fade' is a loss of effectiveness of the brakes, caused by their continuous use. When would this be most likely to happen?

■ On a long journey

■ On a long downhill gradient

■ On the approach to hazards

■ On a long uphill gradient

Answer

☑ **On a long downhill gradient**

Continuous use of the brakes will cause them to overheat, and in extreme cases they'll become ineffective. When you're going downhill, the momentum of your vehicle will cause you to gather speed very quickly. Don't underestimate the importance of the correct use of your brakes.

questions   answers

Q. 3.39

Mark two answers

When driving down a steep hill the driver of a large vehicle should

- ⬛ partly apply the parking brake
- ⬛ have changed to a lower gear
- ⬛ use an endurance brake (retarder)
- ⬛ put the gear lever into neutral
- ⬛ use as high a gear as possible

Answers

- ☑ **have changed to a lower gear**
- ☑ **use an endurance brake (retarder)**

Forward planning to deal with hazards is important at all times. When approaching a long hill you should take note of any early warning signs. Reduce your speed and select the appropriate gear in good time. Using an endurance brake (retarder), if fitted, will help control your speed.

Q. 3.40

Mark one answer

Your vehicle has anti-lock brakes. When stopping in an emergency this should allow you to

- ⬛ brake more gently
- ⬛ brake much later
- ⬛ maintain steering control
- ⬛ stop over a long distance

Answer

- ☑ **maintain steering control**

Anti-lock brakes are a driver aid; they shouldn't be used to get you out of trouble. Don't rely on being able to make sudden direction changes when braking.

Q. 3.41

Mark one answer

Your vehicle is fitted with an anti-lock braking system. When braking normally you should press the brake pedal

- ⬛ in the usual way
- ⬛ on and off rapidly
- ⬛ quickly and firmly
- ⬛ later than usual

Answer

- ☑ **in the usual way**

Anti-lock brakes don't remove the need for good driving practices, such as anticipating hazards and assessing road and weather conditions.

questions   answers

Q. 3.42

Mark one answer

Your vehicle has anti-lock brakes. This means that when you brake normally you will

- ☐ not need to alter the way you brake
- ☐ be able to brake much later
- ☐ need to brake more firmly
- ☐ not need to brake so early

Answer

 not need to alter the way you brake

Plan well ahead to enable you to brake normally. You shouldn't rely on anti-lock brakes to make up for deficiencies in your driving.

Q. 3.43

Mark one answer

You would see an escape lane

- ☐ outside a fire station
- ☐ alongside a bus lane
- ☐ before a motorway exit
- ☐ down a steep hill

Answer

 down a steep hill

The sign shows you the direction of the road. A chequered area, usually straight ahead, defines the escape route, which is for use in emergencies such as brake failure.

Q. 3.44

Mark one answer

You would use an escape lane

- ☐ where motorways merge
- ☐ when carrying a dangerous cargo
- ☐ when your brakes have failed
- ☐ for emergency vehicle repairs

Answer

☑ **when your brakes have failed**

On steep downhill sections of road you will sometimes see an escape lane. This is designed to give a 'run-off' area, usually straight ahead, to allow you to stop your vehicle in the event of an emergency.

questions

answers

Q. 3.45

Mark one answer

On steep hills an emergency area to be used only when your brakes have failed is called

■ a buffer lane

■ an escape lane

■ a rumble strip

■ the hard shoulder

Answer

✓ **an escape lane**

Do not park in the area designated as an escape lane; this would put yourself and others in danger if a vehicle needed to use the 'run-off' area in an emergency. Do NOT use it as a viewing area or for taking a rest period. Find an appropriate place to stop where you will not endanger other road users.

Q. 3.46

Mark one answer

What causes brake fade?

■ Continuous use of the brakes

■ Repeated pumping of the brakes

■ Loss of air pressure in the system

■ Badly worn brake pads

Answer

✓ **Continuous use of the brakes**

The continuous use of the brakes on a long downhill gradient can cause them to overheat and could result in them becoming ineffective. You should engage a low gear to enable the engine's braking effect to assist with controlling your speed. This also allows air pressure to be maintained in the tanks.

Q. 3.47

Mark one answer

The main cause of brake fade is

■ the brakes overheating

■ moisture in the air tanks

■ oil on the brake linings

■ the brakes out of adjustment

Answer

✓ **the brakes overheating**

Planning ahead will enable you to select an appropriate gear and use your endurance brake (retarder) to control the speed of your vehicle when travelling downhill. This will help prevent your brakes overheating on long downhill gradients.

Q. 3.48

Mark one answer

An endurance brake (retarder) can be especially useful

- ■ when driving down long hills
- ■ when driving on steep cambers
- ■ to reduce gear changes
- ■ to improve fuel consumption

Answer

☑ **when driving down long hills**

Plan ahead and use your endurance brake (retarder) to help hold your speed in check on long downhill gradients. This can help prevent your brakes from overheating.

Q. 3.49

Mark one answer

You are driving down a long hill and want to avoid the brakes overheating. The vehicle's speed should be controlled by using the

- ■ anti-lock braking system
- ■ footbrake
- ■ secondary brake
- ■ endurance brake (retarder)

Answer

☑ **endurance brake (retarder)**

Systems that assist in controlling a vehicle's speed without using the wheel brakes are called endurance brakes or 'retarders'. Retarders operate by applying resistance via the transmission to the rotation of the vehicle's driven wheels. This may be achieved by

- increased engine braking
- exhaust braking
- transmission-mounted electromagnetic or hydraulic devices.

Q. 3.50

Mark one answer

A system for controlling the vehicle's speed without using the footbrake is

- ■ a secondary brake
- ■ an endurance brake (retarder)
- ■ a differential lock
- ■ an emergency air system

Answer

☑ **an endurance brake (retarder)**

If your vehicle is fitted with any of these devices, you must become familiar with them before you make your journey. Don't be afraid to ask a colleague to show you. Don't risk an accident through ignorance.

questions   answers

Q. 3.51

Mark two answers

An endurance brake (retarder) may work in which TWO of the following ways?

- ☐ Increasing engine braking
- ☐ Using an extra transmission device
- ☐ Sensing wheel speed
- ☐ Using the parking brake
- ☐ Using the secondary brake

Answers

- ☑ **Increasing engine braking**
- ☑ **Using an extra transmission device**

These systems provide a way of controlling a vehicle's speed without using the wheel-mounted brakes. When descending long hills the vehicle speed can be stabilised without using the service brakes.

Q. 3.52

Mark one answer

An endurance brake (retarder), when not combined with the footbrake, should be used

- ☐ on motorways only
- ☐ on long downhill slopes
- ☐ when braking quickly
- ☐ all the time when stopping

Answer

- ☑ **on long downhill slopes**

Mechanically operated endurance brakes (retarders) alter the engine exhaust gas flow. They are usually operated by a floor-mounted switch. Electrically operated endurance brakes (retarders) can be combined with the use of the footbrake. Alternatively, they may be operated via a multi-position dashboard-mounted lever which offers predefined stages of retardation.

Q. 3.53

Mark one answer

An endurance brake (retarder) should be used

- ☐ on motorways only
- ☐ when braking quickly
- ☐ when you stop or park
- ☐ on long downhill slopes

Answer

- ☑ **on long downhill slopes**

Using an endurance brake on long downhill slopes will help control your speed, without using the service brake. Reducing the demand on the service brake helps prevent the brakes overheating and so reduces the risk of brake fade.

questions answers

Q. 3.54

Mark one answer

You are driving down a snow-covered hill. You should take extra care when using an independent endurance brake (retarder) because

■ your brakes could overheat

■ your speed could increase

■ compressed air could escape

■ the rear wheels could lock

Answer

 the rear wheels could lock

Select an appropriate gear in good time and, if your vehicle has a dashboard mounted lever, apply the endurance brake (retarder) in stages. Careful use is necessary when driving on extremely slippery surfaces to avoid braking too much too soon with the result that you lock your drive wheels.

Q. 3.55

Mark two answers

An anti-lock braking system is most useful when you are driving in

■ misty conditions

■ falling snow

■ drifting fog

■ high winds

■ heavy rain

■ bright sunshine

Answers

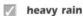 **falling snow**

heavy rain

Do not rely on your anti-lock braking system to keep you out of trouble. It is your responsibility to plan ahead and drive according to the road and weather conditions at all times.

Q. 3.56

Mark one answer

When using an independent endurance brake (retarder) on slippery roads, you should take care to avoid the

■ front wheels spinning

■ rear wheels locking

■ four wheels sliding

■ four wheels spinning

Answer

 rear wheels locking

The endurance brake (retarder) usually operates by applying resistance via the transmission to the rotation of the vehicle's driven wheels.

questions

answers

Q. 3.57

Mark one answer

An electromagnetic endurance brake (retarder) operates by applying resistance to the

- hydraulic lines
- starter motor
- air lines
- transmission

Answer

 transmission

Electromagnetic retarders work by applying a magnetic resistance to the prop shaft which, in turn, slows down the wheels. This allows the service brake to stay cool for optimum performance when required. Retarders are particularly useful when going down long steep hills.

Q. 3.58

Mark one answer

When using an exhaust brake (retarder), extra care must be taken on

- uneven roads
- slippery roads
- downhill gradients
- uphill gradients

Answer

 slippery roads

The exhaust brake (retarder) is usually a mechanical device. It works by either altering the engine exhaust gas flow or amending the valve timing to create a 'compressor' effect. The result is enhanced engine braking which helps to slow your vehicle.

Q. 3.59

Mark two answers

Your vehicle is fully loaded. When dealing with bends all braking should be done

- as close to the bend as possible
- smoothly and in good time
- when driving in a straight line
- as you start to turn the wheel
- when halfway round the bend

Answers

✓ **smoothly and in good time**

✓ **when driving in a straight line**

Braking should always be

- progressive
- correctly timed
- smooth
- sensitive.

When a vehicle changes direction, forces are applied to it and its load. Sudden, excessive or badly timed braking can result in loss of control.

Q. 3.60

Mark one answer

A lorry is overtaking you on a two-lane motorway. It does not have the speed to get past. What should you do?

- Continue at the same speed
- Be prepared to reduce your speed
- Increase your speed and force the lorry to drop back
- Brake hard to allow the other driver to cut in

Answer

☑ **Be prepared to reduce your speed**

Always be prepared to give way to overtaking lorries or buses. Maintaining your speed will only block the motorway to other traffic unnecessarily. Remember, you may find yourself in a similar situation if the limiter on your vehicle does not allow you enough speed to complete an overtaking manoeuvre.

Q. 3.61

Mark one answer

At 50 mph (80 kph) what gap should you leave behind the vehicle in front on a dry, level road?

- One vehicle length
- Two vehicle lengths
- A minimum one-second gap
- A minimum two-second gap

Answer

☑ **A minimum two-second gap**

'Tailgating' – travelling too close to the vehicle in front – is a very dangerous practice. Don't do it.

It's essential that you understand the distance it will take for you to stop in an emergency. Leave at least a two-second gap in good conditions and increase this to four seconds in wet weather.

Q. 3.62

Mark one answer

You are behind a large vehicle. How can you improve your view ahead?

- Stay further back
- Move over to the right
- Move over to the left
- Overtake as soon as you can

Answer

☑ **Stay further back**

Leaving a safety margin will improve your view of the road ahead. Staying back from the vehicle in front will allow you more room to react to hazards that might occur.

Check whether you're too close to another vehicle by using the two-second rule. Pick a fixed object some distance ahead, such as a bridge, sign or lamp-post. As the vehicle in front passes it, begin to say, 'Only a fool breaks the two-second rule'. If you pass the object before you've finished saying it YOU'RE TOO CLOSE. Drop back and try the test again.

questions

answers

Q. 3.63

Mark two answers

You should overtake at night only when

- [ ] you can see well ahead
- [ ] you can do so without cutting in
- [ ] there is an overtaking lane
- [ ] you are outside built-up areas
- [ ] the road is well lit

Answers

- ☑ **you can see well ahead**
- ☑ **you can do so without cutting in**

It is more difficult to judge speed and distance accurately in the dark. Darkness can also hide bends and dips in the road. Plan ahead, and be sure that you have time and space to complete your overtaking safely.

Q. 3.64

Mark one answer

When driving in snow, stopping distances may be increased by up to how many times, compared with a dry road?

- [ ] Two
- [ ] Four
- [ ] Five
- [ ] Ten

Answer

- ☑ **Ten**

In icy or snowy weather your stopping distance can increase by up to ten times. Because snowy weather increases the distance needed to stop, you must look well ahead and leave a good safety margin. It's easy to underestimate the different stopping distances needed in bad weather.

Q. 3.65

Mark one answer

When required to slow down or stop on an icy road you should make sure that

- [ ] braking is gentle and in good time
- [ ] retarders are always used
- [ ] downward gear changes are made
- [ ] the parking brake is used in a rapid on-and-off movement

Answer

- ☑ **braking is gentle and in good time**

When you have to slow down or stop you should avoid harsh, late braking. If you're planning ahead with good anticipation you can reduce the need to brake harshly. Brake gently and in good time to ensure control of your vehicle. This is particularly important on icy or slippery roads.

Q. 3.66

Mark two answers

You are driving a vehicle in icy weather. All braking must be done

■ suddenly

■ by 'pumping' the brakes

■ gently

■ by using the gears first

■ over longer distances

Answers

☑ **gently**

☑ **over longer distances**

All braking should be controlled, in good time and when travelling in a straight line. Avoid braking and turning at the same time. Look well ahead to assess and plan your actions.

Q. 3.67

Mark one answer

After driving through a flood what should you do?

■ Carry out an emergency stop

■ Drive in low gear with the footbrake lightly applied

■ Avoid braking until the brakes are dried out

■ Pump the footbrake when approaching hazards

Answer

☑ **Drive in low gear with the footbrake lightly applied**

If you have to drive through a flood, do so with caution.

Once out of the flood you need to test the brakes on your vehicle to make sure that they are working properly. To do this drive in a low gear with the brakes gently applied. Don't forget to check what's behind you before you do this.

Q. 3.68

Mark one answer

Coasting downhill could seriously affect the correct working of the

■ air brakes

■ cooling system

■ tachograph

■ electrical systems

Answer

☑ **air brakes**

Air brake systems rely on an engine-driven compressor to replenish the air in the brake reservoir tanks. Coasting downhill and relying on the brakes to control your speed could result in loss of sufficient air pressure to operate the brakes effectively, particularly if the compressor is worn.

questions   answers

Q. 3.69

Mark one answer

Your vehicle has power-assisted steering. Its main purpose is to

- [ ] reduce tyre wear
- [ ] assist with braking
- [ ] reduce driver effort
- [ ] assist road holding

Answer

- [✓] **reduce driver effort**

The main purpose of power-assisted steering is to reduce driver effort. When cornering it is possible to oversteer and scrub the front tyres, resulting in excessive wear.

Q. 3.70

Mark three answers

Many vehicles are fitted with power-assisted steering. You need to be aware that this

- [ ] causes less tyre wear
- [ ] prevents you from oversteering
- [ ] makes it easier for you to steer
- [ ] senses when you start to turn the wheel
- [ ] only works at high speeds
- [ ] makes the steering seem light

Answers

- [✓] **makes it easier for you to steer**
- [✓] **senses when you start to turn the wheel**
- [✓] **makes the steering seem light**

Power-assisted steering only operates when the engine is running. If a fault develops, much greater effort is required to turn the steering wheel. Do not attempt to drive a vehicle if you are aware of a fault in the power steering system.

Q. 3.71

Mark two answers

You hit the kerb at speed. You should, as soon as possible, check your vehicle for any damage to the

- [ ] exhaust
- [ ] brakes
- [ ] tyres
- [ ] steering
- [ ] lights

Answers

- [✓] **tyres**
- [✓] **steering**

Hitting the kerb at speed can split the tyre or put the steering and suspension geometry out of alignment. You should have it checked as soon as possible, as a sudden puncture in a front tyre could result in a loss of steering control and a serious accident.

Q. 3.72

Mark one answer

Which of the following is most likely to cause a burst tyre when driving?

- Frequent gear changing in varying conditions
- Running at a constant high speed
- Always operating in cool weather
- Mixing tyres with different tread depth

Answer

✓ **Running at a constant high speed**

Tyres can become very hot and disintegrate under sustained high-speed running. Check for excessive heat when you stop for a break.

Q. 3.73

Mark one answer

When can a 'selective' or 'block' gear change be used?

- To change gear down only
- To change gear up only
- To change gear to a low speed only
- To change gear either up or down

Answer

✓ **To change gear either up or down**

Recognising the opportunities to make selective gear changes can reduce driver effort. Planning ahead will enable you to make the most of any opportunities to put this into practice.

Q. 3.74

Mark one answer

You are driving a vehicle which has a two-speed axle. This

- halves the number of gears
- doubles the number of gears
- engages the diff-lock
- releases the diff-lock

Answer

✓ **doubles the number of gears**

An electrical switch actuates a mechanism in the rear axle which doubles the choice of gear ratios. This can significantly improve the performance of a heavily-laden vehicle.

questions   answers

Q. 3.75

Mark one answer

On a vehicle with automatic transmission you would use 'kickdown' to

- give quicker acceleration
- apply the emergency brakes
- stop more smoothly
- go down a steep hill

Answer

☑ **give quicker acceleration**

Dependent upon road speed, depressing the accelerator pedal firmly to the floor will activate a switch which allows the gearbox to select a lower gear for improved acceleration.

Q. 3.76

Mark one answer

You are driving a modern vehicle. You notice the steering feels heavy. What is the most likely cause?

- Faulty power steering
- An icy road
- A burst rear tyre
- A wet road

Answer

☑ **Faulty power steering**

Many large vehicles are fitted with power-assisted steering. Any fault should be investigated and repaired as soon as possible.

Q. 3.77

Mark one answer

Your vehicle suffers a tyre blow-out. What is likely to create a hazard for other road users?

- Scattered debris
- Skid marks
- Suspension failure
- Axle damage

Answer

☑ **Scattered debris**

When a tyre explodes, fragments are thrown over a wide area. This can create a serious hazard for other drivers. Always check your tyre pressures and look for cuts or damage to the tyres. Frequent checks and proper maintenance can prevent a blow-out.

questions   answers

Q. 3.78 🚌

Mark one answer

You are about to set off in your bus in very frosty weather. You notice a lack of brake air pressure. What is the likely cause of this?

■ Engine temperature too low

■ Weak engine anti-freeze mixture

■ Brake pedal needs adjustment

■ Frozen moisture in the storage tanks

Answer

☑ **Frozen moisture in the storage tanks**

Air braking systems use air from the atmosphere which contains moisture. All air braking systems are fitted with manual or automatic drain valves. Ensure the air tanks are drained daily to help prevent the system freezing in cold weather.

Q. 3.79 🚌

Mark one answer

What could prevent the build-up of brake air pressure on a bus in frosty weather?

■ Lack of anti-freeze in storage tanks

■ Insufficient lagging of tanks and pipes

■ Low engine revolutions

■ Moisture freezing in the system

Answer

☑ **Moisture freezing in the system**

When the weather is frosty, any moisture in the storage tanks may freeze and prevent pressure building up properly.

Q. 3.80 🚌

Mark one answer

An anti-lock braking system warning light fitted to a bus should go out

■ when the brakes are used for the first time

■ immediately after the anti-lock braking system comes into operation

■ when road speed is 10 kph (6 mph) or more

■ when the secondary braking system is used

Answer

☑ **when road speed is 10 kph (6 mph) or more**

Every vehicle fitted with anti-lock brakes must have a warning light fitted in the cab of the vehicle. Check this as part of your routine. Driving with defective anti-lock brakes may constitute an offence.

Anti-lock warnings may differ between manufacturers, but all types should come on with the ignition and should go out when the vehicle reaches 6 mph (10 kph). Make yourself familiar with the warnings and gauges when you're driving a vehicle for the first time and don't carry on any further if the light fails to go out. The safety of your passengers and all other road users will be at risk.

questions

answers

Q. 3.81

Mark one answer

The MOST powerful brake on a bus is normally the

- secondary brake
- anti-lock braking system
- endurance brake (retarder)
- service brake

Answer

☑ **service brake**

The most powerful and effective brakes on the vehicle are the service brakes, and these should be used in normal circumstances. Well-maintained brakes should apply an even pressure to all the wheels, providing an efficient, controlled stop.

Q. 3.82

Mark one answer

When making a short stop, facing uphill, you should

- hold the vehicle on the clutch
- hold the vehicle on the footbrake
- select neutral and apply the parking brake
- apply the parking brake after stopping

Answer

☑ **apply the parking brake after stopping**

If you have to make a stop on an uphill gradient, wait until the vehicle has come to a stop before applying the parking brake, just as you would normally.

Q. 3.83

Mark one answer

You are about to move off. Your vehicle has automatic transmission. Before you select drive (D) you must

- put your foot on the footbrake
- signal to move off
- alter your seat position
- adjust your mirrors

Answer

☑ **put your foot on the footbrake**

It is important to apply the footbrake before you engage 'D' or drive so your vehicle does not creep forward or roll back out of control when you are about to move away. This can be dangerous, for example if there's another road user close behind.

Q. 3.84 🚌

Mark three answers

Which THREE of the following are advantages of progressive braking when driving a bus?

- Passenger safety and comfort
- Increased air brake pressure
- Lower fuel consumption
- Reduced tyre wear
- Avoidance of 'brake fade'

Answers

- ☑ **Passenger safety and comfort**
- ☑ **Lower fuel consumption**
- ☑ **Reduced tyre wear**

As the driver of a bus, the safety and comfort of the passengers is your first priority. If you have the correct attitude when you're driving, your passengers will be assured of a comfortable and pleasant journey.

Good forward planning and anticipation will enable you to avoid harsh braking and late, sharp steering.

Badly driven vehicles cost more to run and maintain.

Q. 3.85 🚌

Mark one answer

The bus you are driving is fitted with an automatic gearbox. When would you use kickdown?

- When stopping in an emergency
- When changing to a higher gear
- When driving at slow speed
- When needing brisk acceleration

Answer

- ☑ **When needing brisk acceleration**

The kickdown facility on an automatic gearbox allows a lower gear to be engaged to allow rapid acceleration (for example, when overtaking). This is achieved by pressing the accelerator to the floor.

Q. 3.86 🚌

Mark one answer

Your coach is fully laden. You notice the steering feels heavy. What is the most likely reason?

- An icy road
- A burst rear tyre
- Faulty power steering
- Too many passengers

Answer

- ☑ **Faulty power steering**

An engine-driven oil pump operates hydraulic rams which assist the movement of steering components. This helps you by reducing the effort required to steer a large vehicle.

The driver

This section looks at the driver and the importance of alertness and attention when you're driving.

The questions will ask you about

- **Consideration**

  considering other road users; being positive and treating them as you would wish to be treated

- **Courtesy**

  not using the size of your vehicle to intimidate other road users

- **Priority**

  being aware that others break the rules or may not understand the position you need to take on the road

- **Vehicle safety equipment**

  correct use of vehicle safety equipment including the use of seat belts and head restraints

- **Tiredness**

  not driving when you are tired, even if you are within your driver's hours

- **Drugs and alcohol**

  being aware of changes in driving behaviour due to alcohol or drugs.

questions   answers

Q. 4.1

Mark one answer

You are approaching a green traffic light and going straight on. Traffic in front of you is stopped and queuing just beyond the junction. What should you do?

- Only go if your vehicle will clear the junction
- Drive slowly across the junction
- Maintain your speed and sound your horn
- Stop in the junction until the traffic clears

Answer

☑ **Only go if your vehicle will clear the junction**

Look well ahead and plan your approach to all junctions. Even though the lights are on green, don't go forward if queuing traffic will cause you to block the junction. Be aware of the length of your vehicle and any inconvenience it may cause other road users.

Q. 4.2

Mark one answer

In rural areas why should you avoid parking on the grass verge?

- When moving off you may leave mud on the road
- There may be sheep or cattle grazing in the area
- You will be blocking an entrance to premises or a driveway
- Your vehicle will probably be blown over by high winds

Answer

☑ **When moving off you may leave mud on the road**

Parking on the grass verge in rural areas should be avoided. The weight of your vehicle may cause damage to the verge and as you drive away you might leave mud and debris on the road.

Q. 4.3

Mark one answer

You are on a wet level road. At 50 mph what gap should you leave from the vehicle in front?

- One second minimum
- Two seconds minimum
- Three seconds minimum
- Four seconds minimum

Answer

☑ **Four seconds minimum**

Stopping distances can at least double on wet roads. Always drive in accordance with the road and weather conditions.

questions

answers

Q. 4.4

Mark one answer

Seat belts are fitted to your lorry. The wearing of them is

- [ ] not advisable
- [ ] advisable
- [ ] required by law
- [ ] not required by law

Answer

- [✓] **required by law**

If seat belts are fitted in your lorry you must wear them unless you are exempt.

Q. 4.5

Mark one answer

You are waiting to turn right in this box van. Just before turning you should

- [ ] wave the pedestrian across
- [ ] check your left mirror and blind spot
- [ ] wave out the green car (arrowed)
- [ ] check your right mirror and blind spot

Answer

- [✓] **check your right mirror and blind spot**

Always make a final check in your mirrors and blind spots before you turn. Another driver or a motorcyclist may have committed themselves to overtaking traffic behind you before they realised you intended to turn.

Q. 4.6

Mark two answers

Extra skills are needed when driving at night. The MAIN problems you will have to deal with are

- [ ] headlight dazzle
- [ ] other drivers speeding
- [ ] cold weather conditions
- [ ] dazzle from shop windows
- [ ] becoming tired

Answers

- [✓] **headlight dazzle**
- [✓] **becoming tired**

You must concentrate even harder than normal when driving at night. The slightest distraction or break in your concentration could result in an accident.

Q. 4.7

Mark one answer

You are driving on a motorway. A moving lorry just ahead of you switches on its hazard warning lights. What does this mean?

■ There are speed cameras ahead

■ The lorry is about to change lanes

■ The lorry is leaving the motorway

■ Traffic further ahead may be stopping

Answer

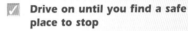 **Traffic further ahead may be stopping**

The driver ahead has spotted a hazard which you may not be able to see yet. Slow down and be ready to stop if necessary.

Q. 4.8

Mark one answer

You are driving in busy traffic. You lose your way. What should you do?

■ Stop at traffic lights and ask pedestrians

■ Shout to other drivers to ask them the way

■ Drive on until you find a safe place to stop

■ Check a map as you keep moving with the traffic

Answer

✓ **Drive on until you find a safe place to stop**

Driving in busy traffic needs 100% concentration. If you become lost, find a safe place to stop before checking a map or asking directions. Don't risk losing concentration by glancing at a map while driving, even if you are in stop-start traffic.

Q. 4.9

Mark three answers

You should show extra consideration for pedestrians when driving past

■ mobile shops

■ open moorland

■ shopping areas

■ ice cream vans

■ wooded areas

■ suspension bridges

Answer

✓ **mobile shops**

✓ **shopping areas**

✓ **ice cream vans**

In all three of these situations, pedestrians may suddenly step out into the road. Vehicles such as mobile shops and ice cream vans require extra care, as there may be children hidden from view who could suddenly run into your path. Always keep your speed down when approaching these situations.

questions

answers

Q. 4.10

Mark three answers

Which of the following are most likely to cause danger to a group of horse riders?

- Powerful brake lights
- Size of your vehicle
- Noise of your vehicle
- The hiss of air brakes
- Leaving plenty of room
- Reacting in good time

Answers

☑ **Size of your vehicle**

☑ **Noise of your vehicle**

☑ **The hiss of air brakes**

The size of your vehicle can be intimidating, as well as reducing the amount of room left for other road users. Any noise can easily startle horses. You should take care to leave as much room as you can for riders. Keep the noise to a minimum by gentle use of the brakes and, if necessary, stopping and turning your engine off.

Q. 4.11

Mark three answers

Which of these should you do when passing sheep on a road?

- Pass quickly and quietly
- Tap your horn once
- Drive very slowly
- Allow plenty of room
- Be ready to stop

Answers

☑ **Drive very slowly**

☑ **Allow plenty of room**

☑ **Be ready to stop**

Animals can be very unpredictable. You should give them as much room as you can, keep speed and noise down to a minimum to avoid panicking them, and always be ready to stop if necessary.

Q. 4.12

Mark one answer

At a toucan crossing you should look out for pedestrians and

- horse riders
- cyclists
- motorcyclists
- trams

Answer

☑ **cyclists**

A toucan crossing is signal-controlled, but unlike a pelican crossing it does not have a flashing amber light in the sequence. Cyclists and pedestrians share the crossing and get the green signal together. Cyclists are permitted to ride across. The signals are push-button operated.

Q. 4.13

Mark one answer

On which of the following pedestrian crossings can a cyclist ride across, without dismounting, when pedestrians are crossing over?

■ Toucan

■ Pelican

■ Puffin

■ Zebra

Answer

 Toucan

Toucans are shared crossings, where cyclists may ride across the road alongside pedestrians. Look out for them where you see signs and markings for cycle tracks.

Q. 4.14

Mark one answer

Your nearside mirror is most likely to endanger pedestrians when

■ using a crawler lane

■ braking hard on a bend

■ driving close to the kerb

■ passing a traffic sign

Answer

 driving close to the kerb

You must be aware that a nearside mirror could strike the head of a pedestrian when you drive close to the kerb. This is a particular hazard in built-up areas and congested shopping centres.

Q. 4.15

Mark one answer

You should use the 'two-second rule'

■ before restarting the engine after it has stalled

■ to keep a safe distance from the vehicle in front

■ before using the 'Mirror - Signal - Manoeuvre' routine

■ when emerging on wet roads

Answer

 to keep a safe distance from the vehicle in front

To measure this, choose a fixed reference point, such as a bridge, sign or tree. When the vehicle ahead passes the object, say to yourself 'Only a fool breaks the two-second rule.' If you reach the object before you finish saying this you're TOO CLOSE.

questions answers

Q. 4.16

Mark one answer

Which of the following can prevent you from obtaining a bus or lorry licence?

- [ ] heart disorders
- [ ] dyslexia
- [ ] skin problems
- [ ] stomach problems

Answer

- [x] **heart disorders**

A number of reasons can prevent you from obtaining, or keeping, a bus or lorry licence. If you develop any serious illness or disability that is likely to last more than three months, and which could affect your driving, you must tell the DVLA Drivers' Medical Group at Swansea immediately. Partial blindness and mental disorders can also prevent you from obtaining a bus or lorry licence.

Q. 4.17

Mark three answers

Before starting your engine your seat should be adjusted for

- [ ] height
- [ ] back support
- [ ] seat belt tension
- [ ] air ventilation
- [ ] distance from the controls
- [ ] leaving the cab

Answers

- [x] **height**
- [x] **back support**
- [x] **distance from the controls**

Being seated properly is very important when driving long distances. A poor driving position can quickly cause fatigue.

Q. 4.18

Mark one answer

A properly adjusted head restraint will

- [ ] make you more comfortable
- [ ] help you to avoid neck injury
- [ ] help you to relax
- [ ] help you to maintain your driving position

Answer

- [x] **help you to avoid neck injury**

The restraint should be adjusted so that it gives maximum protection to the head, in the event of a rear end collision.

Q. 4.19

Mark one answer

What could reduce the risk of neck injury in a collision?

- An air-sprung seat
- Anti-lock brakes
- A collapsible steering wheel
- A properly adjusted head restraint

Answer

 A properly adjusted head restraint

Head restraints can help to reduce the risk of neck injury if you're in a collision. They must be properly adjusted. Make sure they aren't positioned too low because in an accident this could cause damage to the neck.

Q. 4.20

Mark one answer

You may remove your seat belt when carrying out a manoeuvre that involves

- reversing
- a hill start
- an emergency stop
- driving slowly

Answer

☑ **reversing**

Don't forget to put your seat belt back on when you've finished reversing.

Q. 4.21

Mark one answer

You are driving along this road. The red van cuts in close in front of you. What should you do?

- Accelerate to get closer to the red van
- Give a long blast on the horn
- Drop back to leave the correct separation distance
- Flash your headlights several times

Answer

☑ **Drop back to leave the correct separation distance**

There are times when other drivers make incorrect or ill-judged decisions. Try to stay calm and don't retaliate or react aggressively. Always consider the safety of other road users, any passengers and yourself.

questions

answers

Q. 4.22

Mark two answers

While driving you approach a large puddle that is close to the left-hand kerb. Pedestrians are close to the water. You should

- ☐ ignore the puddle
- ☐ brake suddenly and sound your horn
- ☐ slow down before the puddle
- ☐ try to avoid splashing the pedestrians
- ☐ wave at the pedestrians to keep back

Answers

- ☑ **slow down before the puddle**
- ☑ **try to avoid splashing the pedestrians**

The effect of your vehicle driving through a puddle will be to throw water onto the pavement. If there are pedestrians close by they could be splashed with the water. Be considerate and, if it's safe to do so, avoid driving through it.

Q. 4.23

Mark one answer

A long, heavily laden lorry is taking a long time to overtake you. What should you do?

- ☐ Speed up
- ☐ Slow down
- ☐ Hold your speed
- ☐ Change direction

Answer

- ☑ **Slow down**

A long lorry with a heavy load will need more time to pass you than a car. It won't be able to accelerate to pass you quickly, especially on an uphill stretch of road. Be considerate to the lorry driver – ease off the accelerator and allow the lorry to pass.

Q. 4.24

Mark one answer

You are driving a slow-moving vehicle on a narrow road. When traffic wishes to overtake you should

- ☐ take no action
- ☐ put your hazard warning lights on
- ☐ stop immediately and wave them on
- ☐ pull in safely as soon as you can do so

Answer

- ☑ **pull in safely as soon as you can do so**

Try not to hold up a queue of traffic. This might lead to other road users becoming impatient. If you're driving a slow-moving vehicle and the road is narrow, look out for a safe place to pull in.

Q. 4.25

Mark one answer

You are driving a slow-moving vehicle on a narrow winding road. In order to let other vehicles overtake you should

■ wave to them to pass

■ pull in when you can

■ show a left turn signal

■ keep left and hold your speed

Answer

 pull in when you can

Don't frustrate other road users by driving for long distances with a queue of traffic behind you. This could cause them to lose concentration or make ill-judged decisions.

Q. 4.26

Mark one answer

What should you use your horn for?

■ To alert others to your presence

■ To allow you right of way

■ To greet other road users

■ To signal your annoyance

Answer

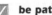 **To alert others to your presence**

Don't use it to greet others, show impatience or to give or claim priority.

Your horn must not be used between 11.30 pm and 7 am in a built-up area, or when your vehicle is stationary, unless another vehicle poses a danger.

Q. 4.27

Mark two answers

You are following a car driven by a learner driver. You cannot overtake it. You should

■ flash your lights so that the driver sees you

■ be patient and stay well behind

■ switch your hazard lights on and stay well behind

■ be ready for mistakes made by the driver

■ drive along the centre line of the road

Answers

 be patient and stay well behind

 be ready for mistakes made by the driver

Learner drivers are often nervous. If you stay well back this will reduce the risk of accidents occurring if mistakes are made by the learner driver. Remember, you were once in that situation yourself.

questions
answers

Q. 4.28

Mark one answer

You are signalled to stop by a police car. You should

■ brake harshly to a stop

■ drive on until you reach a side road

■ pull up on the left when it is safe to

■ stop immediately wherever you are

Answer

☑ **pull up on the left when it is safe to**

If a police car signals for you to stop you should always find a safe place on the left and pull over.

Q. 4.29

Mark one answer

A police car is following you. The police would like you to stop. They will do this by flashing their headlights and

■ signalling with the right indicator

■ signalling with the left indicator

■ switching their hazard flashers on

■ switching their rear fog lights on

Answer

☑ **signalling with the left indicator**

Indicating to the left shows that the police want you to pull in. You should find a safe place to stop before doing so.

Q. 4.30

Mark one answer

Large vehicles have many blind spots. What does 'blind spot' mean?

■ An area of road covered by your right-hand mirror

■ An area of road covered by your left-hand mirror

■ An area of road that cannot be seen in your mirrors

■ An area of road that is not lit by your headlights

Answer

☑ **An area of road that cannot be seen in your mirrors**

Blind spots can occur when bodywork restricts your view through the mirrors. You should be aware that different types of vehicles have different blind spots.

questions   answers

Q. 4.31

Mark one answer

You are driving a vehicle fitted with a hand-held telephone. To answer it you should

- find a safe place to stop
- reduce your speed to less than 30 mph
- steer your vehicle with one hand
- be very careful when dealing with junctions

Answer

☑ **find a safe place to stop**

Telephone calls can distract you, which means that you are not in proper control of your vehicle. You must have full control of your vehicle at all times. If you need to use any telecommunications equipment when driving, find a safe place to stop first.

Q. 4.32

Mark one answer

You have a mobile telephone fitted in your vehicle. It should only be used when you are

- stopped in a safe place
- travelling slowly
- on a motorway
- in light traffic

Answer

☑ **stopped in a safe place**

Once you have stopped your vehicle, you can concentrate on your telephone call or message. If you use your phone while driving, you do not have control of your vehicle and could be distracted, causing it to be involved in an accident.

Q. 4.33

Mark one answer

A pelican crossing that crosses the road in a STRAIGHT line and has a central island must be treated as

- one crossing in daylight only
- one complete crossing
- two separate crossings
- two crossings during darkness

Answer

☑ **one complete crossing**

The lights that control the crossing show to both directions of traffic. If a pedestrian from either side is still crossing when the amber light is flashing, you must wait until they have finished crossing before moving off.

questions answers

Q. 4.34

Mark one answer

At a pelican crossing the flashing amber light means you should

- stop, if you can do so safely
- give way to pedestrians already on the crossing
- stop and wait for the green light
- give way to pedestrians waiting to cross

Answer

☑ **give way to pedestrians already on the crossing**

Pelican crossings are light-controlled crossings where pedestrians use push-button controls to change the signals. Pelican crossings have no red-and-amber stage before green. Instead, they have a flashing amber light, which means you must give way to pedestrians on the crossing. If it's clear, you may proceed with caution.

Q. 4.35

Mark one answer

At a zebra crossing you should

- rev your engine to encourage pedestrians to cross quickly
- park only on the zigzag lines on the left
- always leave it clear in traffic queues
- wave pedestrians to cross if you intend to wait for them

Answer

☑ **always leave it clear in traffic queues**

Look well ahead down the line of traffic so that you don't stop on the crossing and block it. Leave it clear so that pedestrians can cross safely.

Q. 4.36

Mark one answer

In fast traffic a two-second gap may be enough only when conditions are

- dry
- wet
- damp
- foggy

Answer

☑ **dry**

You must be aware that when the weather is bad, you will have to keep a greater distance from the vehicle in front because it will take you further to stop. In wet weather it will take twice as far; in icy weather this could increase to ten times the distance.

Q. 4.37

Mark one answer

At puffin crossings which light will not show to a driver?

- Flashing amber
- Red
- Steady amber
- Green

Answer

☑ **Flashing amber**

A flashing amber light is shown at pelican crossings, but not at puffin crossings. These are controlled electronically and automatically detect when pedestrians are on the crossing. The red phase for traffic is shortened or lengthened according to the position of the pedestrians.

Q. 4.38

Mark one answer

You are approaching a red light at a puffin crossing. Pedestrians are on the crossing. The red light will stay on until

- you start to edge forward onto the crossing
- the pedestrians have reached a safe position
- the pedestrians are clear of the front of your vehicle
- a driver from the opposite direction reaches the crossing

Answer

☑ **the pedestrians have reached a safe position**

The electronic device will automatically detect that the pedestrians have reached a safe position. Don't proceed until the green light shows and it's safe to do so.

Q. 4.39

Mark one answer

Following a large goods vehicle too closely is dangerous because

- your field of vision is seriously reduced
- slipstreaming will reduce wind effect
- your engine will overheat
- your brakes need a constant cooling effect

Answer

☑ **your field of vision is seriously reduced**

Staying back will increase your view of the road ahead. This will help you to see any hazards that might occur and allow you more time to react.

questions   answers

Q. 4.40

Mark one answer

You are following a vehicle on a wet road. You should leave a time gap of at least

- [ ] one second
- [ ] two seconds
- [ ] three seconds
- [ ] four seconds

Answer

✓ **four seconds**

Wet roads will increase the time it will take you to stop. Four seconds is the MINIMUM gap you should leave on wet roads, this is double the gap you should normally keep from the vehicle in front on good, dry roads.

Q. 4.41

Mark one answer

You are overtaking a lorry. You see the driver flash the headlights. What should you do?

- [ ] Move back to the left when it is safe to do so
- [ ] Indicate left and move back slowly
- [ ] Act immediately on the other driver's signal
- [ ] Flash your rear lights on and off twice

Answer

✓ **Move back to the left when it is safe to do so**

Never presume what someone means when they flash their headlights. Wait until it is safe to complete your manoeuvre.

Q. 4.42

Mark one answer

A coach is overtaking you. When it is safe for the coach to move back to the left you should

- [ ] do nothing and let the driver decide
- [ ] switch your sidelights on and off
- [ ] flash your headlights once
- [ ] flash your headlights twice

Answer

✓ **do nothing and let the driver decide**

Allow the coach driver to make the decision to complete the manoeuvre.

Q. 4.43

Mark three answers

Which THREE of the following emergency vehicles will use blue flashing beacons?

- ■ Motorway maintenance
- ■ Bomb disposal team
- ■ Blood transfusion
- ■ Police vehicle
- ■ Breakdown recovery vehicle

Answers

- ☑ **Bomb disposal team**
- ☑ **Blood transfusion**
- ☑ **Police vehicle**

Try to move out of the way of emergency vehicles with blue flashing beacons. Do so safely and without delay.

Q. 4.44

Mark one answer

When being followed by an ambulance showing a flashing blue beacon you should

- ■ pull over as soon as safely possible to let it pass
- ■ accelerate hard to get away from it
- ■ ignore it if possible, let it pass if forced to
- ■ brake harshly and immediately stop in the road

Answer

- ☑ **pull over as soon as safely possible to let it pass**

Pull over safely in a place where the ambulance can pass you. Check that there are no bollards or obstructions in the road that will prevent it doing so.

Q. 4.45

Mark one answer

You see a car showing a flashing green beacon. Should you give way to it?

- ■ Yes, it is a doctor going to an emergency
- ■ Yes, it is a fire crew support vehicle
- ■ No, it is a slow-moving vehicle
- ■ No, it is a breakdown vehicle

Answer

- ☑ **Yes, it is a doctor going to an emergency**

Give way by pulling over and letting the vehicle pass, but don't just stop suddenly. Choose a safe place as soon as you can to let the doctor's car pass safely.

questions answers

Q. 4.46

Mark one answer

What type of emergency vehicle is fitted with a green flashing beacon?

- Fire engine
- Road gritter
- Ambulance
- Doctor's car

Answer

 Doctor's car

A green flashing light on a vehicle means the driver or passenger is a doctor on an emergency call. Give way to them if it's safe to do so. Be aware that the vehicle may be travelling quickly or may stop suddenly.

Q. 4.47

Mark one answer

A bus is stopped at a bus stop ahead of you. Its right-hand indicator is flashing. You should

- flash your headlights and slow down
- slow down and give way if it is safe to do so
- sound your horn and keep going
- slow down and then sound your horn

Answer

slow down and give way if it is safe to do so

Give way to buses whenever you can do so safely, especially when they signal to pull away from bus stops. Look out for people leaving the bus and crossing the road without looking. They may run out from behind the bus. Also look out for people running to catch a bus who may be more concerned about catching it than watching for traffic.

questions   answers

Q. 4.48

Mark one answer

A bus lane on your left shows no times of operation. This means it is

- not in operation at all
- only in operation at peak times
- in operation 24 hours a day
- only in operation in daylight hours

Answer

☑ **in operation 24 hours a day**

You should always be aware of the times when bus lanes are operating. If there is no plate indicating any times of operation, this means that the bus lane operates all the time.

Q. 4.49

Mark one answer

At a puffin crossing what colour follows the green signal?

- Steady red
- Flashing amber
- Steady amber
- Flashing green

Answer

☑ **Steady amber**

Puffin crossings have infra-red sensors which detect when pedestrians are crossing and hold the red traffic signal until the crossing is clear. This means there is no flashing amber phase as there is with a pelican crossing.

Q. 4.50

Mark one answer

You stop for pedestrians waiting to cross at a zebra crossing. They do not start to cross. What should you do?

- Be patient and wait
- Sound your horn
- Drive on
- Wave them to cross

Answer

☑ **Be patient and wait**

If you stop for pedestrians and they don't start to cross, don't wave them across or sound your horn. This could be dangerous if an approaching vehicle is not aware of them. The driver may not have seen or heard your signal and it would be very dangerous for the pedestrians to start to cross.

questions answers

Q. 4.51

Mark one answer

You should beckon pedestrians to cross the road at

- [ ] pedestrian crossings
- [ ] no time
- [ ] junctions
- [ ] school crossings

Answer

✓ **no time**

Beckoning pedestrians to cross can be dangerous. Other road users may not have seen your signal and you might encourage the pedestrians in danger.

Q. 4.52

Mark one answer

You should never wave people across at pedestrian crossings because

- [ ] there may be another vehicle coming
- [ ] they may not be looking
- [ ] it is safer for you to carry on
- [ ] they may not be ready to cross

Answer

✓ **there may be another vehicle coming**

If it's safe you should always stop for pedestrians waiting at pedestrian crossings. Don't wave them to cross the road since another driver may not

- have seen them
- have seen your signal
- be able to stop safely.

Q. 4.53

Mark three answers

You are driving close to the kerb in a busy shopping area. What dangers should you be most aware of?

- [ ] Traffic lights suddenly changing to green
- [ ] The amount of fuel being used when driving slowly
- [ ] Pedestrians stepping off the edge of the pavement
- [ ] The nearside mirror striking the heads of pedestrians
- [ ] Cyclists moving up the left side of your vehicle

Answers

✓ **Pedestrians stepping off the edge of the pavement**

✓ **The nearside mirror striking the heads of pedestrians**

✓ **Cyclists moving up the left side of your vehicle**

When you need to drive close to the kerb, be aware of the dangers.

- Pedestrians may step off the kerb.
- The nearside mirror may be at a pedestrian's head height.
- Cyclists may be tempted to pass you on your left if you are driving slowly in congested conditions.

questions   answers

Q. 4.54

Mark one answer

You have stopped for an elderly pedestrian who is slowly crossing the road. Traffic behind you is being held up. What should you do?

- ■ Edge slowly forward and make them hurry
- ■ Remain where you are and allow them to cross in their own time
- ■ Steer slowly around them to ease the build up of traffic
- ■ Get out of your vehicle and wave them across

Answer

☑ **Remain where you are and allow them to cross in their own time**

Elderly pedestrians can be hesitant and may move slowly when crossing the road. Also, their awareness of traffic may be limited. Be patient and show courtesy and understanding.

Q. 4.55

Mark three answers

You should NOT park your vehicle or trailer

- ■ at an overnight service area
- ■ near the brow of a hill
- ■ opposite a traffic island
- ■ in front of an entrance to a property
- ■ in a factory yard

Answers

☑ **near the brow of a hill**

☑ **opposite a traffic island**

☑ **in front of an entrance to a property**

Do not park where you would endanger or inconvenience others. If your choice of parking place obstructs drivers, riders or pedestrians, move to a more suitable area.

Q. 4.56

Mark two answers

Mirrors fitted to your vehicle MUST be

- ■ clean
- ■ properly adjusted
- ■ convex
- ■ tinted
- ■ concave

Answers

☑ **clean**

☑ **properly adjusted**

It is important to know what is happening behind as well as ahead. Your mirrors must be clean and properly adjusted.

questions   answers

Q. 4.57

Mark one answer

You are driving a slow moving vehicle along a narrow road. You should let other vehicles overtake by

- maintaining a steady speed
- waving them past
- giving a left turn signal
- pulling in when you can

Answer

☑ **pulling in when you can**

Drivers queuing behind you may make hasty or ill-judged decisions in an effort to overtake. If you see a queue of traffic building up behind give way as soon as you can do so safely by pulling in to the left.

Q. 4.58

Mark one answer

As you drive past a group of school children standing close to the kerb you should

- check your offside mirror
- check your nearside mirror
- switch on your headlights
- switch on your hazard lights

Answer

☑ **check your nearside mirror**

On approach you should consider if you need to use the horn as a warning (this may not be appropriate where animals are around). Always check your nearside mirror as you pass potential hazards on the left.

Q. 4.59

Mark one answer

You are driving at the legal speed limit. A vehicle comes up quickly behind, flashing its headlights. You should

- accelerate to maintain a gap behind you
- touch the brake pedal sharply to show your brake lights
- maintain your speed and prevent the vehicle from overtaking
- allow the vehicle to overtake

Answer

☑ **allow the vehicle to overtake**

Don't enforce the speed limit by blocking another vehicle's progress. This is likely to cause the other driver to become more frustrated. Slow down or move over when it is safe to do so and allow the other vehicle to pass.

questions

answers

Q. 4.60

Mark one answer

You are approaching a pelican crossing. The amber light is flashing. You MUST

- ☐ give way to pedestrians who are crossing
- ☐ encourage pedestrians to cross
- ☐ not move until the green light appears
- ☐ stop even if the crossing is clear

Answer

☑ **give way to pedestrians who are crossing**

When the amber light is flashing, you must give way to any pedestrians on the crossing.

DON'T encourage pedestrians to cross by waving or flashing your headlights; they or other road users may misunderstand your signal.

DON'T rev your engine impatiently or edge forward.

Q. 4.61

Mark one answer

A vehicle pulls out in front of you at a junction. What should you do?

- ☐ Swerve past it and sound your horn
- ☐ Flash your headlights and drive up close behind
- ☐ Slow down and be ready to stop
- ☐ Accelerate past it immediately

Answer

☑ **Slow down and be ready to stop**

Try to be ready for the unexpected. Plan ahead and learn to anticipate hazards. You'll then give yourself more time to react to any problems that might occur. Be tolerant of other road users who don't behave correctly.

Q. 4.62

Mark one answer

Which road users are more vulnerable at night in built up areas?

- ☐ Runners
- ☐ Drivers of black taxi cabs
- ☐ Double-deck vehicle drivers
- ☐ Ambulance drivers

Answer

☑ **Runners**

Take extra care. Runners may be difficult to see in the dark.

questions

answers

Q. 4.63

Mark one answer

Which road users are more vulnerable at night in built up areas?

- Drivers of black taxi cabs
- Pedestrians in dark clothing
- Double-deck vehicle drivers
- Ambulance drivers

Answer

 Pedestrians in dark clothing

Look out for pedestrians wearing dark clothing.

Q. 4.64

Mark one answer

Which road users are more vulnerable at night in built up areas?

- Drivers of black taxi cabs
- Double deck vehicle drivers
- Cyclists
- Ambulance drivers

Answer

✓ **Cyclists**

Look out for cyclists who may not have lights on.

Q. 4.65

Mark one answer

You are driving a vehicle on a motorway. A front tyre bursts. You should

- loosen your grip on the steering wheel
- brake firmly to a stop
- hold the steering wheel firmly
- drive to the next service area

Answer

✓ **hold the steering wheel firmly**

A front wheel blow-out can be a heart-stopping moment. Keep calm and resist the temptation to brake hard or swerve. Allow the vehicle to slow down gradually. Be aware of anything on your left. Try to get the vehicle onto the hard shoulder, as far to the left as possible. Switch on your hazard warning lights.

questions answers

Q. 4.66

Mark one answer

Your mobile phone rings while you are driving. You should

- stop immediately
- answer it immediately
- pull up in a suitable place
- pull up at the nearest kerb

Answer

☑ **pull up in a suitable place**

Never risk losing control of your vehicle through any distractions to your driving. It is not worth taking the risk of endangering other road users. Make sure that you pull up in a place that does not obstruct other road users. The safest option of all is to use a message service. This enables you to complete your journey without interruptions and you can catch up with your calls when you take your rest breaks.

Q. 4.67

Mark one answer

NI EXEMPT

You break down on a motorway. You need to call for help. Why may it be better to use an emergency roadside telephone rather than a mobile phone?

- It connects you to a local garage
- Using a mobile phone will distract other drivers
- It allows easy location by the emergency services
- Mobile phones do not work on motorways

Answer

☑ **It allows easy location by the emergency services**

On a motorway it is best to use a roadside emergency telephone so that the emergency services are able to locate you easily.

Q. 4.68

Mark one answer

On the motorway the hard shoulder should be used

- to answer a mobile phone
- when an emergency arises
- for a short rest when tired
- to check a road atlas

Answer

☑ **when an emergency arises**

Pull onto the hard shoulder and use the emergency telephone to report your problem. The telephone connects you to police control, who will put you through to an emergency breakdown service. Never cross the carriageway or a slip road to use a telephone on the other side.

THE DRIVER

questions

Q. 4.69

Mark one answer

You are allowed to stop on a motorway when you

- ☐ need to walk and get fresh air
- ☐ wish to pick up hitch hikers
- ☐ are told to do so by flashing red lights
- ☐ need to use a mobile phone

Answer

☑ **are told to do so by flashing red lights**

If any of the other lanes show a green arrow you may move into that lane and continue if it is safe to do so. If there are red lights above every lane you must stop.

Q. 4.70

Mark one answer

You are most likely to lose concentration when driving if you

- ☐ use a mobile phone
- ☐ switch on the windscreen wipers
- ☐ switch on the heated rear window
- ☐ look at the door mirrors

Answer

☑ **use a mobile phone**

Using a mobile phone will distract you from your driving to the point where you are paying more attention to the phone call or message than you are to your driving.

Q. 4.71

Mark one answer

You should not use a mobile phone whilst driving

- ☐ until you are satisfied that no other traffic is near
- ☐ unless you are able to drive one handed
- ☐ because it might distract your attention from the road ahead
- ☐ because reception is poor when the engine is running

Answer

☑ **because it might distract your attention from the road ahead**

Driving requires your total attention and concentration at all times. Don't be distracted by taking or making mobile phone calls. Be safe, switch off your phone while driving.

Q. 4.72

Mark one answer

Your vehicle is fitted with a hands free phone system. Using this equipment whilst driving

- is quite safe as long as you slow down
- could distract your attention from the road
- is recommended by The Highway Code
- could be very good for road safety

Answer

☑ **could distract your attention from the road**

Using a hands free system doesn't mean that you can safely drive and use a mobile phone. You may still be distracted, reducing your level of concentration. Your responsibility is to keep yourself and other road users safe at all times.

Q. 4.73

Mark one answer

Using a hands free phone is likely to

- improve your safety
- increase your concentration
- reduce your view
- divert your attention

Answer

☑ **divert your attention**

Unlike a passenger, the person speaking to you is unable to see the traffic situations you are dealing with. They will continue to speak to you even if you are approaching a hazardous situation. You need to be concentrating on your driving all of the time, and especially when dealing with a hazard.

Q. 4.74

Mark one answer

You should ONLY use a mobile phone when

- receiving a call
- suitably parked
- driving at less than 30 mph
- driving an automatic vehicle

Answer

☑ **suitably parked**

It is far more convenient for you, as well as being safer, if you are parked in a suitable place when receiving or making a call or using text messaging. You will be free to take notes or refer to papers, for example, which would not be possible while driving.

questions

answers

Q. 4.75

Mark one answer

Using a mobile phone while you are driving

- ☐ is acceptable in a vehicle with power steering
- ☐ will reduce your field of vision
- ☐ could distract your attention from the road
- ☐ will affect your vehicle's electronic systems

Answer

- ☑ **could distract your attention from the road**

Driving today requires all of your attention, all of the time. Any distraction, however brief, is dangerous.

Q. 4.76

Mark one answer

NI EXEMPT

Your vehicle breaks down on the hard shoulder of a motorway. You decide to use your mobile phone to call for help. You should

- ☐ stand at the rear of the vehicle while making the call
- ☐ try to repair the vehicle yourself
- ☐ get out of the vehicle by the right hand door
- ☐ check your location from the marker posts on the left

Answer

- ☑ **check your location from the marker posts on the left**

In an emergency, time can be of the essence. The emergency services need to know your exact location. Look at the marker posts on the edge of the hard shoulder before you phone, there is a number on them. Tell this to the services as it will help them to locate you. Be ready to describe where you are, for example by reference to the last place or junction you passed.

Q. 4.77

Mark one answer

To answer a call on your mobile phone while driving you should

- ☐ reduce your speed wherever you are
- ☐ stop in a proper and convenient place
- ☐ keep the call time to a minimum
- ☐ slow down and allow others to overtake

Answer

- ☑ **stop in a proper and convenient place**

No phone call is important enough to endanger someone's life. If you must be contactable when driving, plan your route to include breaks where you can catch up on telephone messages in safety. Always choose a proper and convenient place to take a break.

Q. 4.78

Mark one answer

NI EXEMPT

Your mobile phone rings while you are on the motorway. Before answering you should

- ■ reduce your speed to 40 mph
- ■ pull up on the hard shoulder
- ■ move into the left hand lane
- ■ stop in a safe place when you can

Answer

☑ **stop in a safe place when you can**

Plan your journey and take breaks to keep in touch if necessary. When driving on motorways, you can't just pull up to answer your mobile phone. You will need to turn off the motorway or wait until you get to the next service area. Be safe, switch it off while driving and use the message facility to listen to any calls when you are parked in a safe and proper place.

Q. 4.79

Mark one answer

You have driven a long distance and feel tired. Your tachograph shows that you have not exceeded your driving hours. What should you do?

- ■ Park in a suitable place and rest
- ■ Reduce your speed and drive more slowly
- ■ Carry on driving to use up your hours
- ■ Increase your speed and reduce your journey time

Answer

☑ **Park in a suitable place and rest**

The smallest lapse in concentration can result in loss of control. If you feel that you may be losing concentration, pull up at the next safe place for a rest.

Q. 4.80

Mark three answers

Which THREE result from drinking alcohol and driving?

- ■ Less control
- ■ A false sense of confidence
- ■ Faster reactions
- ■ Poor judgement of speed
- ■ Greater awareness of danger

Answers

☑ **Less control**

☑ **A false sense of confidence**

☑ **Poor judgement of speed**

You must understand the dangers of mixing alcohol with driving. One drink is too many if you're going to drive. Alcohol will reduce your ability to drive safely.

questions answers

Q. 4.81

Mark three answers

Which THREE of these are likely effects of drinking alcohol on driving?

- ■ Reduced coordination
- ■ Increased confidence
- ■ Poor judgement
- ■ Increased concentration
- ■ Faster reactions
- ■ Colour blindness

Answers

- ☑ **Reduced coordination**
- ☑ **Increased confidence**
- ☑ **Poor judgement**

Alcohol can increase confidence to a point where a driver's behaviour might become 'out of character'. Someone who normally behaves sensibly suddenly takes risks and enjoys it. Never let yourself or your friends get into this situation.

Q. 4.82

Mark three answers

Drinking any amount of alcohol is likely to

- ■ reduce your ability to react to hazards
- ■ increase the speed of your reactions
- ■ worsen your judgement of speed
- ■ increase your awareness of danger
- ■ give a false sense of confidence

Answers

- ☑ **reduce your ability to react to hazards**
- ☑ **worsen your judgement of speed**
- ☑ **give a false sense of confidence**

Never drink if you are going to drive. It's always the safest option not to drink at all.

If you are convicted of drink-driving you will certainly lose your job, so don't be tempted – it isn't worth it.

Q. 4.83

Mark three answers

What else can seriously affect your concentration when driving, other than alcoholic drinks?

- ■ Drugs
- ■ Tiredness
- ■ Tinted windows
- ■ Contact lenses
- ■ Loud music

Answers

- ☑ **Drugs**
- ☑ **Tiredness**
- ☑ **Loud music**

The least distraction can allow your concentration to drift. Focus on your driving so you stay in full control of your vehicle at all times.

Q. 4.84

Mark one answer

How does alcohol affect your driving?

- It speeds up your reactions
- It increases your awareness
- It improves your coordination
- It reduces your concentration

Answer

☑ It reduces your concentration

Concentration and good judgement at all times are needed to be a good, safe driver.

Q. 4.85

Mark one answer

You have been convicted of driving whilst unfit through drink or drugs. You will find this is likely to cause the cost of one of the following to rise considerably. Which one?

- Road fund licence
- Insurance premiums
- Vehicle test certificate
- Driving licence

Answer

☑ Insurance premiums

You have proved yourself to be a risk to yourself and others on the road. For this reason insurance companies may charge you a high premium for the use of your own vehicle. You will certainly lose your job.

questions

answers

Q. 4.86

Mark one answer

What advice should you give to a driver who has had a few alcoholic drinks at a party?

- ▪ Have a strong cup of coffee and then drive home
- ▪ Drive home carefully and slowly
- ▪ Go home by public transport
- ▪ Wait a short while and then drive home

Answer

☑ **Go home by public transport**

Drinking black coffee or waiting a few hours won't make any difference. Alcohol takes time to leave the body. You might even be unfit to drive the following morning.

Q. 4.87

Mark one answer

A driver attends a social event. What precaution should the driver take?

- ▪ Drink plenty of coffee after drinking alcohol
- ▪ Avoid busy roads after drinking alcohol
- ▪ Avoid drinking alcohol completely
- ▪ Avoid drinking alcohol on an empty stomach

Answer

☑ **Avoid drinking alcohol completely**

This is always going to be the safest option. One drink could be too many.

Q. 4.88

Mark two answers

It is eight hours since you last had an alcoholic drink. Which of the following applies?

- ▪ You will certainly be under the legal limit
- ▪ You will have no alcohol in your system
- ▪ You may still be unfit to drive
- ▪ You may still be over the legal limit

Answers

☑ **You may still be unfit to drive**
☑ **You may still be over the legal limit**

Alcohol can take a long time to leave the body. You may feel all right to drive, but its effect will last for many hours.

questions   answers

Q. 4.89

Mark one answer

Persistent misuse of drugs or alcohol may lead to

■ better concentration

■ better eyesight

■ withdrawal of a driving licence

■ faster reactions

Answer

☑ **withdrawal of a driving licence**

Persistent misuse of drugs and or alcohol may lead to the withdrawal of your driving licence. Your insurance premiums will probably increase as well.

Q. 4.90

Mark one answer

Your doctor has given you a course of medicine. Why should you ask if it is OK to drive?

■ Drugs make you a better driver by quickening your reactions

■ You will have to let your insurance company know about the medicine

■ Some types of medicine can cause your reactions to slow down

■ The medicine you take may affect your hearing

Answer

☑ **Some types of medicine can cause your reactions to slow down**

Always check the label of any medication container. The contents might affect your driving. If you aren't sure, ask your doctor or pharmacist.

Q. 4.91

Mark one answer

You have been taking medicine for a few days which made you feel drowsy. Today you feel better, but still need to take the medicine. You should only drive

■ if your journey is necessary

■ at night on quiet roads

■ if someone goes with you

■ after checking with your doctor

Answer

☑ **after checking with your doctor**

Take care, it's not worth taking risks. Always check to be really sure. The medicine may have an effect on you later in the day.

questions

Q. 4.92

Mark two answers

You are not sure if your cough medicine will affect your driving. What TWO things could you do?

- ■ Ask your doctor
- ■ Check the medicine label
- ■ Drive if you feel all right
- ■ Ask a friend or relative for advice

Q. 4.93

Mark one answer

You take some cough medicine given to you by a friend. What must you do before driving?

- ■ Drink some strong coffee
- ■ Ask your friend if taking the medicine affected their driving
- ■ Check the label to see if the medicine will affect your driving
- ■ Make a short journey to see if the medicine is affecting your driving

Q. 4.94

Mark two answers

You are driving along a motorway and become tired. You should

- ■ stop at the next service area and rest
- ■ leave the motorway at the next exit and rest
- ■ increase your speed and turn up the radio volume
- ■ close all your windows and set heating to warm
- ■ pull up on the hard shoulder and change drivers

answers

Answers

☑ **Ask your doctor**
☑ **Check the medicine label**

If you're taking medicine or drugs prescribed by your doctor, check to ensure that they won't make you drowsy. If you forget to ask at the time of your visit to the surgery, check with your pharmacist.

Answer

☑ **Check the label to see if the medicine will affect your driving**

Never drive having taken drugs you don't know about. They might affect your judgement and perception and, therefore, endanger lives.

Answers

☑ **stop at the next service area and rest**
☑ **leave the motorway at the next exit and rest**

If you have planned your journey properly to include rest stops, you will arrive at your destination in good time.

Q. 4.95

Mark one answer

You are about to drive home. You feel very tired and have a severe headache. You should

- ■ wait until you are fit and well before driving
- ■ drive home, but take a tablet for headaches
- ■ drive home if you can stay awake for the journey
- ■ wait for a short time, then drive home slowly

Answer

☑ **wait until you are fit and well before driving**

All your concentration should be on your driving. Any pain you feel will distract you. Change your plans and be safe.

Q. 4.96

Mark one answer

If you are feeling tired it is best to stop as soon as you can. Until then you should

- ■ increase your speed to find a stopping place quickly
- ■ ensure a supply of fresh air
- ■ gently tap the steering wheel
- ■ keep changing speed to improve concentration

Answer

☑ **ensure a supply of fresh air**

If you're travelling on a long journey, plan your route before you leave. This will help you to

- be decisive at intersections and junctions
- plan your rest stops
- know approximately how long the journey will take.

Make sure that the vehicle you're travelling in is well ventilated. A warm, stuffy atmosphere can make you drowsy, which will impair your judgement and perception.

Q. 4.97

Mark one answer

Your reactions will be much slower when driving

- ■ if tired
- ■ in fog
- ■ too quickly
- ■ in rain

Answer

☑ **if tired**

Try to avoid becoming tired by taking plenty of rest stops and allowing fresh air into your vehicle.

questions answers

Q. 4.98

Mark one answer

You are driving on a motorway. You feel tired. You should

- carry on but drive slowly
- leave the motorway at the next exit
- complete your journey as quickly as possible
- stop on the hard shoulder

Answer

✓ **leave the motorway at the next exit**

If you do feel tired and there's no service station for many miles, leave the motorway at the next exit. Find a place off the motorway where you can pull up and stop safely for a rest.

Q. 4.99

Mark one answer

You are taking medication that could affect your driving. What should you do?

- Seek medical advice
- Make short journeys only
- Drive only at night
- Drink plenty of water

Answer

✓ **Seek medical advice**

Check all medicines. Consult your doctor or pharmacist if you are not sure.

Q. 4.100

Mark one answer

You are driving on a motorway and feel tired. You should

- stop on the hard shoulder for a rest
- carry on, but drive slowly
- leave at the next exit
- try to complete your journey more quickly

Answer

✓ **leave at the next exit**

Don't continue to drive without taking your proper rest periods. Walking around in the fresh air during your break will help before setting off again.

Q. 4.101

Mark two answers

The driver of a bus should wear a seat belt if one is fitted UNLESS .

- ☐ the seat belt is particularly uncomfortable
- ☐ the vehicle is being reversed
- ☐ a valid medical exemption certificate is held by the driver
- ☐ the belt is of the lap-only type
- ☐ the passengers carried are children

Answers

- ☑ **the vehicle is being reversed**
- ☑ **a valid medical exemption certificate is held by the driver**

If your vehicle is fitted with a seat belt you must wear it, unless you're exempt for medical reasons. Seat belts save lives. If the fitting of the belt is uncomfortable and it prevents you obtaining a safe driving position, report this to your employer. If it isn't right for you, it's likely that it won't be right for other drivers either.

Carrying passengers

This section looks at the rules concerning carrying passengers.

The questions will ask you about

- **Passenger comfort**

  ensuring the safety and comfort of your passengers

- **Vehicle stability**

  being aware that high and long vehicles must not be allowed to become unstable

- **Driver attitude and responsibility**

  developing a responsible attitude to passengers and other road users

- **Special passengers**

  looking after passengers with special needs.

Q. 5.1

Mark one answer

What would you have to be especially aware of when driving a double-deck bus on a road with a steep camber?

■ Keep Left islands

■ A smooth road surface

■ Pedestrian crossings

■ Overhanging trees

Answer

☑ **Overhanging trees**

A road which has a steep camber will slope sharply towards the kerb. You must be aware of the dangers this can present. The nearside wheels will be lower than the offside causing your bus to lean towards the pavement or verge. This brings a risk of collision with objects such as overhanging trees, lamp posts and bus stop roofs.

Q. 5.2

Mark one answer

As a bus driver your first consideration is to your

■ timetable

■ passengers

■ employer

■ workmates

Answer

☑ **passengers**

Consideration for your passengers can be shown in lots of ways. Be courteous at all times. Give people time to get seated before moving away. Some passengers have special needs: allow them to be independent, but be prepared to help if necessary. Look out for people by the side of the road who may not be able to see or hear your bus coming.

Q. 5.3

Mark two answers

You are driving a double-deck bus. Passenger care is important. You should

■ assist passengers with special needs

■ provide a commentary of the route

■ listen to passengers while driving

■ help passengers unfamiliar with the service

■ carry passengers luggage upstairs

Answers

☑ **assist passengers with special needs**

☑ **help passengers unfamiliar with the service**

Always show consideration to passengers whether they have special needs or not. Try to imagine what assistance you would like if you were in their position.

questions   answers

Q. 5.4 🚌

Mark one answer

As a bus driver your main responsibility is

- ■ the safety and comfort of your passengers
- ■ keeping to a strict timetable
- ■ the collecting of fares
- ■ the issuing of tickets

Answer

☑ **the safety and comfort of your passengers**

You should deliver them to their destination
- safely
- on time
- efficiently
- courteously.

Q. 5.5 🚌

Mark two answers

As a bus driver you should show care to your passengers. You can do this by

- ■ stopping close to the kerb
- ■ reaching destinations early
- ■ not speaking when taking fares
- ■ giving them time to get seated

Answers

☑ **stopping close to the kerb**

☑ **giving them time to get seated**

Ensure that you stop the vehicle where it is safe and convenient for your passengers to get on and off. Accelerating as you move off can easily unsteady a passenger; try to wait until all passengers are seated or settled before moving off.

Q. 5.6 🚌

Mark one answer

What is the MAIN reason for using smooth acceleration when driving your bus?

- ■ To reduce wear on the tyres
- ■ To reduce wear on the engine
- ■ To improve fuel consumption
- ■ To improve passenger comfort

Answer

☑ **To improve passenger comfort**

Operators often publicise journeys as being
- comfortable
- convenient
- fast
- trouble-free.

You play an important part in delivering this standard of service.

questions answers

Q. 5.7

Mark two answers

When driving a bus, your main priorities should be

- the safety of your passengers
- the comfort of your passengers
- keeping strictly to your timetable
- greeting all passengers with a smile
- making sure passengers take their luggage

Answers

- ☑ **the safety of your passengers**
- ☑ **the comfort of your passengers**

A bus driver should set a good example for others to follow. Adopting the correct attitude will help you fulfil your main priority, which is the safety and comfort of your passengers.

Q. 5.8

Mark one answer

For the comfort of your passengers harsh braking should be avoided. You should

- pump the brakes when approaching a bus stop or hazard
- use the gears to slow down
- use the parking brake just before stopping to avoid throwing passengers forward
- plan ahead and take early action on all stops and hazards

Answer

- ☑ **plan ahead and take early action on all stops and hazards**

As the driver of a bus, your first duty is to your passengers. You are delivering a service to paying customers who wish to reach their destination comfortably and safely. Set yourself a high professional standard and take pride in your work. You must ensure that you have a thorough knowledge of *The Highway Code* and other matters relating to vehicle and passenger safety.

Q. 5.9

Mark one answer

A bus driver brakes harshly. Passengers may be thrown towards

- the front of the bus
- the rear of the bus
- the nearside
- the offside

Answer

- ☑ **the front of the bus**

When approaching hazards or bus stops you should always be aware of what your passengers are doing. Late, harsh braking as they leave their seats can take passengers by surprise and cause them to fall over, possibly injuring themselves or others.

questions

answers

Q. 5.10

Mark one answer

How can you avoid harsh braking?

- Gently apply the parking brake
- Plan ahead and take early action
- Slow down by using your gears only
- Pump the brake pedal several times

Answer

☑ **Plan ahead and take early action**

Always look well ahead. Early planning and anticipation will help you to avoid braking harshly. Your passengers won't want to be thrown around every time you deal with a hazard.

Q. 5.11

Mark two answers

On which TWO occasions would passengers be most likely to notice weight transfer?

- Braking
- Cornering
- Reversing
- Overtaking

Answers

☑ **Braking**

☑ **Cornering**

A smooth ride at all times is not always easy to achieve. However, scanning ahead for hazards will help you avoid such things as late braking and taking corners too fast.

Q. 5.12

Mark one answer

Well ahead of you are traffic lights on green. What should you do in case the lights change to red?

- Accelerate to make sure you can cross before they change
- Slow down to avoid the need to stop suddenly
- Accelerate, but warn your passengers you may have to stop
- Carry on at a constant speed, but be ready to sound your horn

Answer

☑ **Slow down to avoid the need to stop suddenly**

If you're approaching a set of traffic lights and they've been on green for a while, be prepared for them to change. Ease off the accelerator and be ready to come to a gradual stop if you need to. Don't try to beat the red light; it may change as you come closer, causing you to brake late and harshly. Think of your passengers.

questions   answers

Q. 5.13

Mark one answer

A bus driver accelerates sharply. Passengers may be thrown towards

■ the rear of the bus

■ the front of the bus

■ the nearside

■ the offside

Answer

☑ **the rear of the bus**

After passengers have boarded, avoid accelerating to build up speed while they are still in the aisle. This can cause them to lose their balance and sustain unnecessary injury. A few seconds' delay to allow passengers time to be seated will make little difference to your overall journey time. BE PROFESSIONAL – BE PATIENT.

Q. 5.14

Mark one answer

A bus driver should avoid stopping harshly MOSTLY for the benefit of the

■ tyres

■ brakes

■ passengers

■ suspension

Answer

☑ **passengers**

Passengers are very vulnerable when they are standing in a moving vehicle. Inconsiderate use of the footbrake can easily cause injury to your passengers, especially the young or infirm, who may not wait until you have stopped before they leave their seat. If you seem to be in a hurry, they may even have left their seat early because they don't want to feel responsible for holding you up.

Q. 5.15

Mark one answer

If a bus takes a bend too fast passengers may be thrown towards

■ the outside of the bend

■ the inside of the bend

■ the front of the bus

■ the rear of the bus

Answer

☑ **the outside of the bend**

Turning corners or travelling around bends too quickly will push passengers sideways. In addition, the weight of the passengers being transferred to one side of the vehicle will make it even more unstable. This in turn will make steering out of the bend more difficult.

questions   answers

Q. 5.16

Mark three answers

For the safety and comfort of your passengers you should

- [ ] brake smoothly
- [ ] think well ahead
- [ ] stop close to the kerb
- [ ] brake hard on a bend
- [ ] give change on the move
- [ ] drive with the door open

Answers

- ✓ **brake smoothly**
- ✓ **think well ahead**
- ✓ **stop close to the kerb**

How well you look after your passengers and drive your bus is a measure of your professionalism. Dealing competently and safely with hazards and other road users is expected. A safe, comfortable ride, even when you are under pressure, will be appreciated by your passengers.

Q. 5.17

Mark two answers

Before moving off from a standstill, a bus driver should be especially aware of passengers who attempt to

- [ ] change seats
- [ ] smoke
- [ ] ask you questions
- [ ] get off
- [ ] get on
- [ ] refuse to pay

Answers

- ✓ **get off**
- ✓ **get on**

Check your nearside external and internal mirrors before you move away for anyone attempting to board or leave your vehicle. Always give passengers time to be seated safely before you move away.

Q. 5.18

Mark one answer

When seat belts are fitted in a bus your passengers SHOULD wear them

- [ ] on journeys over distances of 25 km (15.5 miles)
- [ ] only when travelling in EC countries
- [ ] only when travelling on motorways
- [ ] at all times

Answer

- ✓ **at all times**

As the driver of a bus you may be responsible for several passengers at any given time. If a situation occurs where you have to brake or steer harshly in an emergency, your passengers could be thrown about the vehicle in different directions. Due to the necessary fittings on board, such as luggage racks, handrails and poles, there's a significant danger of injury. If seat belts are provided for passengers, they should wear them. In certain situations they must be worn by law.

Seat belts save lives.

Q. 5.19

Mark one answer

Which of the following is a legal requirement for every bus?

■ A fire extinguisher

■ A current timetable

■ A mobile phone or radio

■ A working tachograph

Answer

☑ **A fire extinguisher**

Every bus must carry a fire extinguisher. Make sure that you know where it's located and how to use it, so that you're fully prepared in the event of a fire.

Q. 5.20

Mark three answers

The location of which of the following MUST be clearly labelled on a bus?

■ Air vents

■ First aid equipment

■ Vehicle length

■ Route timetables

■ Fuel cut-off switch

■ Fire extinguisher

Answers

☑ **First aid equipment**

☑ **Fuel cut-off switch**

☑ **Fire extinguisher**

It is essential to know the location of first aid equipment, the fuel cut-off device and the fire extinguisher on every PCV that you drive. Take time to familiarise yourself with their location whenever you drive a different vehicle. When you take your PCV test you will be asked questions on safety.

Q. 5.21

Mark one answer

If a passenger carries a white stick with a red ring painted on it this shows the person is

■ blind and deaf

■ deaf only

■ unable to climb steps

■ blind only

Answer

☑ **blind and deaf**

Give extra care to those passengers who require more time or help to get on or off the vehicle. Recognise their disability and help them as much as you can. There's a lot of competition these days and passengers often have a choice of how they travel. Take pride in your work and this will show through in the way that you deal with your passengers. They'll appreciate this and may travel with your company again.

CARRYING PASSENGERS

questions

answers

Q. 5.22

Mark one answer

A passenger is boarding your bus. They are carrying a white stick with a red ring painted on it. What does this mean?

- They have a learning difficulty
- They have poor vision and hearing
- They have a physical disability
- They have a speech problem

Answer

☑ **They have poor vision and hearing**

Be prepared to help if they appear to need it, or ask for it. Always do your best to provide a smooth and comfortable ride for your passengers.

Q. 5.23

Mark one answer

A disabled passenger is boarding your bus. They tell you that getting on board is not a problem to them. You should

- let them board without help
- ask a passenger to help them
- leave your cab and help them
- do nothing, you cannot leave your seat

Answer

☑ **let them board without help**

Always be prepared to offer assistance if they ask for it, but allow them to show their independence, even if it delays you for a few seconds longer.

Q. 5.24

Mark three answers

As a bus driver, which of the following should you not do?

- Signal if necessary when pulling in
- Drive on before people are seated
- Issue tickets without looking at customers' faces
- Use smooth acceleration and anticipate braking needs
- Give time to passengers and show consideration
- Always rush to keep to a timetable

Answers

☑ **Drive on before people are seated**

☑ **Issue tickets without looking at customers' faces**

☑ **Always rush to keep to a timetable**

Nobody likes to be late; but you should not let the pressure of your timetable make you feel you have to rush people. Being pleasant to your passengers and showing them some common courtesies will encourage them to use your service again.

questions answers

Q. 5.25

Mark three answers

While you are collecting fares you should look at passengers when speaking to them. This will

- help you to recognise someone having difficulty

- show people you are in a rush to keep to a timetable

- show common courtesy and help the image of your company

- help deaf and hearing-impaired people to understand you

- help you decide whether people with a disability should get on the bus

Answers

✓ **help you to recognise someone having difficulty**

✓ **show common courtesy and help the image of your company**

✓ **help deaf and hearing-impaired people to understand you**

You are a representative of your company, so showing passengers that their custom is appreciated will encourage them to travel with you again.

Q. 5.26

Mark two answers

When dealing with passengers who are hard of hearing it is important that you

- shout as loudly as you can

- look at them when speaking to them

- hurry them to get seated

- are as helpful as possible

Answers

✓ **look at them when speaking to them**

✓ **are as helpful as possible**

Hard-of-hearing passengers may want to lip read. Make sure that they are able to see your face clearly as you speak.

questions

answers

Q. 5.27

Mark one answer

Your bus is fitted with lifts or ramps for the less able bodied. The equipment should only be operated by

☐ wheel chair attendants

☐ fully-trained people

☐ bus company employees

☐ accompanying nurses

Answer

☑ **fully-trained people**

Make sure that you are fully trained in the safe use of lifts, ramps and securing devices. If you drive a vehicle fitted with this equipment, never let untrained people operate it. Look out for the safety of others at all times.

Q. 5.28

Mark one answer

The purpose of a 'kneeling bus' is to

☐ improve passenger comfort on bumpy roads

☐ help with access under low bridges

☐ allow the step height to be raised and lowered

☐ give more clearance over speed ramps

Answer

☑ **allow the step height to be raised and lowered**

This type of bus can be especially useful for disabled passengers. Using air suspension, the front entrance can be lowered for easier access. Make sure you are properly trained to operate this equipment. Only use it for the intended purpose, and make sure it is in the correct position before continuing your journey.

Q. 5.29

Mark one answer

This sign fitted to the front and rear of a bus means that

☐ the bus may be carrying children

☐ children must be accompanied by an adult

☐ the bus is carrying blind people

☐ the driver will help disabled people

Answer

☑ **the bus may be carrying children**

If you're carrying children on your vehicle and it isn't on a scheduled route used by the general public, it must have this sign displayed to the front and rear. When carrying children to and from school it's likely that you'll have to make several stops in places other than recognised bus stops. Think carefully before you stop. Don't cause unnecessary inconvenience to other road users.

Q. 5.30

Mark one answer

Hazard warning lights may only be used at certain times. In addition, a bus displaying this sign may use them when

- ◼ stopped at a pedestrian crossing
- ◼ stopped and children are getting on or off the vehicle
- ◼ approaching a school crossing patrol
- ◼ there is a sign warning of a school ahead

Answer

- ☑ **stopped and children are getting on or off the vehicle**

You may be driving in the rush hour, when traffic is heavy, so when you stop you're permitted to show your hazard warning lights. This will show other road users that children are getting on and off the vehicle. Look out for passing traffic and try to ensure that all your passengers get on and off safely.

Q. 5.31

Mark one answer

You are driving a bus. The bell rings four times. This means

- ◼ continue past the next bus stop
- ◼ the bus is full
- ◼ move off when safe
- ◼ there is an emergency

Answer

- ☑ **there is an emergency**

Four bell rings indicate that someone on the bus considers an emergency situation has occurred. As the driver, you must stop the vehicle safely, with consideration for your passengers, before investigating further.

questions   answers

Q. 5.32

Mark one answer

Your conductor rings the bell twice. This means

▪ carry on past the next bus stop

▪ stop immediately for an emergency stop

▪ pull in at the next bus stop

▪ move off when safe to do so

Answer

☑ **move off when safe to do so**

Make sure that you are both familiar with the correct signals. The conductor should ensure that all passengers are settled before signalling.

Q. 5.33

Mark one answer

You are driving a bus. The bell rings three times. This means

▪ pull in at the next stop

▪ move away when safe

▪ an emergency on board

▪ your vehicle is full

Answer

☑ **your vehicle is full**

The bell system is used to inform you using a predetermined set of codes. Never allow anyone to use the bells other than in the accepted way.

Q. 5.34

Mark one answer

Your bus has broken down at night in heavy rain. Why should you move your passengers to the front of the bus?

▪ To keep the bus stable

▪ To help you see clearly out of the back window

▪ To limit injuries in case of a rear-end collision

▪ To keep them informed about the breakdown

Answer

☑ **To limit injuries in case of a rear-end collision**

The safety of your passengers should be your first priority. You should take every possible precaution to ensure they are out of danger.

166

questions

answers

Q. 5.35

Mark one answer

You are driving a half-cab bus and have no contact with the passengers. This is only allowed if

- ▪ it is fitted with an interior mirror
- ▪ there is a chain or strap across the doorway
- ▪ a responsible person is in charge of them
- ▪ you make sure no one stands on the platform

Answer

☑ **a responsible person is in charge of them**

It's essential that the passengers on the vehicle are able to report any problems to a responsible person. This person should be aware of the correct bell signals so that they are able to communicate with the driver.

Q. 5.36

Mark one answer

You are driving a coach at night with passengers on board. You should never

- ▪ stop at service stations
- ▪ switch the radio on
- ▪ leave the interior in darkness
- ▪ close any curtains

Answer

☑ **leave the interior in darkness**

Passengers should be able to move about the vehicle in safety. You should ensure that all interior lights are in working order before you start your journey.

questions

answers

Q. 5.37

Mark three answers

There is a fire on the upper deck of your double-deck bus. You should

☐ stop safely and quickly

☐ get everyone off the bus

☐ contact emergency services

☐ open all the windows

☐ move the passengers into the lower deck

☐ make sure passengers have their belongings

Answers

☑ **stop safely and quickly**

☑ **get everyone off the bus**

☑ **contact emergency services**

Fire can spread extremely quickly. Your first priority is the safety of your passengers. If at all possible disconnect electrical lines and cut off the fuel supply. Fire can destroy a vehicle in an alarmingly short time.

Q. 5.38

Mark one answer

Frequent tyre checks are advised on three axle double deck vehicles because

☐ their tyres are more likely to deflate

☐ punctures can be difficult to detect

☐ blow-outs are more common on these vehicles

☐ their tyre air pressures are difficult to maintain

Answer

☑ **punctures can be difficult to detect**

Frequent tyre checks are advisable on multi-axled vehicles. The inside wheels on the rear twin-axle are the most difficult to check. A deflated tyre will transfer the weight to the second tyre on a twin-axle pair and could cause it to burst as they are not designed to run on their own.

questions   answers

Q. 5.39

Mark one answer

The driver of a coach should always wear gloves when

- loading and stowing passengers' luggage
- operating a disabled passenger lift
- checking the fuel cut off switch
- ☑ topping up the oil or water levels

Answer

☑ **topping up the oil or water levels**

Even the best maintained vehicles accumulate a certain amount of grime around the engine oil filler. By wearing gloves you can keep your hands and cuffs clean to present a smart appearance to your customers.

Q. 5.40

Mark two answers

The driver of a coach should always wear gloves when

- emptying the ticket machines
- ☑ emptying waste systems
- driving in cold weather
- driving a vehicle without power steering
- checking the fuel gauge
- ☑ checking battery levels

Answers

☑ **emptying waste systems**

☑ **checking battery levels**

A few simple precautions are necessary when carrying out regular maintenance tasks. Wearing gloves will help eliminate the risk of infections or conditions such as eczema or dermatitis.

Q. 5.41

Mark one answer

A bus driver should never allow passengers to

- smoke in the saloon
- stand in the aisle
- stow their own luggage
- ☑ ride on an open platform

Answer

☑ **ride on an open platform**

A bus driver is responsible for the safety of passengers on board. Anyone standing on an open platform is at risk should the driver have to brake suddenly or take a corner at speed.

questions answers

Q. 5.42

Mark one answer

Kneeling buses are specifically designed to improve access for

◼ the driver

◼ extra luggage

◼ elderly passengers

◼ low bridges

Answer

☑ **elderly passengers**

Some buses are equipped with air or hydraulic systems that allow the step level to be lowered. They are known as kneeling buses. Don't forget to raise the step again before moving off.

Q. 5.43

Mark one answer

What are kneeling buses designed to improve?

◼ Access for the disabled

◼ Stability when cornering

◼ Passenger comfort at higher speeds

◼ Access for the driver

Answer

☑ **Access for the disabled**

Kneeling buses are equipped with air or hydraulic systems that allow the step level to be lowered. This improves access for disabled and elderly passengers; remember to raise the step before moving off.

Q. 5.44

Mark one answer

Your double deck bus breaks down on a busy road. You should ask your passengers to move to the

◼ rear of the bus

◼ top deck

◼ lower deck

◼ front of the bus

Answer

☑ **front of the bus**

The greatest risk to a stationary bus is being hit from behind. Moving your passengers forward could reduce the risk of injury.

questions   answers

Q. 5.45

Mark one answer

You are driving a bus carrying passengers at night. Why should you always put the interior lights on?

- ▪ It will help you see the road ahead
- ▪ So that passengers can see to move around
- ▪ It will help passengers to see outside
- ▪ So that you can see your controls

Answer

✓ **So that passengers can see to move around**

Passengers need a properly lit area so they can move around safely.

Q. 5.46

Mark one answer

As you move off watch out, in particular, for any passengers who attempt to

- ▪ smoke in the lower saloon
- ▪ stand in the upper saloon
- ▪ avoid paying the correct fare
- ▪ board the bus

Answer

✓ **board the bus**

Always check your nearside mirror before moving away as a passenger may be attempting to open the door to board the bus or running to jump aboard an open platform. Also check for passengers trying to get off the bus as you move away.

Q. 5.47

Mark one answer

When you pull away from a bus stop watch out in particular, for passengers who attempt to

- ▪ avoid paying the correct fare
- ▪ smoke in the lower saloon
- ▪ alight from the bus
- ▪ use an expired travel pass

Answer

✓ **alight from the bus**

Even though you have started to move off, passengers may still try to get off the bus. You should also check your nearside mirror for any passengers trying to get on.

questions answers

Q. 5.48 🚌

Mark one answer

A passenger finds walking difficult. What could you do to help?

▪ Drive quickly so that passengers will not be on for long

▪ Wait until the passenger is sitting down before moving away

▪ Make sure they have a window seat

▪ Suggest they stand near the door

Answer

☑ **Wait until the passenger is sitting down before moving away**

Try to wait until your passengers have sat down before you move off. This is even more important if they are elderly or have difficulty walking. Don't forget the personal touch. Offer help when you think it might be needed and remember, a smile goes a long way.

Q. 5.49 🚌

Mark two answers

You are the driver of a bus displaying reflective yellow signs. You are permitted to use hazard warning lights when

▪ stationary and parked to take a rest period

▪ stationary and children are boarding

▪ stationary and children are getting off

▪ slowing down to find a parking space

▪ slowing down in town centre traffic queues

▪ slowing down approaching a bus stop

Answers

☑ **stationary and children are boarding**

☑ **stationary and children are getting off**

Buses carrying children must display a distinctive yellow reflective sign on the front and rear, unless running a scheduled service for the general public. Buses displaying the sign are permitted to use hazard warning lights when they have stopped for children to get on or off.

questions   answers

Q. 5.50 🚌

Mark two answers

You are parking your coach at a coastal resort. Your passengers will still have access. You should make sure

- ◼ the cab area is isolated
- ◼ the gear lever is in neutral
- ◼ the storage lockers are open
- ◼ a responsible person is on the coach

Answers

- ☑ **the cab area is isolated**
- ☑ **a responsible person is on the coach**

Your coach must never be left unattended if passengers still have access to it. In particular, they must not be able to get into the cab area of the vehicle. You or another responsible person must always be there to supervise the coach.

Q. 5.51 🚌

Mark two answers

You have parked and left your bus. The public will still have access to it. You should make sure that

- ◼ the door key is different to the ignition key
- ◼ the cab area is shut off
- ◼ a responsible person is on board
- ◼ all interior lights are on

Answers

- ☑ **the cab area is shut off**
- ☑ **a responsible person is on board**

Your bus must never be left unsupervised when passengers are still able to get back on board. The cab area must be protected, and either you or another responsible person must remain on board to ensure everyone's safety.

Q. 5.52 🚌

Mark three answers

When driving a double-deck bus on a steep camber you should be especially aware of

- ◼ lamp posts
- ◼ parking meters
- ◼ parked cars
- ◼ shop awnings
- ◼ litter bins
- ◼ traffic signs

Answers

- ☑ **lamp posts**
- ☑ **shop awnings**
- ☑ **traffic signs**

When driving high-sided vehicles, such as double-deck buses, you must be aware of how road camber changes can affect your vehicle. As the bus leans towards the kerb, shop awnings, trees and street furniture, such as lamp posts, can get frighteningly close to passengers sitting on the top deck.

questions   answers

Q. 5.53

Mark three answers

A bus driver MUST not drive whilst

- ■ issuing tickets
- ■ the doors are open
- ■ wearing sunglasses
- ■ giving change
- ■ passengers are standing
- ■ luggage is being carried

Answers

- ✓ **issuing tickets**
- ✓ **the doors are open**
- ✓ **giving change**

On regular services, traffic congestion can soon put you behind schedule. Nevertheless, you have a responsibility to your passengers at all times not to take shortcuts or jeopardise their safety. They are paying you for a service which must always deliver them safely to their destination.

Q. 5.54

Mark one answer

What is the likely weight difference between an empty bus and a bus with 75 passengers on board?

- ■ 5 tonnes
- ■ 10 tonnes
- ■ 15 tonnes
- ■ 20 tonnes

Answer

- ✓ **5 tonnes**

The way that your vehicle handles will be very different when it's full compared with when it's empty. Having 75 passengers on board could increase the weight of the bus by up to about 5 tonnes and the passengers may also have luggage.

All extra weight will have an effect on inertia and momentum: it will take longer to build up speed and the vehicle will maintain forward momentum. Advanced planning and controlled braking will be required to allow for this extra weight.

Q. 5.55

Mark one answer

It is important to be able to work out the weight difference between a full bus and an empty one. About how many passengers will equal 1 tonne in weight?

◼ 8
◼ 15
◼ 25
◼ 30

Answer

☑ **15**

You should also make allowances for any luggage your passengers may bring on board. An average of two cases per passenger on a 50-seat coach will add about 1.5 tonnes to the overall weight of your bus or coach.

Q. 5.56

Mark one answer

It is only legal to drive an empty, half-cab bus when the passenger access has

◼ a vertical pole
◼ no high steps
◼ no obstructions
◼ a chain or strap

Answer

☑ **a chain or strap**

You should never drive a half-cab bus in which you have no contact with the passengers unless a responsible person is in charge of the passenger saloon. If you do not have a responsible person in charge of the passenger saloon, the entrance should be secured with a chain or strap.

Always keep an eye on your nearside mirror when you are travelling slowly or are stationary in areas where pedestrians may attempt to jump aboard.

questions   answers

Q. 5.57 🚌

Mark one answer

You are driving a double-deck half-cab bus. Passengers can only be carried if

- ◼ no one uses the upper deck
- ◼ you can see them in your mirror
- ◼ a responsible person is in charge of them
- ◼ they are all travelling to the same destination

Answer

- ☑ **a responsible person is in charge of them**

Under no circumstances should you drive a half-cab bus with passengers on board unless there is a responsible person in charge of them.

Q. 5.58 🚌

Mark one answer

While driving your half-cab bus you hear the three-bell signal from the conductor. This means

- ◼ stop when safe
- ◼ bus empty
- ◼ bus full
- ◼ move off when safe

Answer

- ☑ **bus full**

One bell means 'stop', two bells mean 'move off when safe', and three bells are used to announce when the bus is full.

Q. 5.59 🚌

Mark one answer

It is legal to drive an empty, half-cab double-deck bus, but the passenger access must have

- ◼ a hand rail
- ◼ a vertical pole
- ◼ a chain or strap
- ◼ a warning notice

Answer

- ☑ **a chain or strap**

The chain or strap will prevent any passengers jumping on board while you're stationary or waiting in traffic queues. You must not carry any passengers unless there's a responsible person on board to supervise.

questions   answers

Q. 5.60

Mark one answer

Buses and coaches used for school contract work MUST have

- ▨ yellow reflective signs
- ▨ only one door
- ▨ a conductor
- ▨ a 'no overtaking' sign

Answer

☑ **yellow reflective signs**

Vehicles carrying school children display this sign to alert other drivers to the possible danger of young children crossing the road. As the bus driver, you must make every effort to ensure their safety when boarding or getting off your bus, as well as during their journey with you.

Q. 5.61

Mark one answer

You are driving a half-cab bus. The correct signal to move off when safe is

- ▨ one bell
- ▨ two bells
- ▨ three bells
- ▨ four bells

Answer

☑ **two bells**

This is the correct signal to move off when safe.

The road

This section looks at safety margins and judgement when you're driving.

The questions will ask you about

- **Anticipation**
  planning ahead to prevent last-second reactions

- **Hazard awareness**
  recognising a hazard ahead and preparing for it

- **Attention**
  looking out for problems ahead when you're driving

- **Speed and distance**
  travelling at the correct speed for the situation, leaving a safe distance to react if a problem arises

- **Reaction time**
  being aware that you need time to react

- **Risk factors**
  knowing how various road and weather conditions affect safety.

questions answers

Q. 6.1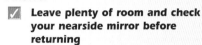

Mark one answer

You overtake a cyclist on a two-way road. What should you do?

☐ Pass closely staying about 1 metre (3 feet 3 inches) from the kerb

☐ Go past quickly and move back to the left sharply

☐ Leave plenty of room and check your nearside mirror before returning

☐ Use a right-turn signal after pulling out

Answer

☑ **Leave plenty of room and check your nearside mirror before returning**

Only overtake when it is safe to do so. Never force other vehicles to move for you. Be patient and stay well back from the cyclist until there is a safe overtaking gap.

Q. 6.2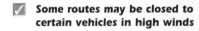

Mark one answer

Your lorry has a curtain-side body. Your route will take you over several high-level bridges. Why is it particularly important to check the weather forecast?

☐ Rain can make crossing bridges very difficult for large vehicles

☐ In hot weather the bridges might be closed to heavy traffic

☐ You won't be able to climb the bridges if it's frosty

☐ Some routes may be closed to certain vehicles in high winds

Answer

☑ **Some routes may be closed to certain vehicles in high winds**

In exposed places such as high-level bridges and roads, viaducts or some motorways, the wind can be particularly strong. If you're driving a high-sided vehicle make sure that you check the weather forecast and plan an alternative route, just in case.

questions   answers

Q. 6.3 🚚

Mark one answer

You want to join a motorway. Traffic is flowing freely on the motorway. What should you do?

☐ Keep to a low speed until you see a gap on the motorway

☐ Build up your speed on the slip road before joining the motorway

☐ Stop at the start of the slip road and move off when there is a gap

☐ Use the hard shoulder if necessary, to build up speed

Answer

☑ **Build up your speed on the slip road before joining the motorway**

Normally you should avoid having to stop before joining a motorway. Use the slip road to build up your speed so that you can emerge safely. If it's extremely busy there may be rare occasions when you have to stop and then filter into the traffic. This is most likely to happen at roadworks and where there are contraflow systems.

Q. 6.4 🚚

Mark one answer

You are driving an articulated lorry on a three-lane motorway. When can you drive in the right-hand lane?

☐ When overtaking a slow moving car in the middle lane

☐ When the escort vehicle of an oversized load signals you to pass

☐ If no speed limiter is fitted to your lorry

☐ If your lorry is unladen

Answer

☑ **When the escort vehicle of an oversized load signals you to pass**

Articulated lorries are prohibited from driving in the right-hand lane of motorways with three or more lanes except when an escort vehicle gives you a signal, when road signs indicate or when directed by a police officer.

Q. 6.5 🚚

Mark one answer

Before driving your lorry in high winds, you should always

☐ check your wind deflector

☐ check your spray suppression equipment

☐ plan your journey well in advance

☐ only half load your lorry

Answer

☑ **plan your journey well in advance**

Plan your route with care. Take into account whether the road will be exposed and if there will be bridges or viaducts to cross. Be sensible and avoid these areas if possible in high winds.

questions   answers

Q. 6.6

Mark one answer

You are overtaking another lorry. Due to an uphill gradient you start to lose speed. You should

- continue at the same speed and position
- try to force the vehicle you were overtaking to drop back
- try to force the vehicle you were overtaking to speed up
- ease off and drop behind the vehicle you were trying to overtake

Answer

✓ **ease off and drop behind the vehicle you were trying to overtake**

If you try to overtake another vehicle and you realise that you're unable to complete the manoeuvre, ease off the accelerator and drop back behind the vehicle. If the vehicle you're trying to overtake is large then it will take longer to pass. You should assess whether you have the time and the power to complete the manoeuvre BEFORE you try to overtake.

Q. 6.7

Mark one answer

When driving an empty curtain-sided vehicle, how could you reduce crosswind problems on exposed bridges?

- Tie just one curtain side back and lock open the rear doors
- Leave both curtain sides closed
- Tie both curtain sides at one end of the vehicle
- Tie the curtain sides halfway back

Answer

✓ **Tie both curtain sides at one end of the vehicle**

If you're driving an empty curtain-sided vehicle, you can help to lower the resistance to side winds if you tie back the curtains. The air will be able to flow across the flat bed of the vehicle and lessen any loss of control, particularly when crossing exposed viaducts or bridges.

Q. 6.8

Mark one answer

A high-sided vehicle will be MOST affected by crosswinds when it is

- stationary
- travelling loaded
- reversing
- travelling empty

Answer

✓ **travelling empty**

Take care if you are driving an empty high-sided vehicle when the wind is blowing across the road you are travelling on. Watch for places where the conditions could suddenly change, such as a gap in the trees or when passing under a bridge.

questions

answers

Q. 6.9

Mark one answer

You are driving an empty curtain-sided vehicle. Why might you consider tying the curtains open?

- To use less fuel
- It is a legal requirement
- To prevent the curtains tearing
- To reduce the effect of crosswinds

Answer

☑ **To reduce the effect of crosswinds**

Closed curtains on large empty vehicles can hold the wind. Strong side winds can actually lift and blow the semi-trailer off course as the vehicle is travelling along the road.

Q. 6.10

Mark one answer

A box van will be MOST affected by crosswinds when it is

- travelling empty
- stationary
- travelling loaded
- reversing

Answer

☑ **travelling empty**

High-sided vehicles such as box vans are affected by strong winds, particularly when unladen. Reduce your speed and stay alert for other road users who are also affected by weather conditions.

Q. 6.11

Mark three answers

In high winds, drivers of lorries approaching high bridges or viaducts should expect

- lower speed limits
- minimum speed limits
- no restrictions for loaded vehicles
- lane closures
- no restrictions for lorries
- diversions

Answers

☑ **lower speed limits**

☑ **lane closures**

☑ **diversions**

You might be delayed by road closures or diversions. Consider this when you're planning your rest stops. Delays will add to your driving time.

Q. 6.12

Mark one answer

Which of these vehicles is MOST at risk from high crosswinds?

- ▪ A laden lorry with box body
- ▪ An unladen lorry with box body
- ▪ An unladen lorry with platform body
- ▪ A laden lorry with platform body

Answer

☑ **An unladen lorry with box body**

The combination of an unladen vehicle with high sides will leave it vulnerable to the effects of strong winds. An evenly distributed load will keep the vehicle more stable and less likely to be blown off course. The higher your vehicle, the more it will be affected by strong winds. Be aware that it may become unstable or difficult to control.

Q. 6.13

Mark one answer

Which vehicle is most at risk when being driven in strong crosswinds?

- ▪ A box van carrying light goods
- ▪ An unladen lorry with platform body
- ▪ A container vehicle with a heavy load
- ▪ A low-loader carrying heavy machinery

Answer

☑ **A box van carrying light goods**

High-sided vehicles catch the wind more than flat-bed vehicles. You should be aware of the places where you are likely to be at risk.

Q. 6.14

Mark one answer

In strong winds an overtaking lorry can affect other road users. Which vehicle is most at risk?

- ▪ A car
- ▪ A furniture van
- ▪ A motorcycle
- ▪ A coach

Answer

☑ **A motorcycle**

Road users, such as motorcyclists, cyclists and vehicles towing caravans could be blown off course by high winds. You should be aware of this when you're following or planning to overtake them. When you overtake your vehicle could cause buffeting to these types of vehicle.

questions answers

Q. 6.15

Mark two answers

Which TWO types of vehicle are most at risk in windy conditions?

- High-sided lorries
- Saloon cars
- Unladen vans
- Single-deck buses
- Tractor units

Answers

- ✓ **High-sided lorries**
- ✓ **Unladen vans**

The higher the sides of your vehicle, the more the vehicle will be buffeted by strong winds. The large area of bodywork will present a resistance to crosswinds, and this in turn will affect the control you have on the vehicle. The risk of loss of control will be increased if your vehicle isn't carrying a load. The vehicle will be lighter and so could be more easily pushed off course by the wind.

Q. 6.16

Mark one answer

When are air deflectors most effective?

- When there is a crosswind
- When there is a headwind
- When reversing
- When there is a strong tailwind

Answer

- ✓ **When there is a headwind**

Cab mounted air deflectors and lower panels will streamline the vehicle and it will, therefore, offer less resistance to the air around it. This will decrease its fuel consumption. Conserving energy and resources should be a concern for all drivers on the road.

Q. 6.17

Mark two answers

You are driving your lorry on the motorway. Visibility is reduced by heavy rain and spray. You should

- maintain a constant speed
- use main beam headlights
- double your dry weather separation distance
- stay in the left-hand lane
- obey advisory speed limit signs

Answers

- ✓ **double your dry weather separation distance**
- ✓ **obey advisory speed limit signs**

Wet roads reduce tyre grip and can make the surface even more slippery. Give yourself plenty of time and room for slowing down and stopping. Keep well back from other vehicles. Advisory signs are set by the police and should be adhered to when they are shown.

questions   answers

Q. 6.18

Mark one answer

Before driving your lorry from a wet construction site at the side of a motorway, you should

- inform the local council
- hose down the road
- hose down the wheels
- inform the lorry operator

Answer

✓ **hose down the wheels**

It is important that you prevent any mud or debris from being deposited on the road. This can cause danger to other road users. If possible, hose the mud off your vehicle before driving on the public road.

Q. 6.19

Mark one answer

You are driving a lorry from a wet construction site onto a motorway. You must take extra precautions before driving because

- your lorry will be unladen and liable to 'bounce'
- it is an offence to emerge from a works site straight onto a motorway
- your lorry's spray suppression equipment will be inoperative
- it is an offence to deposit mud on a road

Answer

✓ **it is an offence to deposit mud on a road**

You should take all possible precautions to prevent any mud being deposited on the road as this is a hazard to other road users. It is also an offence for which you could be prosecuted.

questions   answers

Q. 6.20

Mark one answer

Before raising the body of a tipper lorry you should make sure the ground is

- soft and level
- soft and downhill
- solid and uphill
- solid and level

Answer

✓ **solid and level**

When discharging a load from a tipper vehicle the centre of gravity is raised to a critical position. It's vitally important the vehicle is on a level, solid surface before engaging the hoist mechanism.

Q. 6.21

Mark two answers

Your lorry has a sleeper cab. A quick sideways glance would be helpful especially

- after driving over a pedestrian crossing
- when traffic is merging from the right or left
- before climbing a steep hill
- when driving round sharp bends
- before changing lanes on a motorway

Answers

✓ **when traffic is merging from the right or left**

✓ **before changing lanes on a motorway**

The size and design of some cabs, especially a sleeper cab, can cause blind spots. A quick sideways glance might show up something you cannot see in your mirrors.

Q. 6.22

Mark one answer

You are driving a lorry in a busy town. A driver pulls out in front of you. You have to brake hard. What should you do?

- Overtake as quickly as possible
- Stay calm and accept the error
- Flash your lights to show your annoyance
- Sound your horn and speed up

Answer

✓ **Stay calm and accept the error**

Some drivers might emerge from a junction when it is not safe to do so. Don't intimidate them by driving up too close or revving the engine. Understand that other drivers might make mistakes.

Q. 6.23

Mark one answer

Baffle plates help reduce the load movement in lorries that are carrying

■ containers

■ cars

■ animals

■ liquids

Answer

 liquids

If the drivers of certain tanker vehicles relax the footbrake when braking to a stop there's a danger that the motion in the fluid load could force their vehicles forward. This is due to the wave effect created in the tank contents and is more likely to happen where baffle plates have not been fitted.

Q. 6.24

Mark one answer

You are driving in snow. Care should be taken when using the endurance brake (retarder) because it may cause

■ the front wheels to lock

■ an increase in speed

■ the rear wheels to lock

■ compressed air to escape

Answer

 the rear wheels to lock

When operating independent retarders, care must be taken when descending snow covered gradients. The retarder could cause the rear wheels to lock.

Q. 6.25

Mark one answer

Wheel nuts should be checked shortly after

■ driving down a steep hill

■ initial tightening

■ driving on a motorway

■ unloading

Answer

✓ initial tightening

Always recheck wheel nuts shortly after their initial tightening. Make sure they are tightened to the torque specified by the manufacturer.

questions

answers

Q. 6.26

Mark one answer

You are driving on a motorway after heavy rain. Visibility is low because of spray being thrown up by other lorries. You should

- use dipped headlights
- use sidelights only
- remove spray suppression equipment
- use the two second rule

Answer

☑ **use dipped headlights**

If visibility is reduced use dipped headlights to make yourself seen. During and after heavy rain you should also reduce speed and increase your distance from the vehicle in front.

Q. 6.27

Mark one answer

You are on a motorway just after heavy rain. Spray is being thrown up causing poor visibility. What should you do?

- Use the two-second rule
- Use sidelights only
- Remove spray suppression equipment
- Leave a greater separation distance

Answer

☑ **Leave a greater separation distance**

When visibility is poor and the road is wet leave a greater separation distance. You should leave at least a four-second time gap from the vehicle in front. You should also reduce speed and use dipped headlights.

Q. 6.28

Mark one answer

Spray is causing poor visibility on the motorway. What should you do?

- Use the two-second rule
- Use sidelights only
- Slow to a safe speed
- Remove spray suppression equipment

Answer

☑ **Slow to a safe speed**

Spray from other vehicles, particularly lorries, will reduce visibility. Slow down and leave a greater separation distance from the vehicle in front. You should also use dipped headlights.

Q. 6.29

Mark one answer

You are driving a lorry weighing more than 7.5 tonnes maximum authorised mass. You may only use the right-hand lane to overtake on a motorway with

⬛ two lanes

⬛ three lanes

⬛ a 50 mph speed limit

⬛ a 40 mph speed limit

Answer

☑ **two lanes**

You may use the right hand lane to overtake only on a two-lane motorway. Lorries weighing more than 7.5 tonnes maximum authorised mass are not allowed to use the far right-hand lane of a motorway with three or more lanes.

Q. 6.30

Mark one answer

You are driving on a motorway. You look in your mirrors and see smoke coming from your rear tyres. What should you do?

⬛ Reduce speed for the rest of your journey

⬛ Drive on the hard shoulder until the smoke stops

⬛ Stop as soon as it's safe to do so

⬛ Ignore it, this is normal when driving at speed

Answer

☑ **Stop as soon as it's safe to do so**

Your tyre may burst or shred if it becomes overheated. This could result in serious loss of control. Stop on the hard shoulder as soon as it's safe to do so and call for help.

Q. 6.31

Mark one answer

The entrances to roundabouts are often slippery when wet. You should always

⬛ keep in the left lane

⬛ brake in good time

⬛ use the handbrake

⬛ stop before emerging

Answer

☑ **brake in good time**

The entrances to roundabouts are often worn which can make the surface slippery, especially when wet. You should always plan your approach and brake in good time.

questions   answers

Q. 6.32

Mark one answer

Braking continuously can make brakes overheat. This will make

- [ ] the brakes work better
- [ ] braking less effective
- [ ] the brake pedal hard
- [ ] the air pressure build up

Answer

✓ **braking less effective**

Whenever you brake, the moving energy of your vehicle is converted into heat. Continuous use of the brakes, particularly from high speed or on long steep descents, can cause the shoes and drums to overheat. This will make them less effective and in some cases they may not work at all.

Q. 6.33

Mark one answer

You are driving on a dual carriageway. Ahead you see a vehicle with an amber flashing light. What may this be?

- [ ] An ambulance
- [ ] A fire engine
- [ ] A doctors car on call
- [ ] A disabled person's vehicle

Answer

✓ **A disabled person's vehicle**

There is a growing number of small battery-powered vehicles being produced for disabled people. On dual carriageways they must have a flashing amber light, but be very careful as they can only travel at a maximum speed of 8 mph. You may also see other vehicles on dual carriageways with amber flashing lights such as agricultural or breakdown vehicles.

Q. 6.34

Mark one answer

You are driving in a high wind. What do you need to be careful of?

- [ ] Fallen trees
- [ ] Poor visibility
- [ ] A risk of grounding
- [ ] Steep gradients

Answer

✓ **Fallen trees**

In severe weather conditions you should be aware of the dangers of fallen trees or damaged branches that may fall on your vehicle. Be aware of the dangers and look out for fallen trees that may be lying across the road just around bends.

Q. 6.35

Mark one answer

You are driving a high-sided vehicle. You are about to drive over a high suspension bridge. What in particular do you need to be aware of?

☐ The swaying of the bridge

☐ The width of the lanes

☐ The effect of strong crosswinds

☐ The overhanging bridge cables

Answer

☑ **The effect of strong crosswinds**

In exposed places the wind can be particularly strong. Make allowances for this especially when passing or being passed by other vehicles.

Q. 6.36

Mark one answer

You are driving through the night. You notice that your steering feels lighter than normal. What could this mean?

☐ That your tyres are losing pressure

☐ There is a leak in the power steering pump

☐ That there is ice or frost on the road

☐ There is not enough tread on your tyres

Answer

☑ **That there is ice or frost on the road**

When you're in a warm cab you may not notice the drop in outside temperature. One of the first signs of an icy road is a lack of 'feel' in the steering.

Q. 6.37

Mark one answer

You are stationary. The air brake pressure warning light comes on. Why should you NOT release the parking brake?

☐ Because the vehicle will suddenly roll backwards

☐ Because it will cause the air pressure to rise

☐ Because the service brake may not stop you

☐ Because the warning light will go out

Answer

☑ **Because the service brake may not stop you**

Even though a warning device indicates low air brake pressure you may still be able to release the parking brake. If you do this and start moving the service brake may be ineffective and you may not be able to stop.

questions answers

Q. 6.38

Mark one answer

You are driving near a school in busy traffic. A group of children are walking close to the kerb on your side of the road. What should you do?

- ◻ Move to the other side of the road
- ◻ Wave at them to move back from the kerb
- ◻ Stop for a moment to see what they do
- ◻ Drive slowly until you are clear of the area

Answer

☑ **Drive slowly until you are clear of the area**

Children can be unpredictable and should be approached with extreme caution. When they are in groups they may 'fool around' and push each other into the road. You need to take extra care because a large vehicle has many blind spots.

Q. 6.39

Mark one answer

You are in the centre lane of a motorway and overtaking another vehicle. What should you do before returning to the left-hand lane?

- ◻ Signal left then check your mirror
- ◻ Wait for the other driver to flash their headlights
- ◻ Check ahead and then your nearside mirror
- ◻ Check behind for fast traffic in the right-hand lane

Answer

☑ **Check ahead and then your nearside mirror**

Never return to the left-hand lane until you are sure that you are well clear of the vehicle you have just overtaken. Don't cut in too soon and don't rely on the other driver flashing you in. Make your own judgement!

Q. 6.40

Mark one answer

Usually, on a motorway, how far from the exit is the first sign showing the junction number?

- ◻ Half a mile
- ◻ One mile
- ◻ Two miles
- ◻ Three miles

Answer

☑ **One mile**

Motorway traffic travels at higher speeds, and advance signs warning of junctions are vital to enable you to be in the correct lane in good time to take your exit. In most cases, one mile before the exit you will see a junction sign with road numbers. Half a mile before the exit the sign will also include the names of places accessible from that junction.

Q. 6.41

Mark one answer

When approaching a zebra crossing you should

- stop before the zigzag lines
- wave pedestrians across the road
- sound the horn and flash headlights
- be prepared to stop in good time

Answer

☑ **be prepared to stop in good time**

Always keep your speed down on the approach to zebra crossings. This will allow you to stop safely if necessary. On the approach look well ahead for anyone about to cross.

Q. 6.42

Mark one answer

You are driving a high-sided vehicle on a motorway. You should be ESPECIALLY aware of the effects of crosswinds

- on high bridges
- in cuttings
- in tunnels
- when passing signs

Answer

☑ **on high bridges**

High-sided vehicles are very vulnerable to strong winds. In bad weather listen to or watch out for weather forecasts. You might need to alter your route or even cancel your journey altogether.

Q. 6.43

Mark one answer

You are on a motorway in a high-sided vehicle. You should be ESPECIALLY aware of the effects of crosswinds

- when passing signs
- on exposed sections
- in contraflow systems
- in service areas

Answer

☑ **on exposed sections**

When the weather is bad, listen to and watch out for weather forecasts. Motorways in particular have exposed sections of road, placing high-sided vehicles at risk.

193

questions answers

Q. 6.44

Mark one answer

You are driving a high-sided vehicle in very windy conditions. Which of the following should you avoid if possible?

- ■ Suspension bridges
- ■ Steep hills
- ■ Country lanes
- ■ Road tunnels

Answer

 Suspension bridges

In windy weather try to avoid routes where you would have to negotiate these and other exposed stretches of road. Think about other factors, such as ferry cancellations, that might lead to changes in your route or rest periods.

Q. 6.45

Mark one answer

The conditions are very windy. You are driving a high-sided vehicle. Which of the following should you avoid if possible?

- ■ Road tunnels
- ■ Steep hills
- ■ Country lanes
- ■ Viaducts

Answer

 Viaducts

Try to avoid routes where you would have to negotiate viaducts and other high and exposed places when it is very windy. You may need to alter your route or rest stops and consider other factors such as ferry cancellations.

questions   answers

Q. 6.46

Mark one answer

You are driving in heavy rain. Your steering suddenly feels very light. What should you do?

- Brake very sharply
- Steer towards the centre line
- Ease off the accelerator
- Increase your speed

Answer

✓ **Ease off the accelerator**

In wet conditions water can build up between your tyres and the road surface. This is known as aquaplaning and will cause your vehicle to slide. Tyres will not grip in this situation. Try to regain control by easing off the accelerator to gradually lose speed. Do not brake or steer until tyre grip is restored.

Q. 6.47

Mark one answer

Why should you be especially aware of parked cars when driving at night?

- There are more of them
- They are more likely to move off
- The drivers may be drunk
- They can park without lights

Answer

✓ **They can park without lights**

Vehicles below 1525 kg are permitted to park without lights on roads with a speed limit no greater than 30 mph. In dark streets you may not be able to see them clearly.

Q. 6.48

Mark one answer

You are waiting at a T-junction. A vehicle is coming from the right with the left signal flashing. What should you do?

- Move out and accelerate hard
- Wait until the vehicle starts to turn in
- Pull out before the vehicle reaches the junction
- Move out slowly

Answer

✓ **Wait until the vehicle starts to turn in**

Try to anticipate the actions of other road users. Their signals might be misleading. When you're waiting at a junction, don't emerge until you're sure of their intentions.

questions   answers

Q. 6.49

Mark one answer

On a motorway what do signs showing a crawler lane suggest?

- Advance warning for a steep downhill section
- Only lorries and buses are allowed to use that lane
- Vehicles fitted with speed limiters must use that lane
- There will be a long, gradual uphill gradient ahead

Answer

☑ **There will be a long, gradual uphill gradient ahead**

Before you overtake another vehicle, there are several things to consider. Due to the size and weight of your vehicle you'll need a long, clear road ahead before you attempt the manoeuvre. There are several factors to think about, but first ask yourself if overtaking is really necessary. You'll have to use your skill and judgement to assess the situation and decide whether you can overtake safely. If you see a crawler lane sign ahead this would indicate an uphill gradient. You shouldn't attempt any manoeuvre that would require an increase in speed, such as overtaking. The combination of a heavy load, a speed limiter and a gradient may leave you without the power to overtake safely.

Q. 6.50

Mark one answer

You become stuck in snow. What might help you to move off?

- Trolley jack
- Can of de icer
- Wheel brace
- Shovel

Answer

☑ **Shovel**

A shovel can be used to clear away deep snow, and to make a clear path for the vehicle to pull away in. Cloth sacks can be placed under the wheels in order for them to have something to grip on while the vehicle pulls clear.

Q. 6.51

Mark one answer

What might help you to move off when you are stuck in snow?

- Trolley jack
- Cloth sacks
- Wheel brace
- Can of de icer

Answer

☑ **Cloth sacks**

Cloth sacks placed under the wheels will provide extra grip. It will also be useful to carry a shovel in your vehicle.

questions

answers

Q. 6.52

Mark two answers

You are about to pass this car. What are the TWO main hazards you should be aware of?

☐ Bright sunshine reflecting off the car windscreen

☐ The driver's side door may suddenly open

☐ The parked car may move off with no warning

☐ The narrow pavement on the right

Answers

✅ **The driver's side door may suddenly open**

✅ **The parked car may move off with no warning**

You do not know what the driver of this car will do. Be prepared for any hazard. The driver may not have seen you. Planning ahead will allow you to be in the correct gear and at the correct speed to be able to deal safely with this hazard.

Q. 6.53

Mark one answer

Before braking in wet conditions you should make sure, as far as possible, that

☐ the gear lever is in neutral

☐ all spray suppression equipment is working

☐ there is no mist on your rear view mirrors

☐ your vehicle is travelling in a straight line

Answer

✅ **your vehicle is travelling in a straight line**

If you need to brake when the road surface is wet, do so while your vehicle is travelling in a straight line. This will lessen the risk of skidding. As a professional driver you should be in the routine of braking in good time, so that you aren't braking and changing direction at the same time.

questions answers

Q. 6.54

Mark one answer

You have parked your vehicle on a two-way road at night. You should

- leave the lights on
- switch off all lights
- leave your lights on if you have parked on the right-hand side
- switch off your lights if you have parked underneath a street lamp

Answer

 leave the lights on

Large vehicles are required by law to leave lights on when parked at night, unless in a designated off-road parking area. Also, unless you're in a one-way street, you must only park on the left-hand side. It's generally much better to park off-road if you can, particularly if you're going to be stationary for a long period of time.

Q. 6.55

Mark two answers

When driving, on which TWO occasions would you be most likely to experience weight transfer?

- Reversing
- Braking
- Overtaking
- Unloading
- Cornering
- Loading

Answers

☑ **Braking**

☑ **Cornering**

You must take extra care when your vehicle is carrying a load. When braking or cornering, the vehicle's weight will transfer. When cornering, weight will be transferred away from the direction in which you're turning. If you are also braking, weight can be transferred in several different directions.

Q. 6.56

Mark three answers

When driving a laden vehicle downhill, the effect of gravity will tend to

- make the vehicle use more fuel
- make the vehicle's speed increase
- require more braking effort
- require less braking effort
- increase stopping distances
- reduce stopping distances

Answers

☑ **make the vehicle's speed increase**

☑ **require more braking effort**

☑ **increase stopping distances**

Always plan ahead; take note of warning signs informing you of the gradient of the hill. Make sure you reduce your speed and select an appropriate lower gear in good time.

questions answers

Q. 6.57

Mark one answer

Long vehicles need to straddle lanes

- to avoid mounting the kerb
- to avoid braking sharply
- when driving on motorways
- when coming to contraflow systems

Answer

☑ **to avoid mounting the kerb**

When driving a long vehicle around corners it's sometimes necessary to adopt a different road position to avoid mounting the kerb or colliding with street furniture such as lamp posts, traffic signs, etc. Other road users may not understand what you intend to do next. Watch them carefully and always signal in good time.

Q. 6.58

Mark one answer

When driving in windy weather, you should

- drive in a normal manner in exposed areas
- anticipate how conditions may affect other road users
- never alter your intended route if this would lengthen a journey
- always overtake smaller or vulnerable vehicles quickly

Answer

☑ **anticipate how conditions may affect other road users**

Cyclists and motorcyclists are very vulnerable in high winds. They can be blown into your path. Plan ahead and give them a wide berth.

Q. 6.59

Mark one answer

You are driving a high-sided vehicle on a motorway. You should be especially aware of the effects of crosswinds on your vehicle

- when travelling in cuttings
- after passing motorway bridges
- after passing motorway signs
- when travelling in tunnels

Answer

☑ **after passing motorway bridges**

Bridges provide shelter from wind. The force of wind after passing a bridge can be stronger than expected. Be prepared for this and be ready to react.

questions   answers

Q. 6.60

Mark two answers

High-sided vehicles can be affected by side winds. In which TWO situations is this most likely?

- Narrow country roads
- Open roads
- Motorway flyovers
- Motorway underpasses
- Built-up areas
- Roads with speed humps

Answers

- ☑ **Open roads**
- ☑ **Motorway flyovers**

As a driver of a large vehicle you should listen to weather forecasts, which will tell you of any severe weather conditions. Plan your route accordingly. You're most likely to be subjected to high winds where there are

- high-level bridges
- high-level roads
- exposed viaducts
- exposed stretches of motorway.

Q. 6.61

Mark two answers

You are driving a high-sided vehicle. Which of these places may cause you problems on a windy day?

- Road tunnels
- High-level roads
- Dead ground
- Ring roads
- Exposed viaducts
- Residential roads

Answers

- ☑ **High-level roads**
- ☑ **Exposed viaducts**

Listen to the weather forecasts and plan your route to avoid exposed roads. If you can delay your journey or take an alternative route you could save yourself, your employer and the emergency services a lot of unnecessary work and expense.

Q. 6.62

Mark one answer

Which of the following vehicles is least likely to be affected by high winds?

Answer

The car is the most stable of the vehicles shown. All vehicles are affected by crosswinds and buffeting from larger vehicles. Be aware that your speed and road position could cause unnecessary turbulence when passing smaller vehicles.

Q. 6.63

Mark one answer

What is a 'buffer' lane?

A lane for large vehicles blown off course

A lane for overtaking

A lane to park in until the wind drops

The only lane to be used in high winds

Answer

☑ **A lane for large vehicles blown off course**

During high winds one of the lanes on high bridges might be closed to traffic to create a 'buffer' lane. This lane is kept free to prevent vehicles being blown into the path of other road users in the next lane. The closure of this lane may cause traffic congestion and delay.

Q. 6.64

Mark one answer

In high winds where would you expect to find 'buffer' lanes?

In built-up areas

On high bridges

On country roads

In roadworks

Answer

☑ **On high bridges**

If your route takes in any locations that are frequently subjected to high winds, such as

- high-level bridges
- high-level roads
- exposed viaducts
- exposed stretches of motorway

listen to the weather forecasts, which will inform you of any need to replan your route.

questions answers

Q. 6.65

Mark one answer

When is a 'buffer' lane most likely to be in use?

- ☐ When windy
- ☐ When raining
- ☐ When foggy
- ☐ When icy

Answer

☑ When windy

A buffer lane is established when the wind begins to cause a risk to high-sided vehicles. At other times it will be a normal lane. Don't use the buffer lane unless your vehicle has been blown off course into it, or you need to use it to avoid an accident. Leave it free, however heavy the traffic.

Q. 6.66

Mark one answer

How can you best control your vehicle when driving on snow in windy conditions?

- ☐ By keeping the engine revs high and spinning the wheels
- ☐ By driving in your very lowest crawler gear
- ☐ By keeping the engine revs high and slipping the clutch
- ☐ By driving slowly in as high a gear as possible

Answer

☑ By driving slowly in as high a gear as possible

Driving slowly will give you better control of your vehicle. By using a high gear you reduce the chance of your wheels spinning and skidding on the snow.

Q. 6.67

Mark one answer

Which of these vehicles is most at risk from strong crosswinds on motorways?

- ☐ A motorcycle
- ☐ An unladen lorry
- ☐ A sports car
- ☐ A road tanker

Answer

☑ A motorcycle

Motorcyclists can be very vulnerable to strong crosswinds. Allow extra room when overtaking them in windy weather. Check your nearside mirror whilst alongside and before moving back to the left.

questions answers

Q. 6.68

Mark one answer

You are driving a large vehicle in gusty conditions. Which of the following is most likely to be affected when you overtake it?

■ A motorcycle

■ A flat-bed lorry

■ A car

■ A loaded tanker

Answer

☑ **A motorcycle**

Give motorcyclists extra room in windy conditions. A combination of gusty conditions and buffeting caused by your vehicle can easily upset the motorcyclist's control and balance.

Q. 6.69

Mark one answer

You are driving on a motorway in high winds. You are overtaking a motorcyclist. You should be especially aware of the effects caused by

■ exhaust smoke

■ engine noise

■ buffeting

■ tyre noise

Answer

☑ **buffeting**

Always watch motorcyclists carefully in your nearside mirror when you overtake them. Give them plenty of room as the rider might wobble or be blown off course.

Q. 6.70

Mark one answer

In gusty winds on a motorway you must be aware of motorcyclists as they may

■ be blown into your path

■ leave at the next exit

■ suddenly stop on the hard shoulder

■ position to turn right

Answer

☑ **be blown into your path**

On motorways there are often exposed stretches of road where there are strong crosswinds. A gust of wind can force a motorcyclist to swerve across the lanes. GIVE THEM PLENTY OF ROOM!

questions   answers

Q. 6.71

Mark three answers

Which road users are in the most danger from the buffeting effects of large vehicles?

- Lorry drivers
- Coach drivers
- Tractor drivers
- Pedestrians
- Horse riders
- Cyclists

Answers

- ☑ **Pedestrians**
- ☑ **Horse riders**
- ☑ **Cyclists**

Remember that buffeting can affect other road users including

- cars towing caravans
- motorcyclists.

Q. 6.72

Mark four answers

Which road users would be most affected by turbulence caused by your vehicle?

- Pedestrians
- Car drivers towing caravans
- Drivers of skip lorries
- Cyclists
- Coach drivers
- Horse riders

Answers

- ☑ **Pedestrians**
- ☑ **Car drivers towing caravans**
- ☑ **Cyclists**
- ☑ **Horse riders**

Be considerate when passing more vulnerable road users. Give them plenty of room, don't use the size of your vehicle to intimidate other road users.

Q. 6.73

Mark four answers

Turbulence is created by large vehicles travelling at speed. This is most likely to be a danger to

- low-loaders
- cyclists
- pedestrians
- motorcyclists
- tankers
- caravans

Answers

- ☑ **cyclists**
- ☑ **pedestrians**
- ☑ **motorcyclists**
- ☑ **caravans**

Passing too close to any of the above will create turbulence which could affect their balance or control. Don't be guilty of putting others in danger through thoughtless or inconsiderate driving.

Q. 6.74

Mark one answer

You are overtaking a motorcycle in windy conditions. Why should you always check your nearside mirror?

- To check your road position
- To see if the rider is still in control of the motorcycle
- To see if other vehicles have been affected
- To check if it is properly adjusted

Answer

☑ **To see if the rider is still in control of the motorcycle**

You must check the nearside mirror during and after overtaking a motorcyclist. Make sure that the rider is still in control and that your vehicle hasn't caused buffeting.

Q. 6.75

Mark three answers

Which THREE of the following are most likely to be affected by high winds?

- Slow-moving vehicles
- Cyclists
- Vehicles towing caravans
- Curtain-sided vehicles
- Track-laying vehicles
- Front-wheel drive vehicles

Answers

☑ **Cyclists**

☑ **Vehicles towing caravans**

☑ **Curtain-sided vehicles**

Very windy conditions can cause certain types of vehicles to be blown off course. Be aware of these and allow extra room when overtaking.

Q. 6.76

Mark one answer

You are driving a high sided vehicle on a motorway. You should be especially aware of the effects of crosswinds on your vehicle when

- travelling in cuttings
- travelling through tunnels
- driving across viaducts
- passing motorway signs

Answer

☑ **driving across viaducts**

On motorways you should be especially careful when driving over bridges and viaducts which are frequently subjected to high winds. Be prepared to reduce your speed.

questions answers

Q. 6.77

Mark one answer

You are following a scooter on an uneven road. You should

- allow extra room, they may swerve to avoid pot holes
- leave less room so they can see you in their mirrors
- drive closely behind and get ready to overtake
- drive close to shield them

Answer

☑ **allow extra room, they may swerve to avoid pot holes**

Never follow any road user too closely. This is particularly important when you are following scooter or motorcycle riders or cyclists. They might brake or swerve suddenly, for example, due to poor road surface conditions. Don't use the size of your vehicle to intimidate them. Be professional and set an example to others.

Q. 6.78

Mark one answer

On a motorway the surface is still wet after rain. You should take extra care when overtaking because

- wet roads may create more buffeting
- other vehicles will have their lights on
- vehicles may be parked on the hard shoulder
- the road may still be slippery

Answer

☑ **the road may still be slippery**

Rain reacts with oil, dirt and debris on the surface, reducing grip between the tyres and the road.

Q. 6.79

Mark one answer

The road is wet. Why might a motorcyclist steer around drain covers on a bend?

- To prevent the motorcycle skidding
- To avoid puncturing the tyres
- To help steer around the bend
- To avoid splashing pedestrians

Answer

☑ **To prevent the motorcycle skidding**

Drain covers usually have a metal surface. When wet they can cause the motorcycle to skid.

questions   answers

Q. 6.80
Mark one answer

In heavy rain what is the least amount of space you should allow for braking?

- The normal distance
- Twice the normal distance
- Three times the normal distance
- Five times the normal distance

Answer

☑ **Twice the normal distance**

Your tyres could lose their grip in wet conditions. If you're travelling in heavy rain you should be aware that it could take twice as long for you to stop as in dry weather. Therefore increase your distance from the vehicle in front.

Q. 6.81
Mark three answers

You are driving on a motorway. Your view ahead is poor due to heavy spray. Which THREE of the following should you do?

- Move into the lane on the right
- Use the four-second rule
- Switch on your dipped headlights
- Switch on your full-beam headlights
- Reduce your speed

Answers

☑ **Use the four-second rule**

☑ **Switch on your dipped headlights**

☑ **Reduce your speed**

If you're travelling on a motorway and your view ahead is poor then you should reduce your speed. Leave about four seconds between you and the vehicle in front, and make sure that others can see you by using your dipped headlights.

Q. 6.82
Mark one answer

When overtaking on motorways in very wet weather, what is the main danger that can affect your vehicle?

- Your engine may get flooded
- Your braking distance may be reduced
- Your steering may become heavy
- Your tyres may lose grip

Answer

☑ **Your tyres may lose grip**

Water can form a layer between the road and the tyre resulting in a loss of contact with the road. This is known as aquaplaning.

questions answers

Q. 6.83

Mark one answer

Overtaking on a motorway in heavy rain needs extra care because of

- slippery manhole covers
- spray from traffic
- reduced braking distances
- bright reflections

Answer

☑ **spray from traffic**

Other drivers can be affected by the spray created by your vehicle, causing them to be temporarily blinded. Always take care when you need to change lanes, give a signal in good time and watch your mirrors carefully before pulling out in these conditions.

Q. 6.84

Mark one answer

Visibility can be worse when driving at higher speeds in wet weather because

- drivers always bunch together
- headlights will dazzle you more easily
- of people driving at different speeds
- more spray is thrown up

Answer

☑ **more spray is thrown up**

The faster a wheel turns, the more spray is thrown up from the road to the side and rear of the vehicle. Always use dipped headlights in poor visibility caused by rain and spray.

Q. 6.85

Mark one answer

You intend to overtake a large vehicle that is throwing up spray. You should

- get much closer before moving out
- wait until the other driver gives a left signal
- move out earlier than normal
- wait for the other vehicle to slow down on a hill

Answer

☑ **move out earlier than normal**

If you wish to overtake a vehicle that's throwing up spray, move out to overtake earlier than normal. This will prevent you being affected by the rear spray as well as the side spray as you pass.

Q. 6.86

Mark one answer

Your vehicle is fitted with spray suppression equipment. What effect will this have on other drivers if it is NOT in good working order?

▪ Their vision will be increased

▪ Their vision will be reduced

▪ They will be able to overtake quickly

▪ They will be able to follow closely

Answer

☑ **Their vision will be reduced**

Spray suppression equipment reduces the amount of spray thrown up to other road users. Check the equipment regularly to make sure it is secure.

Q. 6.87

Mark one answer

The purpose of the brushes fitted to this vehicle is to

▪ clear mud from the tyres on building sites

▪ remove objects from the tyre tread

▪ stop snow building up behind the wheel

▪ reduce spray and increase visibility

Answer

☑ **reduce spray and increase visibility**

The brushes are part of a spray suppression system which stops water from being thrown up at the sides and to the rear of the vehicle. Check them regularly for security, and if they become worn make sure they are replaced.

questions answers

Q. 6.88

Mark one answer

You should check your vehicle's spray suppression equipment

- [ ] only when you will be using a motorway
- [ ] before setting out on a journey
- [ ] only at the start of winter as a pre-winter check
- [ ] yearly before the MOT test

Answer

☑ **before setting out on a journey**

You should check all your spray suppression equipment before setting out. Bear in mind that the weather may change during the course of the journey.

Q. 6.89

Mark one answer

In wet weather, following drivers will be able to see better if your vehicle is fitted with

- [ ] spray reducers
- [ ] side-panel skirts
- [ ] wind deflectors
- [ ] a catalytic converter

Answer

☑ **spray reducers**

Spray reducers or spray suppression equipment are attachments fitted around the wheel arch area of large vehicles. They effectively trap the water thrown up from the wheels when driving on wet roads. This improves visibility for you and other drivers who wish to overtake.

Q. 6.90

Mark one answer

This vehicle is fitted with spray suppression equipment. This will be most useful when it is

- [ ] raining
- [ ] snowing
- [ ] windy
- [ ] foggy

Answer

☑ **raining**

The spray suppression equipment helps prevent water being thrown up and causing reduced visibility. Driving at a reduced speed in wet weather conditions will also help to reduce the amount of water thrown up by your vehicle.

questions   answers

Q. 6.91

Mark one answer

When driving through deep water you should drive

- slowly in a low gear with engine speed high
- slowly in a high gear with engine speed low
- as quickly as possible to cause less delay
- at normal speed if you have spray reducers fitted

Answer

☑ **slowly in a low gear with engine speed high**

It is important to keep the engine speed high to prevent water entering the engine through the exhaust system. It may be necessary to slip the clutch in these circumstances to keep the road speed as low as possible.

Q. 6.92

Mark one answer

You are approaching a working snow plough on a motorway. You should not overtake because

- it is illegal to overtake snow ploughs
- snow ploughs are left-hand drive only
- your speed could cause snow to drift behind
- there may be deep snow ahead

Answer

☑ **there may be deep snow ahead**

There is no way of knowing how deep the snow could be ahead. If you overtake and then become stuck in the snow you may cause problems for the snow plough, particularly if you block the road.

Q. 6.93

Mark three answers

You are driving in heavy rain. Why is there a need to increase your distance from the vehicle in front?

- To prevent rain entering the vehicle's braking system
- The tyres will have less grip on the road surface
- Spray from traffic will make it difficult to see ahead
- To reduce the risk of water spraying into filters
- Normal stopping distances could be doubled

Answers

☑ **The tyres will have less grip on the road surface**

☑ **Spray from traffic will make it difficult to see ahead**

☑ **Normal stopping distances could be doubled**

Extra care is needed when driving in adverse weather conditions. Reduce your speed and switch on dipped headlights. Tyres will have less grip on a wet road so it will take longer to stop. Spray from large vehicles will be an added hazard, especially on motorways.

questions   answers

Q. 6.94

Mark one answer

You are driving a large vehicle on a motorway. Why should you slow down when the roads are very wet?

☐ To force other drivers to act properly and slow down

☐ To reduce the amount of spray thrown up

☐ To prevent water entering the braking system

☐ To stop the electrics getting wet

Answer

☑ **To reduce the amount of spray thrown up**

Driving at high speed on a wet motorway can seriously reduce vision. Spray thrown up by large, fast-moving vehicles can make it very difficult for other drivers to see ahead.

Q. 6.95

Mark one answer

You are driving on a motorway in heavy rain. When would you be allowed to use high-intensity rear fog lights?

☐ When visibility is more than 100 metres (328 feet)

☐ Only when the national speed limit applies

☐ Only when you are being followed closely by other traffic

☐ When visibility is reduced to 100 metres (328 feet) or less

Answer

☑ **When visibility is reduced to 100 metres (328 feet) or less**

Heavy rain and the resulting spray from higher speeds and large vehicles can seriously affect visibility on the motorway. Reduce your speed and use your headlights. Do not use high-intensity rear lights UNLESS visibility is reduced to 100 metres (328 feet) or less.

Q. 6.96

Mark one answer

You are driving on a motorway in heavy rain. What could cause your steering to be less responsive?

☐ Water reducing the tyre grip on the road

☐ Tyres becoming hotter in the bad weather

☐ Braking gently and in good time

☐ Water entering the braking system

Answer

☑ **Water reducing the tyre grip on the road**

Be careful when driving in bad weather. Steering can be less responsive when the roads are wet because water prevents the tyres from gripping the road. If this happens, ease off the accelerator and slow down gradually.

Q. 6.97

Mark one answer

What causes extra danger when overtaking in rain?

- Other vehicles driving slowly
- Vehicles wandering across lanes
- Increase in vehicle noise
- Spray from large vehicles

Answer

✓ **Spray from large vehicles**

Other vehicles might create heavy spray, so you must be cautious when you're overtaking. Severe spray can result in a complete loss of vision as you overtake. Be aware of this and anticipate it happening. Spray from your vehicle could cause the driver of an overtaking vehicle to lose visibility. You should be aware of this as smaller vehicles overtake you.

Q. 6.98

Mark one answer

A driver pulls out of a side road in front of you. You have to brake hard. You should

- ignore the error and stay calm
- flash your lights to show your annoyance
- sound your horn to show your annoyance
- overtake as soon as possible

Answer

✓ **ignore the error and stay calm**

If you're driving where there are a number of side roads, be alert. Drivers approaching or emerging from the side road might not be able to see you. Be especially careful if there are a lot of parked vehicles. If a vehicle does emerge and you have to stop quickly, try to be tolerant and learn from the experience.

Q. 6.99

Mark one answer

A car driver pulls out causing you to brake. You should

- keep calm and not retaliate
- overtake and sound your horn
- drive close behind and sound your horn
- flag the driver down and explain the mistake

Answer

✓ **keep calm and not retaliate**

You have to understand that others on the road might disobey the rules or make an error of judgement at times. Try to accept this calmly and learn from other people's mistakes.

questions answers

Q. 6.100

Mark one answer

Another driver's behaviour has upset you. It may help if you

- ☐ stop and take a break
- ☐ shout abusive language
- ☐ gesture to them with your hand
- ☐ follow their car, flashing your headlights

Answer

☑ **stop and take a break**

Tiredness may make you more irritable than you would be normally. You might react differently to situations because of it. If you feel yourself becoming tense, take a break.

Q. 6.101

Mark three answers

A vehicle travelling downhill will

- ☐ need more engine power
- ☐ need more braking effort
- ☐ take longer to stop
- ☐ need a shorter stopping distance
- ☐ require less braking effort
- ☐ increase speed quickly

Answers

☑ **need more braking effort**

☑ **take longer to stop**

☑ **increase speed quickly**

When a vehicle is stationary on level ground the only force acting on it is the downward pull of gravity. When travelling on a downhill gradient the effect of gravity will tend to make the vehicle's speed increase, require more braking effort and increased stopping distances.

Q. 6.102

Mark one answer

The road is wet. Why should you slow down as you approach this pedestrian?

- ☐ Because there are no road markings
- ☐ To avoid splashing them
- ☐ Because they have priority
- ☐ To encourage them to cross

Answer

☑ **To avoid splashing them**

Drive with consideration along wet roads, especially if pedestrians are walking or standing near the kerb.

questions

answers

Q. 6.103

Mark two answers

Tailgating another vehicle is dangerous because

- ▪ your job could be at risk
- ▪ your braking time is increased
- ▪ your view to the rear is reduced
- ▪ your view ahead is reduced
- ▪ your room for braking is reduced

Answers

- ☑ **your view ahead is reduced**
- ☑ **your room for braking is reduced**

Tailgating is very dangerous because there is no safety distance in which to stop between yourself and the driver in front. It also intimidates the driver you are following.

Q. 6.104

Mark one answer

Hazard warning lights may be used while moving when

- ▪ you have just overtaken another vehicle
- ▪ you need to reverse for some distance
- ▪ traffic ahead is slowing quickly on a motorway
- ▪ one of your lights has failed

Answer

- ☑ **traffic ahead is slowing quickly on a motorway**

While moving, hazard warning lights may only be used on a motorway or unrestricted dual carriageway to warn drivers behind of a need to slow down, due to a temporary obstruction ahead.

Q. 6.105

Mark one answer

You are driving in town and see these lights flashing. What would you expect to see ahead?

- ▪ Contraflow system
- ▪ Uneven road surface
- ▪ Children crossing the road
- ▪ Roadworks ahead

Answer

- ☑ **Children crossing the road**

These lights warn of children likely to be crossing the road on their way to and from school. Slow down and watch out for them.

questions answers

Q. 6.106

Mark one answer

Where are these lights found?

▨ On approach to a level crossing

▨ Near a fire station

▨ On approach to a motorway

▨ Near a school

Answer

☑ **Near a school**

Flashing amber lights are found near schools. They warn you that children are likely to be crossing the road to and from school. Drive slowly until you are clear of the area.

Q. 6.107

Mark one answer

You are allowed to use hazard warning lights while moving when

▨ towing another vehicle

▨ an overtaking lorry has cleared the front of your vehicle

▨ being towed by another vehicle

▨ traffic ahead on a motorway is slowing down quickly

Answer

☑ **traffic ahead on a motorway is slowing down quickly**

Hazard warning lights may only be used while moving when driving on motorways, or unrestricted dual carriageways. You can only use them to warn drivers behind you of a hazard or obstruction ahead.

questions answers

Q. 6.108

Mark three answers

What extra problems may you have when driving at night?

- Increased overtaking distances
- An increase in traffic
- Reduced visibility
- Reduced braking distances
- Dazzle from other vehicles
- Becoming tired

Answers

- ☑ **Reduced visibility**
- ☑ **Dazzle from other vehicles**
- ☑ **Becoming tired**

Make sure that you drive within the speed limit, even if the roads appear to be empty. You must be able to stop safely in the distance that you can see clear ahead, which will be the distance illuminated by your headlights or by street lights.

Q. 6.109

Mark one answer

Another driver does something that upsets you. You should

- try not to react
- let them know how you feel
- flash your headlights several times
- sound your horn

Answer

- ☑ **try not to react**

There are occasions when other drivers or riders make a misjudgement or a mistake. If this happens, try not to let it worry you. Don't react by showing anger. Sounding the horn, flashing your headlights or shouting at the other driver won't help the situation. Good anticipation will help to prevent these incidents becoming accidents.

Q. 6.110

Mark one answer

You should take extra care when overtaking at night because

- every driver will normally be tired
- large vehicles are subject to a 10% speed reduction
- speed and distance are harder to judge
- most towns are not adequately lit

Answer

- ☑ **speed and distance are harder to judge**

In the darkness it will be difficult to assess the road ahead, especially if there are bends or hills which may prevent you from seeing an oncoming vehicle.

questions

answers

Q. 6.111

Mark one answer

You are driving along a motorway in thick fog at night. The reflective studs are red on your left and white on your right. You are driving

- [ ] in the right-hand lane
- [ ] on the hard shoulder
- [ ] in the left-hand lane
- [ ] in the middle lane

Answer

☑ **in the left-hand lane**

The red studs indicate the hard shoulder. Always use more than one reference point at all times. This will help you to be more certain of your position.

Q. 6.112

Mark one answer

You are driving on a three-lane motorway. You are about to move into the middle lane to overtake a slower vehicle. You should check

- [ ] for traffic in the right-hand lane returning to the middle lane
- [ ] for traffic which is intending to leave at the next exit
- [ ] the nearside mirror before pulling out
- [ ] for any traffic behind that is trying to pass you on the left

Answer

☑ **for traffic in the right-hand lane returning to the middle lane**

Traffic returning from the right-hand lane can be a hazard to be aware of when overtaking. Always check your blind spot before changing lanes.

questions

answers

Q. 6.113

Mark one answer

Before overtaking or changing lanes on a motorway you should always

- ■ check your mirrors carefully
- ■ change to a lower gear
- ■ look over your left shoulder
- ■ increase your speed gently

Answer
 check your mirrors carefully

Check your mirrors to ensure that it is safe to overtake. Remember that traffic coming up behind you will be travelling at a faster speed.

Q. 6.114

Mark one answer

You are driving at the maximum speed limit for your vehicle on a clear motorway. You should keep to

- ■ any one of the lanes
- ■ the middle lane
- ■ the right-hand lane
- ■ the left-hand lane

Answer
✓ **the left-hand lane**

You should remain in the left-hand lane unless you are overtaking other vehicles. Don't be inconsiderate and hog the centre or right-hand lane of a two-lane motorway.

Q. 6.115

Mark one answer

You are driving in the left-hand lane of a motorway. You see another large vehicle merging from a slip road. It is travelling at the same speed as you. You should

- ■ try to race and get ahead of it
- ■ leave the other vehicle to adjust its speed
- ■ stay at the maximum speed allowed for your vehicle
- ■ be ready to adjust your speed

Answer
✓ **be ready to adjust your speed**

Be alert for this type of situation developing; it is not always possible to change lanes safely. The merging driver has a responsibility to give way if necessary. Don't change lanes if it will inconvenience or endanger other road users on the main carriageway.

Q. 6.116

Mark two answers

When driving in the left-hand lane of a motorway you see merging vehicles travelling at the same speed as you. You should

- ☐ try and accelerate past them
- ☐ move to the next lane if safe
- ☐ allow the traffic to merge by adjusting your speed
- ☐ expect the traffic to let you pass

Answers

- ☑ **move to the next lane if safe**
- ☑ **allow the traffic to merge by adjusting your speed**

Only change lanes if doing so will not inconvenience other road users on the main carriageway. Merging drivers have a responsibility to give way, if necessary, and not force their way into the main carriageway. Planning ahead will ensure you are well prepared to deal with these situations.

Q. 6.117

Mark three answers

You should take extra care before moving into the centre lane of a three-lane motorway because

- ☐ the centre lane is narrower
- ☐ another vehicle might be planning to use the same lane
- ☐ other drivers need time to react
- ☐ car drivers might not know they must give way to large vehicles
- ☐ the bridge height clearance will be less in that lane
- ☐ traffic from behind may be travelling much faster than you

Answers

- ☑ **another vehicle might be planning to use the same lane**
- ☑ **other drivers need time to react**
- ☑ **traffic from behind may be travelling much faster than you**

You should plan ahead to assess the actions of other vehicles using the road. Always indicate your intentions in good time, this will allow others to revise their course of action if necessary. Always check your blind spots before changing lanes.

questions   answers

Q. 6.118

Mark one answer

Normally, vehicles over 7.5 tonnes maximum authorised mass may use the right-hand lane of a motorway only when

- ■ it is a three-lane motorway
- ■ there are vehicles on the hard shoulder
- ■ it is a two-lane motorway
- ■ other vehicles are turning right

Answer

 it is a two-lane motorway

Goods and passenger vehicles with a MAM of more than 7.5 tonnes must not use the right-hand lane on motorways with more than two lanes, unless there are exceptional circumstances.

Q. 6.119

Mark one answer

You have just overtaken another vehicle on a motorway. When moving back to the left you should avoid

- ■ cutting in
- ■ increasing your speed
- ■ changing gear
- ■ signalling

Answer

☑ **cutting in**

Always check your nearside mirror carefully before moving back to the left after overtaking. Don't rely on the other driver flashing their headlights. Remember, *The Highway Code* explains that the correct interpretation of this is simply 'I am here'.

Q. 6.120

Mark one answer

What is a crawler lane for?

- ■ To enable other traffic to overtake on the nearside
- ■ To enable large vehicles to pull over and park out of the way
- ■ To enable slow-moving traffic to move further over to the left on uphill gradients
- ■ To enable emergency vehicles to get to the scene of an accident quicker

Answer

☑ **To enable slow-moving traffic to move further over to the left on uphill gradients**

On a motorway where there's long uphill gradients there may be a crawler lane. This type of lane helps the traffic to flow by diverting the slower, heavy vehicles into an extra lane on the left.

questions answers

Q. 6.121

Mark one answer

You see this sign on a motorway. It means you are coming to a

- long downhill slope
- long uphill slope
- 'lorries only' lane
- service area

Answer

☑ **long uphill slope**

The term 'crawler lane' doesn't mean the lane is only for extremely slow vehicles. It is advising you of an extra lane on the left. Crawler lanes are usually built on sections of road where the length of the gradient is such that some large vehicles will be slowed to the point where they become a hazard for other road users.

Q. 6.122

Mark one answer

You should use a crawler lane

- to let faster traffic overtake you
- when turning right from major roads
- for parking when having a break
- when slowing down for a motorway exit

Answer

☑ **to let faster traffic overtake you**

Many vehicles are very powerful and can maintain speed even when climbing a gradient. Even if your vehicle is capable of maintaining speed, you can still use the crawler lane to allow other road users to overtake safely.

Q. 6.123

Mark one answer

Before overtaking you should

- flash your headlights to oncoming traffic
- look ahead for right-turn lane markings
- drive very close to the vehicle in front
- make a final check in your left mirror

Answer

☑ **look ahead for right-turn lane markings**

Before overtaking look well ahead for road markings and traffic signs which indicate a right turn ahead. If a vehicle is turning right you could risk a collision.

questions   answers

Q. 6.124

Mark three answers

You should not overtake when

- there are signs and road markings that allow you to
- you are unable to see clearly ahead
- you would have to break the speed limit
- your view of the road ahead is clear
- approaching motorway exits or slip roads
- other road users would have to slow down

Answers

☑ **you are unable to see clearly ahead**

☑ **you would have to break the speed limit**

☑ **other road users would have to slow down**

Never commit yourself to an overtaking manoeuvre with a large vehicle unless you are absolutely certain you have the time and space to see it through safely. Don't take unnecessary risks which endanger other road users.

Q. 6.125

Mark one answer

You are driving a fully laden vehicle. You are approaching an uphill gradient as you are overtaking another vehicle. Which of the following is NOT correct?

- You will be able to get past quicker
- The extra weight will make you slower
- It will take you longer to get past
- You will need more power from the engine

Answer

☑ **You will be able to get past quicker**

Always plan well ahead before overtaking. Take into consideration the size of your vehicle. The load on your vehicle will influence its handling and speed characteristics.

Q. 6.126

Mark one answer

After overtaking another large vehicle how would you know when it was safe to move back to the nearside lane?

- By waiting for the driver you have just overtaken to flash the headlights
- By checking your nearside mirror
- By using your hazard warning lights as a signal
- By moving over to the nearside in the hope that the other vehicle will slow down

Answer

☑ **By checking your nearside mirror**

While overtaking you'll need to judge carefully when to pull back into the nearside lane. Don't cut in too soon on the vehicle you've overtaken – leave a safety margin. Check your left-hand (nearside) mirror to make sure the rear of your vehicle is well clear. You should allow for the length of both vehicles and take into account the speed difference. Don't rely on signals from other drivers. They may be signalling to someone else.

questions answers

Q. 6.127

Mark one answer

Because of its size and design a large vehicle will have

- less blind spots than smaller vehicles
- more blind spots than smaller vehicles
- the same blind spots as smaller vehicles
- no blind spots at all

Answer

☑ **more blind spots than smaller vehicles**

Always take the time to check where your blind spots are at the earliest opportunity when driving a vehicle that is unfamiliar to you. If you are aware of the point when a vehicle disappears from view in your mirrors, then you can take steps to prevent an accident by checking that blind spot area before changes of direction. Good use of the mirrors when driving will help you to be aware of a vehicle in your blind spot areas.

Q. 6.128

Mark one answer

You are driving on a dual carriageway and intend to overtake the vehicle ahead. Behind there is a car approaching quickly in the right-hand lane. You should

- keep behind the slower vehicle
- signal and move out
- move up closer to the slower vehicle
- stay on the left, large vehicles cannot use the right-hand lane

Answer

☑ **keep behind the slower vehicle**

This will allow the faster-moving vehicle to overtake safely. If you pull out to overtake at this time, you will cause the car behind to brake sharply. Don't use the size of your vehicle to intimidate. Be professional and show consideration to other road users.

Q. 6.129

Mark one answer

What should you do after overtaking on a dual carriageway?

- Move back to the left as soon as possible
- Indicate left then right
- Wait until the other driver flashes their headlights
- Switch your rear lights on and off

Answer

☑ **Move back to the left as soon as possible**

When you are sure it is safe, signal if necessary and move back to the left. Don't drive for long distances in the centre or right-hand lane unnecessarily.

questions answers

Q. 6.130

Mark one answer

You are turning right at a roundabout driving a long vehicle. You need to occupy the left-hand lane. You should check mirrors and

- signal left on approach
- signal right on approach
- avoid giving a signal on approach
- signal right after entering the roundabout

Answer

☑ **signal right on approach**

There are times when, due to the size of your vehicle, you'll have to take up part of another lane. If you need to do this, make sure that you use effective observation all around. Be aware that other road users might not understand the reasons for your position on the road. You should signal your intentions and take up your position in good time.

Q. 6.131

Mark one answer

Long vehicles need to straddle lanes

- to avoid braking sharply
- when driving on motorways
- to avoid mounting the kerb
- when coming to contraflow systems

Answer

☑ **to avoid mounting the kerb**

When you have to straddle the lanes at small roundabouts or junctions, always signal in good time. Be alert for inexperienced road users who may, without realising, put themselves into a dangerous position.

Q. 6.132

Mark two answers

When approaching these roadworks, you should NOT

- start to overtake
- increase speed
- flash your headlights
- give any signals

Answers

☑ **start to overtake**

☑ **increase speed**

Slow down and look out for warning signs. Always obey speed limits at roadworks. Look for workers stepping into the road.

Don't use the size of your vehicle to force your way through. If the obstruction is on your side of the road, give way to oncoming traffic. Look for and act according to signals given by the person in charge of a 'Stop-Go' board or temporary traffic lights.

questions answers

Q. 6.133

Mark one answer

It is very windy. You are about to overtake a motorcyclist. You should

■ allow extra room
■ overtake slowly
■ sound your horn as you pass
■ keep close as you pass

Answer

 allow extra room

Cyclists and motorcyclists may become unbalanced by your vehicle passing too close. Plan ahead and give them plenty of room. Remember that your large vehicle can cause a vacuum which will suck the rider towards it. The noise and close proximity of your vehicle can also startle them, which could cause them to swerve suddenly.

Q. 6.134

Mark one answer

You are driving behind two cyclists. They are approaching a roundabout in the left-hand lane. What should you expect them to do?

■ Go in any direction
■ Turn left
■ Turn right
■ Go straight ahead

Answer

 Go in any direction

When following cyclists into a roundabout be aware that they might not take the exit you expect them to. Cyclists approaching in the left-hand lane may be turning right. They may not have been able to get into the correct lane due to busy traffic. Be courteous and give them room.

Q. 6.135

Mark one answer

You should never attempt to overtake a cyclist

■ on a roundabout
■ before you turn left
■ before you turn right
■ on a one-way street

Answer

 before you turn left

When you are driving a large vehicle always make good use of your nearside mirror before you turn left. Cyclists don't always understand the reasons why a large vehicle will adopt a position away from the kerb before turning left. Wait for them to pass the junction before you turn left.

questions

answers

Q. 6.136

Mark one answer

You are about to overtake a lorry. You should

- look well ahead for uphill gradients
- check your position in the left mirror
- quickly change to a higher gear
- close right up before pulling out

Answer

✓ **look well ahead for uphill gradients**

Plan your overtaking carefully. The weight of your vehicle combined with the restrictions imposed by a speed limiter are factors you should take into consideration.

Q. 6.137

Mark one answer

You are in the left-hand lane on a three-lane motorway. Before you overtake you should check for any vehicles in the right-hand lane that might be about to

- move to the right
- move back to the left
- cut in sharply behind you
- accelerate briskly in front of you

Answer

✓ **move back to the left**

Vehicles overtaking in the right-hand lane may return to the centre lane when they have finished their manoeuvre. You should look for this before starting to pull out. Don't rely on the size of your vehicle to claim right of way.

Q. 6.138

Mark three answers

Normally white lights on a vehicle at night show you that the vehicle is

- moving away from you
- moving towards you
- ahead of you and braking
- stationary facing you
- stationary and facing away from you
- reversing towards you

Answers

✓ **moving towards you**
✓ **stationary facing you**
✓ **reversing towards you**

Other road users must be able to recognise the size of your vehicle and which way you are going.

questions answers

Q. 6.139

Mark three answers

When driving at night you should make sure all your lights are clean and working correctly. Why is this?

- To enable you to see ahead properly
- To prevent the battery from overcharging
- So that other road users can see the size of your vehicle
- So that the intensity of street lighting can be reduced
- To allow following drivers to use dipped headlights
- So that other road users are aware of your direction of travel

Answers

- ☑ **To enable you to see ahead properly**
- ☑ **So that other road users can see the size of your vehicle**
- ☑ **So that other road users are aware of your direction of travel**

See and be seen. Driving at night when your vehicle is poorly lit is dangerous for you and other road users and pedestrians.

Q. 6.140

Mark one answer

High-intensity rear fog lights should be used when visibility is less than

- 100 metres (328 feet)
- 200 metres (656 feet)
- 300 metres (984 feet)
- 400 metres (1312 feet)

Answer

- ☑ **100 metres (328 feet)**

Large vehicles are no more visible than other vehicles in dense fog. If visibility is seriously reduced, use your fog lights to help other drivers see you.

Q. 6.141

Mark one answer

You should switch off fog lights when visibility is more than

- 10 metres (32 feet)
- your stopping distance
- your separation distance
- 100 metres (328 feet)

Answer

- ☑ **100 metres (328 feet)**

Do not drive with front or rear fog lights switched on unnecessarily. The glare from them can dazzle other drivers.

questions   answers

Q. 6.142

Mark one answer

You are driving at night in a built up area. To ensure that you can be seen you should use

- ■ dipped beam headlights
- ■ main beam headlights
- ■ side lights only
- ■ front fog lights only

Answer

☑ **dipped beam headlights**

Using dipped headlights will help others see you and also aids your visibility if the street lighting changes or isn't working.

Q. 6.143

Mark one answer

You should switch off rear fog lights when visibility is more than

- ■ 10 metres (32 feet)
- ■ 50 metres (164 feet)
- ■ 75 metres (246 feet)
- ■ 100 metres (328 feet)

Answer

☑ **100 metres (328 feet)**

Be professional; switch off your fog lights when visibility improves. Don't cause unnecessary glare or distraction to other drivers.

Q. 6.144

Mark one answer

You will be driving a high-floor coach. You will be going over several high bridges. Why should you check the weather forecast?

- ■ Rain can make crossing bridges very difficult for buses and coaches
- ■ In hot weather the bridges might be closed to heavy traffic
- ■ You won't be able to climb the bridges if it's frosty
- ■ Some roads may be closed to certain vehicles in high winds

Answer

☑ **Some roads may be closed to certain vehicles in high winds**

Some exposed places are frequently subject to high winds. These can include high-level bridges and roads, viaducts and some motorways. Check the weather forecast and plan an alternative route. Remember, you are responsible for your passengers' safety. DON'T ignore warnings of severe winds.

questions

answers

Q. 6.145
Mark one answer

As a bus driver, what should you do when overtaking a motorcyclist in strong winds?

- Sound the horn
- Pass close
- Use the nearside mirror
- Move back in early

Answer

☑ **Use the nearside mirror**

Motorcyclists can be blown into your path in strong winds. Check your nearside mirror and allow them PLENTY of room as you overtake.

Q. 6.146
Mark one answer

You are driving a bus in strong winds. What should you do when overtaking a motorcyclist?

- Pass close
- Move back early
- Give a thank you wave
- Pass wide

Answer

☑ **Pass wide**

In strong winds motorcyclists and cyclists are particularly vulnerable. When overtaking give them PLENTY of room and also check your nearside mirror as you pass.

Q. 6.147
Mark one answer

When overtaking a cyclist in heavy rain extra care has to be taken because of

- spray from your vehicle
- exhaust fumes from your vehicle
- noise from your vehicle
- the height of your vehicle

Answer

☑ **spray from your vehicle**

When passing other road users, especially motorcyclists and cyclists, the spray from your vehicle could affect their control. Pass them leaving plenty of room, and check in your left-hand mirror as you pass to see whether they're still in control.

questions   answers

Q. 6.148

Mark two answers

What TWO effects will a strong side wind have on a bus?

- Steering will be easier
- The bus will tend to go off course
- Braking will be affected
- Stopping distance will be increased
- Steering will be more difficult
- Stopping distance will be decreased

Answers

- ☑ **The bus will tend to go off course**
- ☑ **Steering will be more difficult**

Be alert for places where the road is shielded from the wind. When you are steering into the wind you may suddenly find yourself making an unintentional change of direction.

Q. 6.149

Mark one answer

Double-deck buses are more likely than single-deck buses to be affected by

- strong winds
- heavy rain
- thick fog
- dense spray

Answer

- ☑ **strong winds**

If you're driving a double-deck bus you'll feel the effect of the wind to a greater degree, due to the vehicle's extra height.

Q. 6.150

Mark one answer

As a bus driver what should you do when overtaking a motorcycle in strong winds?

- Pass close
- Move back early
- Pass wide
- Signal left

Answer

- ☑ **Pass wide**

Motorcycles can be blown into your path in strong winds. Allow them plenty of room when you are overtaking.

questions answers

Q. 6.151

Mark one answer

Spray suppression equipment fitted to buses is particularly useful when it is

- [ ] raining
- [ ] icy
- [ ] foggy
- [ ] windy

Answer

☑ **raining**

If there's heavy rain the spray suppression equipment fitted on your vehicle will protect other road users from loss of vision when following or passing your vehicle. Check the wheel arches to ensure that the fitments haven't worked loose and that no parts have broken off. Well-maintained equipment will force the spray back down onto the road instead of to the rear and the sides of the vehicle.

Q. 6.152

Mark two answers

Your bus breaks down on the motorway. You have several passengers on board. You should

- [ ] move the passengers to the rear
- [ ] place a warning triangle in front of the bus
- [ ] stop on the hard shoulder
- [ ] move the passengers to the front

Answers

☑ **stop on the hard shoulder**

☑ **move the passengers to the front**

Stop as far to the left as possible on the hard shoulder. Make sure all your passengers have moved as far as possible to the front of the vehicle. Send a responsible person to the nearest telephone; you will be directed to this by small arrows on marker posts.

questions

Q. 6.153

Mark four answers

Which of the following MUST be clearly displayed on your bus?

- Seating and standing capacity
- Location of all bus stops
- Emergency exit location
- The route timetable
- Fuel cut-off switch
- Electrical isolator switch

Q. 6.154

Mark one answer

On a six wheel double deck bus rear wheel punctures are

- much easier to detect
- more likely to happen
- more difficult to detect
- less likely to happen

Q. 6.155

Mark one answer

With a long bus, under normal driving conditions, when is it acceptable to straddle lanes?

- Only when joining a bus lane
- On all bends and corners
- On the approach to all roundabouts
- To avoid mounting the kerb

answers

Answers

- ☑ **Seating and standing capacity**
- ☑ **Emergency exit location**
- ☑ **Fuel cut-off switch**
- ☑ **Electrical isolator switch**

Ensure that all information required on the vehicle, by law referred to as the 'legal lettering', is displayed – seating/standing capacity, emergency exit location, fuel cut-off switch and electrical isolator.

Answer

☑ **more difficult to detect**

The handling of a six-wheel bus or coach is not much different from a two-axle vehicle, except that punctures can be more difficult to detect.

Answer

☑ **To avoid mounting the kerb**

There are times when you might have to take up part of another lane in order to make a turn or manoeuvre. Be on your guard for other road users by using your mirrors to check all around your vehicle. Other traffic might try to move up alongside in the gap you've left to make your turn. Good planning and anticipation will allow you to signal your intentions to other road users and take up your position in good time.

questions   answers

Q. 6.156

Mark one answer

When parked on the road at night, buses and coaches must

- [ ] be under street lights
- [ ] be within 25 metres (82 feet) of a street light
- [ ] have all of the interior lights switched on
- [ ] have their sidelights on

Answer

✓ **have their sidelights on**

Make sure that all your lights are working, and that they are clean. Your vehicle may cause other road users to slow down or stop, so they must be able to see you in good time.

Q. 6.157

Mark one answer

Unless there is street lighting, why could it be dangerous to overtake at night when driving a bus?

- [ ] There may be unseen dips or bends in the road
- [ ] You may dazzle other drivers
- [ ] It is harder to concentrate
- [ ] It is harder to keep control in the dark

Answer

✓ **There may be unseen dips or bends in the road**

On unlit roads it is more difficult to see where the road bends or if there are junctions or dips. This could also prevent you from seeing oncoming traffic. Don't endanger your passengers. Unless the road is well lit or you are on a dual carriageway, ask yourself if overtaking is absolutely necessary.

Q. 6.158

Mark one answer

Why do some buses have marker lights along their sides?

- [ ] To make them easier to overtake
- [ ] To help the driver when reversing
- [ ] To help any passengers getting on or off
- [ ] To make them easier to see at junctions

Answer

✓ **To make them easier to see at junctions**

Newer buses and coaches have marker lights along the side; these ensure that they are visible as they emerge from junctions and roundabouts, and in other situations.

Accident handling

This section looks at how to behave in the event of an accident.

The questions will ask you about

- **Reducing risk**

  good planning and anticipation, to lessen the risk of an accident

- **Injuries**

  what to do if someone is injured

- **Casualties**

  treatment and reporting procedures.

questions

answers

Q. 7.1

Mark two answers

There is a fire in your engine compartment. Which TWO of the following should you do?

- Open all windows
- Disconnect electrical leads
- Flag down a passing motorist
- Cut off the fuel supply
- Try to remove the load

Answers

☑ **Disconnect electrical leads**

☑ **Cut off the fuel supply**

If you suspect a fire, try to isolate the source. If at all possible, disconnect leads and cut off the fuel supply.

Q. 7.2

Mark one answer

Your vehicle breaks down in a tunnel. What should you do?

- Stay in your vehicle and wait for the Police
- Stand in the lane behind your vehicle to warn others
- Stand in front of your vehicle to warn oncoming drivers
- Leave your vehicle immediately and call for help

Answer

☑ **Leave your vehicle immediately and call for help**

A broken down vehicle in a tunnel can cause serious congestion and danger to other traffic and drivers. If your vehicle breaks down you should get help without delay. Switch on your hazard warning lights and then go to an emergency telephone point to call for help.

Q. 7.3

Mark one answer

In the UK the headroom under bridges, unless otherwise shown, is AT LEAST

- 4.8 metres (16 feet)
- 5 metres (16 feet 6 inches)
- 6 metres (19 feet 8 inches)
- 8 metres (26 feet 3 inches)

Answer

☑ **5 metres (16 feet 6 inches)**

You must always be aware of the height of the vehicle you're driving. There are about 800 incidents a year where vehicles or their loads hit railway or other bridges. Every effort should be made to prevent this happening. If you hit a bridge you must report it to the police and if it's a railway bridge you must also report it to the relevant railway authority. Failure to report an incident involving a railway bridge is an offence.

questions answers

Q. 7.4

Mark one answer

NI EXEMPT

You are approaching a bridge that has NO height restriction on it. The height of the bridge will be at least

◼ 3.6 metres (11 feet 10 inches)

◼ 4.4 metres (14 feet 5 inches)

◼ 4.8 metres (16 feet)

◼ 5 metres (16 feet 6 inches)

Answer

☑ **5 metres (16 feet 6 inches)**

The headroom under bridges in the UK is at least 5 metres (16 feet 6 inches), unless otherwise indicated. Where the overhead clearance is arched, this headroom is normally only between the limits marked.

Q. 7.5

Mark two answers

A laminated windscreen is one which

◼ will not shatter

◼ does not mist up

◼ has a plastic layer

◼ cuts down on glare

Answers

☑ **will not shatter**

☑ **has a plastic layer**

Windscreens are either laminated or toughened. The main difference is that toughened screens shatter, whereas a laminated screen will crack. A small crack may quickly become larger if the screen flexes as the vehicle is being driven.

Q. 7.6

Mark three answers

You are the first to arrive at the scene of an accident. Someone is unconscious. Which of the following should be given urgent priority to help them?

◼ Try to get them to drink water

◼ Look for any witnesses

◼ Clear the airway and keep it open

◼ Check that they are breathing

◼ Stop any bleeding

◼ Take the numbers of any vehicles involved

Answers

☑ **Clear the airway and keep it open**

☑ **Check that they are breathing**

☑ **Stop any bleeding**

Gently tilt the head to clear the airway. Check for at least ten seconds that the casualty is breathing by looking for movement in the chest, listening for sounds and feeling for breath on your cheek. Apply pressure to any wound that is bleeding, using the cleanest material available; avoid pressing on anything caught in the wound.

questions

answers

Q. 7.7

Mark one answer

What must you do if you are involved in an accident?

- Drive on for help
- Inform the police within seven days
- Stop at the scene of the accident
- Drive to the nearest police station

Answer

 Stop at the scene of the accident

If your vehicle is involved in an accident you must stop. If the accident causes any injury or damage to any other person or vehicle, to any animals not in your vehicle or to roadside property, you must stop at the scene and comply with certain legal obligations specified in *The Highway Code*.

Q. 7.8

Mark one answer

NI EXEMPT

Your vehicle has been involved in an accident where someone is injured. You do not produce the required insurance certificate at the time of the accident. You must report the accident to the police as soon as possible, or in any case within

- 24 hours
- 48 hours
- 72 hours
- seven days

Answer

 24 hours

If you don't give your name and address at the time of the accident, report the accident to the police as soon as reasonably practicable, or in any case within 24 hours. If any other person is injured and you don't produce your insurance certificate at the time of the accident to the police, or to any other person who has reasonable grounds to request it, you must also

- report the accident to the police as soon as possible, or in any case within 24 hours

- produce your insurance certificate to the police either when reporting the accident or within seven days (five days in Northern Ireland) at any police station you select.

questions   answers

Q. 7.9

Mark one answer

At the scene of an accident you see a plain orange rectangle displayed on one of the vehicles. This tells you that the vehicle

- is carrying dangerous goods
- is carrying a First Aid kit
- is carrying medical supplies
- is unladen

Answer

☑ **is carrying dangerous goods**

Vehicles that carry dangerous goods have badges displayed on the side and rear. These are coloured orange and show the type of material that's being carried. Make a note of this and report it to the emergency services when you contact them.

Q. 7.10

Mark one answer

You arrive at an accident where someone is suffering from severe burns. Which of the following would help?

- Douse the burns with cold water
- Remove anything stuck to the burns
- Burst blisters that form on the burns
- Apply ointment to the burns

Answer

☑ **Douse the burns with cold water**

Cold water will cool the burning tissue, help prevent further damage, reduce swelling, minimise shock and alleviate pain. Use water, or another liquid, that is clean and non-toxic.

Q. 7.11

Mark one answer

A vehicle has rolled over and caught fire. The drivers hands and arms have been burned. You should NOT

- douse the burns with cold water
- lay the casualty down
- remove smouldering clothing
- remove anything sticking to the burns

Answer

☑ **remove anything sticking to the burns**

Do not remove anything sticking to a burn. You may cause further damage and introduce infection into the wound.

questions   answers

Q. 7.12

Mark one answer

You arrive at the scene of an accident. A pedestrian is bleeding heavily from a leg wound. What should you do?

- Apply firm pressure to the wound
- Dab the wound to stop the bleeding
- Keep both legs flat on the ground
- Wrap an ice pack near the wound

Answer

☑ **Apply firm pressure to the wound**

Control blood loss by applying pressure over the wound and raising the leg if possible.

Q. 7.13

Mark one answer

An accident has just happened. An injured person is lying in the busy road. What is the first thing you should do to help?

- Treat the person for shock
- Warn other traffic
- Place them in the recovery position
- Make sure the injured person is kept warm

Answer

☑ **Warn other traffic**

You could do this by displaying an advanced warning signal, if you have one, or switching on hazard warning or other lights. You could also use any other means that does not put you at risk.

Q. 7.14

Mark three answers

You are the first person to arrive at an accident where people are badly injured. Which THREE should you do?

- Switch on your own hazard warning lights
- Make sure that someone telephones for an ambulance
- Try and get people who are injured to drink something
- Move the people who are injured clear of their vehicles
- Get people who are not injured clear of the scene

Answers

☑ **Switch on your own hazard warning lights**

☑ **Make sure that someone telephones for an ambulance**

☑ **Get people who are not injured clear of the scene**

If you're the first to arrive at the scene of an accident, further collisions and fire are the first concerns. Switching off vehicle engines will reduce the risk of fire. Your hazard warning lights will let approaching traffic know that there's a need for caution. Don't assume someone else has called the emergency services. Do it yourself.

questions   answers

Q. 7.15

Mark two answers

You are at the scene of an accident and there are several bystanders. Which TWO of the following should you do first?

▪ Always pull people who are hurt out of their vehicles

▪ Ask the bystanders to check the casualties for signs of bleeding

▪ Make sure that the emergency services have been called for

▪ Keep the bystanders clear as they do not know first aid

▪ Clear a parking area for ambulance and fire service crews

Answers

☑ **Ask the bystanders to check the casualties for signs of bleeding**

☑ **Make sure that the emergency services have been called for**

If any of the bystanders have first aid skills, encourage them to help. Otherwise try to keep them away from the accident scene.

Q. 7.16

Mark three answers

You arrive at a serious motorcycle accident. The motorcyclist is unconscious and bleeding. Your main priorities should be to

▪ try to stop the bleeding

▪ make a list of witnesses

▪ check the casualty's breathing

▪ take the numbers of the vehicles involved

▪ sweep up any loose debris

▪ check the casualty's airways

Answers

☑ **try to stop the bleeding**

☑ **check the casualty's breathing**

☑ **check the casualty's airways**

At a road accident the danger of further collisions and fire need to be dealt with first. Injuries should be dealt with in the order: Airway, Breathing, Circulation and bleeding. Do not remove a motorcyclist's helmet unless it is essential to do so.

Q. 7.17

Mark one answer

You arrive at an accident. A motorcyclist is unconscious. Your first priority is the casualty's

■ breathing
■ bleeding
■ broken bones
■ bruising

Answer

☑ **breathing**

The first priority when dealing with an unconscious person is to make sure they can breathe. This may involve clearing their airway if they're having difficulty or some obstruction is obvious but don't attempt to remove a motorcyclist's safety helmet unless it's essential – serious injury could result.

At the scene of an accident make sure there is no danger from further collisions or fire before dealing with any casualties.

Q. 7.18

Mark three answers

At an accident a casualty is unconscious. Which three of the following should you check urgently?

■ Circulation
■ Airway
■ Shock
■ Breathing
■ Broken bones

Answers

☑ **Circulation**
☑ **Airway**
☑ **Breathing**

An unconscious casualty may have difficulty breathing. Check that their tongue has not fallen back, blocking their airway. Do this by gently tilting the head back.

Q. 7.19

Mark three answers

In first aid what does ABC stand for?

■ Airway
■ Bleeding
■ Conscious
■ Breathing
■ Circulation
■ Alert

Answers

☑ **Airway**
☑ **Breathing**
☑ **Circulation**

To check if a casualty is breathing put your face close to their mouth. Look, listen and feel for any sign of breathing.

questions

answers

Q. 7.20

Mark three answers

You arrive at the scene of an accident. It has just happened, and someone is unconscious. Which of the following should be given urgent priority to help them?

- ▮ Clear the airway and keep it open
- ▮ Try to get them to drink water
- ▮ Check that they are breathing
- ▮ Look for any witnesses
- ▮ Stop any heavy bleeding
- ▮ Take the numbers of vehicles involved

Answers

- ☑ **Clear the airway and keep it open**
- ☑ **Check that they are breathing**
- ☑ **Stop any heavy bleeding**

Stay with the casualty and make sure someone rings for an ambulance.

Q. 7.21

Mark three answers

At an accident someone is unconscious. Your main priorities should be to

- ▮ sweep up the broken glass
- ▮ take the names of witnesses
- ▮ count the number of vehicles involved
- ▮ check the airway is clear
- ▮ make sure they are breathing
- ▮ stop any heavy bleeding

Answers

- ☑ **check the airway is clear**
- ☑ **make sure they are breathing**
- ☑ **stop any heavy bleeding**

Remember this procedure by saying ABC

- • Airway
- • Breathing
- • Circulation.

questions   answers

Q. 7.22

Mark three answers

You have stopped at the scene of an accident to give help. Which THREE things should you do?

- [ ] Keep injured people warm and comfortable

- [ ] Keep injured people calm by talking to them reassuringly

- [ ] Keep injured people on the move by walking them around

- [ ] Give injured people a warm drink

- [ ] Make sure that injured people are not left alone

Answers

- [x] **Keep injured people warm and comfortable**

- [x] **Keep injured people calm by talking to them reassuringly**

- [x] **Make sure that injured people are not left alone**

If you stop at the scene of an accident to give help and there are casualties, don't move injured people unless further danger is threatened or give them anything to drink.

Q. 7.23

Mark three answers

You arrive at the scene of an accident. It has just happened and someone is injured. Which of the following should be given urgent priority?

- [ ] Stop any severe bleeding

- [ ] Get them a warm drink

- [ ] Check that their breathing is OK

- [ ] Take numbers of vehicles involved

- [ ] Look for witnesses

- [ ] Clear their airway and keep it open

Answers

- [x] **Stop any severe bleeding**

- [x] **Check that their breathing is OK**

- [x] **Clear their airway and keep it open**

Where possible call the emergency services first. If you are able to give first aid, remember the ABC: check their airway first, then their breathing and then circulation (and bleeding).

If you feel you are not capable of carrying out first aid, then consider doing some training. It could save a life.

questions   answers

Q. 7.24

Mark two answers

At an accident a casualty has stopped breathing. You should

- remove anything that is blocking the mouth
- keep the head tilted forwards as far as possible
- raise the legs to help with circulation
- try to give the casualty something to drink
- keep the head tilted back as far as possible

Answers

- ✓ **remove anything that is blocking the mouth**
- ✓ **keep the head tilted back as far as possible**

These actions will ensure that the casualty has clear airways and is in the correct position if mouth-to-mouth resuscitation is required.

Q. 7.25

Mark four answers

You are at the scene of an accident. Someone is suffering from shock. You should

- reassure them constantly
- offer them a cigarette
- keep them warm
- avoid moving them if possible
- loosen any tight clothing
- give them a warm drink

Answers

- ✓ **reassure them constantly**
- ✓ **keep them warm**
- ✓ **avoid moving them if possible**
- ✓ **loosen any tight clothing**

The effects of trauma may not be immediately obvious. Prompt treatment can help to minimise the effects of shock.

- Lay the casualty down.
- Loosen tight clothing.
- Call an ambulance.
- Check their breathing and pulse.

Q. 7.26

Mark one answer

Which of the following should you not do at the scene of an accident?

- Warn other traffic by switching on your hazard warning lights
- Call the emergency services immediately
- Offer someone a cigarette to calm them down
- Ask drivers to switch off their engines

Answer

- ✓ **Offer someone a cigarette to calm them down**

Keeping casualties or witnesses calm is important, but never offer a cigarette because of the risk of fire. Check for any signs of shock, such as

- sweating or clammy skin
- giddiness
- rapid or shallow breathing
- a weak pulse.

questions

answers

Q. 7.27

Mark two answers

When treating someone for shock you should

- reassure them
- loosen tight clothes
- walk them around
- give them a hot drink
- offer them an alcoholic drink

Answers

- ☑ **reassure them**
- ☑ **loosen tight clothes**

Keep talking to the casualty to help them stay calm. Don't leave them alone.

Q. 7.28

Mark two answers

There has been an accident. The driver is suffering from shock. You should

- give them a drink
- reassure them
- not leave them alone
- offer them a cigarette
- ask who caused the accident

Answers

- ☑ **reassure them**
- ☑ **not leave them alone**

They could have an injury that is not immediately obvious. Loosen any tight clothing and check that their breathing is not rapid or shallow.

Q. 7.29

Mark one answer

You have to treat someone for shock at the scene of an accident. You should

- reassure them constantly
- walk them around to calm them down
- give them something cold to drink
- cool them down as soon as possible

Answer

- ☑ **reassure them constantly**

You should lay the casualty down and speak to them reassuringly. If possible, get someone else to call an ambulance to avoid leaving the casualty alone.

questions answers

Q. 7.30

Mark one answer

You arrive at the scene of a motorcycle accident. No other vehicle is involved. The rider is unconscious, lying in the middle of the road. The first thing you should do is

- move the rider out of the road
- warn other traffic
- clear the road of debris
- give the rider reassurance

Answer

 warn other traffic

The motorcyclist is in an extremely vulnerable position, exposed to further danger from traffic. The traffic needs to slow right down and be aware of the hazard in good time.

Q. 7.31

Mark one answer

At an accident a small child is not breathing. When giving mouth to mouth you should blow

- sharply
- gently
- heavily
- rapidly

Answer

✓ **gently**

With a small child, breathe gently into the nose and mouth until you see the chest rise. Give five breaths, allowing two seconds for the lungs to inflate.

Q. 7.32

Mark three answers

To start mouth to mouth on a casualty you should

- tilt the head forward
- clear the airway
- turn them on their side
- tilt their head back
- pinch the nostrils together
- put their arms across their chest

Answers

✓ **clear the airway**

✓ **tilt their head back**

✓ **pinch the nostrils together**

Use your finger to check for and move any obvious obstruction in the mouth. It's important to ensure that the airway is clear.

questions

answers

Q. 7.33

Mark one answer

You are giving mouth to mouth to a casualty. They are still not breathing on their own. You should

- give up if you think they are dead
- only keep trying for up to two minutes
- carry on until an ambulance arrives
- only keep trying for up to four minutes

Answer

 carry on until an ambulance arrives

Make sure that someone has called the emergency services. They have the expertise and equipment to deal with the situation.

Q. 7.34

Mark one answer

When you are giving mouth to mouth you should only stop when

- you think the casualty is dead
- the casualty can breathe without help
- the casualty has turned blue
- you think the ambulance is coming

Answer

☑ **the casualty can breathe without help**

Don't give up and never assume someone is dead. Look for signs of recovery and check the casualty's pulse.

Q. 7.35

Mark one answer

You arrive at the scene of an accident. There has been an engine fire and someones hands and arms have been burnt. You should NOT

- douse the burn thoroughly with cool liquid
- lay the casualty down
- remove anything sticking to the burn
- remove smouldering clothing

Answer

☑ **remove anything sticking to the burn**

This could cause further damage and introduce infection to the wound. Your first priorities are to cool the burn and check the patient for shock.

questions answers

Q. 7.36

Mark one answer

You arrive at an accident where someone is suffering from severe burns. You should

- apply lotions to the injury
- burst any blisters
- remove anything stuck to the burns
- douse the burns with cool liquid

Answer

☑ **douse the burns with cool liquid**

Try to find fluid that is clean, cold and non-toxic. It will help to cool the burn and relieve the pain. Keep the wound doused for at least ten minutes. If blisters appear, don't attempt to burst them, as this could lead to infection.

Q. 7.37

Mark two answers

You arrive at the scene of an accident. A pedestrian has a severe bleeding wound on their leg, although it is not broken. What should you do?

- Dab the wound to stop bleeding
- Keep both legs flat on the ground
- Apply firm pressure to the wound
- Raise the leg to lessen bleeding
- Fetch them a warm drink

Answers

☑ **Apply firm pressure to the wound**

☑ **Raise the leg to lessen bleeding**

As soon as you can, apply a pad to the wound with a bandage or a clean length of cloth. Raising the leg will lessen the flow of blood. Be aware that any restriction of blood circulation for more than a short period of time may result in long-term injury.

Q. 7.38

Mark one answer

You arrive at the scene of an accident. A passenger is bleeding badly from an arm wound. What should you do?

- Apply pressure over the wound and keep the arm down
- Dab the wound
- Get them a drink
- Apply pressure over the wound and raise the arm

Answer

☑ **Apply pressure over the wound and raise the arm**

If possible, lay the casualty down. Raising the arm above the level of the heart will reduce the flow of blood.

questions answers

Q. 7.39

Mark one answer

You arrive at the scene of an accident. A pedestrian is bleeding heavily from a leg wound, but the leg is not broken. What should you do?

- Dab the wound to stop the bleeding
- Keep both legs flat on the ground
- Apply firm pressure to the wound
- Fetch them a warm drink

Answer

☑ **Apply firm pressure to the wound**

Lift the casualty's leg so that the wound is higher than their heart. This should reduce the flow of blood.

Q. 7.40

Mark one answer

At an accident a casualty is unconscious but still breathing. You should only move them if

- an ambulance is on its way
- bystanders advise you to
- there is further danger
- bystanders will help you to

Answer

☑ **there is further danger**

Moving them could cause further injury. So it's important that this is only done if there is obvious danger to the casualty.

Q. 7.41

Mark one answer

At an accident you suspect a casualty has back injuries. The area is safe. You should

- offer them a drink
- not move them
- raise their legs
- offer them a cigarette

Answer

☑ **not move them**

Talk to the casualty and keep them calm. If you attempt to move them it could cause further injury. Call an ambulance straight away.

ACCIDENT HANDLING

questions answers

Q. 7.42

Mark one answer

At an accident it is important to look after the casualty. When the area is safe, you should

- get them out of the vehicle
- give them a drink
- give them something to eat
- keep them in the vehicle

Answer

☑ **keep them in the vehicle**

Don't move casualties who are trapped in vehicles unless they are in danger.

Q. 7.43

Mark one answer

You are driving on a motorway. A large box falls onto the carriageway from a lorry ahead of you. The lorry does not stop. You should

- drive to the next emergency telephone and inform the police
- catch up with the lorry and try to get the driver's attention
- stop close to the box and switch on your hazard warning lights until the police arrive
- pull over to the hard shoulder, then try and remove the box

Answer

☑ **drive to the next emergency telephone and inform the police**

Lorry drivers are sometimes unaware of objects falling from their vehicles. If you see something fall off a lorry onto the motorway, watch to see if the driver pulls over. If the lorry doesn't stop you should

- pull over onto the hard shoulder near an emergency telephone
- report the hazard to the police.

Q. 7.44

Mark three answers

You are stopped by a police officer. Which of the following documents are the police most likely to ask you to produce?

- Insurance certificate
- Vehicle registration document
- Road fund licence
- Theory test certificate
- Driving licence
- Test certificate (MOT)

Answers

☑ **Insurance certificate**

☑ **Driving licence**

☑ **Test certificate (MOT)**

These documents must be produced at the time when asked for. If you cannot do this you may be asked to take them to a police station within seven days.

questions

answers

Q. 7.45

Mark one answer

You have been involved in an accident and damaged some property. Your vehicle is still road worthy. Nobody else is present. What should you do?

- ☑ Stop, then report the accident to the police within 24 hours
- ☐ Leave the scene. Do not report the accident if there are no witnesses
- ☐ Stop, then report the accident to the police after 48 hours
- ☐ Leave the scene. Do not report the accident if there were no injuries

Answer

☑ **Stop, then report the accident to the police within 24 hours**

If you are involved in an accident that causes damage or injury to a person or property, you must stop. You are also obliged to give your details to anyone who has reasonable grounds to ask for them. If you don't do this, you must inform the police as soon as possible and in any case within 24 hours.

Q. 7.46

Mark one answer

At the scene of an accident a person has become hysterical. You should calm them by

- ☐ leaving them to quietly recover
- ☐ shouting at them loudly
- ☐ giving them a hot drink
- ☐ talking quietly and firmly to them

Answer

☑ **talking quietly and firmly to them**

Try to calm somebody who is hysterical by talking quietly and firmly to them.

Q. 7.47

Mark one answer

You are at an accident. Why may it be unwise to move a casualty?

- ☐ You could damage your back
- ☐ You could get blood on your hands
- ☐ You could be accused of an assault
- ☐ You could cause more injury

Answer

☑ **You could cause more injury**

Be especially careful about moving casualties at the scene of an accident. Inexperienced handling of a casualty could cause more injury, or even prove to be fatal.

253

questions   answers

Q. 7.48

Mark one answer

There has been an accident. The driver is in contact with live electrical cables. Do not touch the driver unless you can use

- ☐ a metal pole
- ☐ your bare hands
- ☐ a damp piece of cloth
- ☐ a length of wood

Answer

☑ **a length of wood**

If you arrive at the scene of an accident, don't touch any casualties who are in contact with live electricity. You should use a dry non-conducting item, such as a wooden sweeping brush or plastic spade. You must not give first aid until you are sure the electrical contact has been broken.

Q. 7.49

Mark two answers

You are at the scene of an accident and someone's arm is bleeding heavily. How could you help stop the bleeding?

- ☐ Raise the arm
- ☐ Lower the arm
- ☐ Place firm pressure on the wound
- ☐ Keep the wound free from pressure

Answers

☑ **Raise the arm**

☑ **Place firm pressure on the wound**

If you notice the limb bleeding heavily, raise it to reduce the flow of blood. Put firm pressure on the wound without pressing on anything that may be caught in it.

Q. 7.50

Mark one answer

When using an emergency telephone on a motorway where should you stand?

- ☐ In front of the barrier
- ☐ Facing the oncoming traffic
- ☐ With your back to the traffic
- ☐ Looking towards the grass verge

Answer

☑ **Facing the oncoming traffic**

Motorway phones are free and easily located. You should face the oncoming traffic while using them, so that you can see what is coming.

questions

Q. 7.51

Mark one answer

Which type of fire extinguisher should NOT be used on flammable liquids?

■ Water (red)

■ Foam (cream)

■ Dry powder (blue)

■ Carbon Dioxide (black)

Answer

☑ **Water (red)**

It's very important to know the correct fire extinguisher to use. Using the wrong one could be dangerous and may spread the fire further.

Q. 7.52

Mark one answer

You have a breakdown on a motorway. You cannot get fully onto the hard shoulder. What should you do?

■ Stand at the edge of the carriageway to warn others

■ Place a warning triangle in the lane behind your vehicle

■ Wear a bright jacket and stand in the lane behind your vehicle

■ Go straight to the nearest emergency telephone

Answer

☑ **Go straight to the nearest emergency telephone**

Standing on or near the edge of the carriageway could be very dangerous. Your first priority is to use the phone to alert the emergency services. Use the emergency telephone, which connects directly to the police, in preference to a mobile phone. This will allow precise location by the emergency services.

Q. 7.53

Mark one answer

Your engine catches fire. Before attempting to put the fire out you should

■ shut off the fuel supply

■ open the engine housing wide

■ drive to the nearest fire station

■ empty the air tanks

Answer

☑ **shut off the fuel supply**

An engine fire is serious enough, but if this reached the fuel tank the results would be disastrous. You should ensure that the fuel supply is cut off as your first priority.

questions   answers

Q. 7.54

Mark one answer

Before driving through a tunnel what should you do?

- Switch your radio off
- Remove your sunglasses
- Close your sunroof
- Switch on windscreen wipers

Answer

☑ **Remove your sunglasses**

Before driving into a tunnel you should remove any sunglasses that you are wearing. If you don't, you'll find that your vision is restricted, even in tunnels that appear to be well lit.

Q. 7.55

Mark one answer

You are driving through a tunnel and the traffic is flowing freely. What should you do?

- Use parking lights
- Use front spot lights
- Use dipped headlights
- Use rear fog lights

Answer

☑ **Use dipped headlights**

Before entering a tunnel you should switch on your dipped headlights, this will allow you to see and be seen. In many tunnels it is a legal requirement.

Other precautions you can take before driving through a tunnel are to remove any sunglasses you are wearing and to tune your radio into a local channel.

Q. 7.56

Mark one answer

Before entering a tunnel it is good advice to

- put on your sunglasses
- check tyre pressures
- change to a lower gear
- tune your radio to a local channel

Answer

☑ **tune your radio to a local channel**

On the approach to many tunnels a board will indicate a local channel or radio frequency that you should tune into. This should give a warning of any accidents or congestion in the tunnel ahead. Severe loss of life has occurred in recent tunnel fires. Getting advanced warning of problems ahead will help you to be prepared and to take appropriate action.

questions   answers

Q. 7.57

Mark one answer

You are driving through a congested tunnel and have to stop. What should you do?

- ■ Pull up very close to the vehicle in front to save space
- ■ Ignore any message signs as they're never up to date
- ■ Keep a safe distance from the vehicle in front
- ■ Do not switch on your hazard warning lights

Answer

☑ **Keep a safe distance from the vehicle in front**

It's important to keep a safe distance from the vehicle in front at all times. This still applies in congested tunnels even if you are moving very slowly or have stopped. If the vehicle in front breaks down you may need room to manoeuvre past it.

Q. 7.58

Mark one answer

You are driving through a tunnel. Your vehicle breaks down. What should you do?

- ■ Switch on hazard warning lights
- ■ Remain in your vehicle
- ■ Wait for the police to find you
- ■ Rely on CCTV cameras seeing you

Answer

☑ **Switch on hazard warning lights**

If your vehicle breaks down in a tunnel it could present a danger to other traffic. First switch on your hazard warning lights. If there are passengers in your vehicle take them to the nearest exit point. You should then call for help from an emergency telephone point. Don't rely on being found by the police or being seen by a CCTV camera. The longer a vehicle stays in an exposed position the more danger it poses to other traffic.

Q. 7.59

Mark one answer

You have an accident while driving through a tunnel. You are not injured but your vehicle cannot be driven. What should you do first?

- ■ Rely on other drivers phoning for the Police
- ■ Switch off the engine and switch on hazard lights
- ■ Take the names of witnesses and other drivers
- ■ Sweep up any debris that is in the road

Answer

☑ **Switch off the engine and switch on hazard lights**

If you are involved in an accident in a tunnel be aware of the danger this can cause to other traffic. You should immediately switch on your hazard lights and switch off your engine.

257

questions

answers

Q. 7.60

Mark one answer

Your vehicle catches fire while driving through a tunnel. It is still driveable. What should you do?

- [ ] Leave it where it is with the engine running
- [ ] Pull up, then walk to an emergency telephone point
- [ ] Park it away from the carriageway
- [ ] Drive it out of the tunnel if you can do so

Answer

- ✓ **Drive it out of the tunnel if you can do so**

If it's possible, and you can do so without causing further danger, it's safer to drive a vehicle that's on fire out of a tunnel. The greatest danger in a tunnel fire is smoke and suffocation.

Q. 7.61

Mark one answer

While driving through a tunnel your vehicle catches fire. It cannot be driven. What should you do first?

- [ ] Wait for the Police, tunnels are regularly patrolled
- [ ] Stay with your vehicle, you will be seen by the CCTV cameras
- [ ] Pull over to the side and switch off the engine
- [ ] Do not put out the fire, wait for the emergency services

Answer

- ✓ **Pull over to the side and switch off the engine**

If your vehicle catches fire pull over to the side and as far away from other vehicles as possible. Warn other traffic by switching on your hazard warning lights.

Q. 7.62

Mark one answer

You are driving through a tunnel in heavy traffic and it is very busy. What should you do?

☐ stay close to the vehicle in front to reduce congestion

☐ switch off your dipped headlights to reduce dazzle

☐ closely follow the tail lights of other vehicles

☐ follow instructions given by variable message signs

Answer

☑ **follow instructions given by variable message signs**

In congested tunnels you should always obey the instructions given by variable message signs and tunnel officials. Listen out for radio announcements and observe the road signs and signals. KEEP YOUR DISTANCE!

Q. 7.63

Mark one answer

You arrive at the scene of a serious accident. Your FIRST priority should be to

☐ your passengers

☐ yourself

☐ the emergency services

☐ accident victims

Answer

☑ **your passengers**

In the event of an accident, keeping calm and in command of the situation could save lives. Your passengers are your first priority. Make sure they are safe and call the emergency services.

Q. 7.64

Mark one answer

You are driving a coach carrying elderly people. You arrive at the scene of an accident. The emergency services have already arrived. You should

☐ ask your passengers to find out what is happening

☐ not tell passengers anything in case you upset them

☐ leave the passengers on the bus and see what is happening yourself

☐ tell the passengers what is happening without upsetting them

Answer

☑ **tell the passengers what is happening without upsetting them**

You should reassure passengers when letting them know what has happened. Confirm to them that the emergency services are in attendance.

questions   answers

Q. 7.65

Mark one answer

Your bus and other vehicles have been involved in an accident. You should

- switch off their headlights
- switch off the fuel supply
- turn vehicles the right way up
- always pull casualties out of their vehicles

Answer

☑ **switch off the fuel supply**

The risk of fire will be reduced if all fuel supplies are switched off.

Q. 7.66

Mark one answer

NI EXEMPT

Your bus has hit a parked vehicle. The owner cannot be found. You must report the accident

- to the police within seven days
- to the owner as soon as possible
- to the owner within seven days
- to the police within 24 hours

Answer

☑ **to the police within 24 hours**

If you damage a parked vehicle and the owner isn't around, you must report it to the police within 24 hours. This applies to any property you might have damaged. In Northern Ireland all accidents must be reported to the police immediately.

Q. 7.67

Mark one answer

You are treating a passenger who is in shock. You should

- give them liquids
- keep them moving
- encourage them to sleep
- keep them warm

Answer

☑ **keep them warm**

Knowing what to do in the event of an accident could save lives. Stay calm and be in command of the situation. Call the emergency services. They're the experts and know how to deal with injured or shocked victims. First aid is very important, but the correct procedure is vital.

Although not obviously injured, passengers may be suffering from shock. Reassure them and keep them warm. Don't give them anything to eat or drink.

questions   answers

Q. 7.68 🚌

Mark one answer

A passenger on your bus has stopped breathing. You help them by giving mouth to mouth resuscitation. When should you stop doing this?

▮ When they can breathe on their own

▮ When you think the passenger has died

▮ When their skin colour has turned blue

▮ When you think the ambulance is coming

Answer

☑ **When they can breathe on their own**

You should only stop resuscitation when the passenger can breathe on their own or a professional medical person can take over.

Q. 7.69 🚌

Mark one answer

Your bus is involved in an accident. You have a passenger who is unconscious but still breathing. What should you do?

▮ Get medical help

▮ Check their pulse

▮ Give them liquid

▮ Lie them on their back

Answer

☑ **Get medical help**

If one of your passengers is unconscious but breathing get medical help immediately. Only move the casualty if there's danger of further injury. Call the experts: dial 999.

Q. 7.70 🚌

Mark one answer

Your bus is stopped at the scene of an accident. Why should you consider moving your passengers to the front of the bus?

▮ To improve weight distribution

▮ To reduce the risk of injury from behind

▮ To be nearer emergency exits

▮ To be witnesses of the accident

Answer

☑ **To reduce the risk of injury from behind**

You'll need to decide whether it's appropriate for passengers to move to a safer position if another vehicle could run into the back of the bus.

questions

answers

Q. 7.71

Mark one answer

NI EXEMPT

Your bus hits a low railway bridge. Nobody is injured. You should report the accident

- [ ] immediately to your employer
- [ ] within 24 hours to the railway authority
- [ ] within seven days to the police
- [ ] immediately to the railway authority

Answer

- [✓] **immediately to the railway authority**

If your bus hits a railway bridge you MUST inform the railway authorities immediately due to the possibility of structural damage to the bridge. You should find the telephone number on or near the bridge. It's very important to do this as soon as possible so that all rail traffic is stopped. You must also inform the police immediately or in any case within 24 hours.

Q. 7.72

Mark one answer

While going through a tunnel your coach catches fire. It cannot be driven any further. What should you do?

- [ ] Move the passengers to the rear of the coach
- [ ] Get the passengers off, keeping them together
- [ ] Make sure the passengers stay in their seats
- [ ] Move the passengers to the front of the coach

Answer

- [✓] **Get the passengers off, keeping them together**

If your coach catches fire and it is unsafe to go any further, pull over to the side, switch the engine off and switch on your hazard warning lights.

Your immediate responsibility is to your passengers. Get them off the coach, keep them together and take them to the nearest emergency exit.

Vehicle condition

This section looks at the condition of your vehicle.

The questions will ask you about

- **Wheels and tyres**

  taking precautions during the removal and replacement of wheels and the correct fitting, use and care of tyres

- **The principles of construction and function of large vehicles**

  the internal combustion engine and its fuel, lubrication, coolant and ignition systems, the vehicle's transmission, lubrication and electrical systems

- **Vehicle coupling mechanisms**

  maintenance and use of coupling systems

- **Breakdowns**

  preventative maintenance, running repairs and locating the cause of breakdowns.

questions

Q. 8.1

Mark one answer

What is the main reason for cleaning your wheels and tyres when leaving a building site?

☐ It helps to keep the tyres in good condition

☐ So that the tyres will not cause damage to the road surface

☐ So that air pressure will not leak from the tyre valves

☐ It is illegal for you to spread mud on the road

Answer

✓ **It is illegal for you to spread mud on the road**

If your wheels leave mud on the road you must arrange for it to be cleared. A slippery, muddy surface could cause danger to other road users.

Q. 8.2

Mark one answer

You should look at the rear wheels before leaving a building site to check that

☐ the diff-lock is engaged

☐ the diff-lock is disengaged

☐ the load-sensing valve is working

☐ bricks are not wedged between them

Answer

✓ **bricks are not wedged between them**

Bricks will damage the tyres and could be thrown out as you increase your road speed, which could be dangerous to the drivers of following vehicles.

Q. 8.3

Mark one answer

You are driving on a muddy building site. Before driving on normal road surfaces you should

☐ disengage the diff-lock

☐ engage the diff-lock

☐ apply the steering lock

☐ disengage the twist lock

Answer

✓ **disengage the diff-lock**

Attempting to drive at normal speeds with the diff-lock engaged is dangerous; it will severely affect your steering control. The diff-lock is designed to be used in slippery conditions, at low speed.

questions

answers

Q. 8.4

Mark one answer

You are driving a lorry along a motorway. You notice that tread is coming away from one of your tyres. What should you do?

▪ Stop on the hard shoulder and phone for assistance

▪ Stop on the hard shoulder and change the wheel

▪ Continue driving to the next service station

▪ Continue driving and leave by the next exit

Answer

☑ **Stop on the hard shoulder and phone for assistance**

It's dangerous to drive a defective vehicle. Continuous high speeds on the motorway can cause the tyres to become hot and shred. If you notice this in your mirrors you must stop on the hard shoulder as soon as it's safe to do so.

If you're on a motorway and you notice any defect on your vehicle, you must stop on the hard shoulder as soon as it's safe. Use the emergency telephone for assistance.

Q. 8.5

Mark one answer

What is the MINIMUM depth of tread required over three-quarters of the breadth of a lorry tyre?

▪ 1 mm

▪ 1.5 mm

▪ 2.5 mm

▪ 5 mm

Answer

☑ **1 mm**

Your tyres are your only contact with the road. It's essential that this contact gives you the grip you need to control your vehicle at all times. If the weather is wet or icy your tyres' grip may be reduced.

Q. 8.6

Mark one answer

After recoupling a trailer, which of the following should you do LAST?

▪ Connect the brake lines

▪ Release the trailer parking brake

▪ Connect the electrical lines

▪ Raise the trailer legs

Answer

☑ **Release the trailer parking brake**

It's important to work methodically when uncoupling or recoupling a tractor unit and trailer. After recoupling, check that all connections, systems and lights are working correctly.

questions   answers

Q. 8.7

Mark one answer

Tyre pressures should be increased when your vehicle is

■ towing a trailer

■ heavily loaded

■ used occasionally

■ unloaded

Answer

 heavily loaded

Generally the tyre pressures should be higher for a heavily loaded vehicle. Check your tyres regularly, at least once a week, for damage or wear as well as for correct pressure.

Q. 8.8

Mark one answer

Your lorry coupling system (fifth wheel) should be checked and lubricated

■ only prior to an MOT

■ every 6 months

■ yearly

■ regularly

Answer

 regularly

Maintenance of the fifth wheel should be carried out regularly, ideally monthly or every 10,000 km.

Q. 8.9

Mark one answer

A fifth wheel type coupling relies on which of the following connecting devices?

■ Suzie

■ Kingpin

■ D link

■ Eyelet

Answer

 Kingpin

It is important to check that the kingpin locking mechanism is secure when recoupling. You should do this by attempting to move forward with the trailer brake applied. Also remember to connect the dog-clip.

questions

Q. 8.10

Mark three answers

You are checking your vehicle's tyres before starting a long motorway drive. Each tyre should be checked for

- air pressure
- tracking
- tread wear
- tread pattern
- bulges
- valve clearance

Answers

- ✓ **air pressure**
- ✓ **tread wear**
- ✓ **bulges**

All tyres must be properly inflated and in good condition. Sometimes on motorways you can see the remains of tyres that have disintegrated due to a failure that might have been avoided if the tyre had been checked before the journey started.

Q. 8.11

Mark one answer

You notice that two wheel nuts are missing from one of the wheels. What should you do?

- Continue your journey
- Drive to the nearest tyre depot
- Use a nut from another wheel
- Park and phone for assistance

Answer

- ✓ **Park and phone for assistance**

If you notice any missing wheel nuts, park and phone for assistance. It's essential that all wheel fixings are tightened to the torque specified by the manufacturer, with an approved calibrated torque wrench. As a professional driver you must ensure that your vehicle is in serviceable condition at all times. Checks should be made before you leave on any journey, but make a visual check every time you start up again after a rest stop. Don't take risks by driving a defective vehicle.

questions

answers

Q. 8.12

Mark three answers

Which THREE of the following items would make a tyre illegal for a large vehicle?

- ■ Different makes of tyres on the same axle
- ■ A lump or bulge
- ■ A deep cut more than 25 mm (1 inch) long
- ■ An exposed ply or cord
- ■ Recut tyres
- ■ A tread depth of 1.3 mm

Answers

- ☑ **A lump or bulge**
- ☑ **A deep cut more than 25 mm (1 inch) long**
- ☑ **An exposed ply or cord**

You should check your tyres as part of your routine check of the vehicle. A damaged or worn tyre can have a major effect on handling and will make your vehicle a danger to you and other road users. It's also an offence to drive with one or more tyres that have these defects.

Q. 8.13

Mark one answer

In very cold weather moisture may freeze in your vehicle's air storage tanks. Which of the following would help to prevent this?

- ■ Covering the air tanks with a blanket
- ■ Draining the tanks daily
- ■ Using the brakes frequently
- ■ Pumping the brakes

Answer

- ☑ **Draining the tanks daily**

In very cold weather moisture can build up in the storage tanks and freeze. Ice can form in the pipes and this will result in loss of pressure or brake failure. Make sure that you drain the tanks daily as part of a routine. Most modern vehicles are fitted with automatic bleed valves. Check that they're working properly and that air-drying systems are effective.

Q. 8.14

Mark one answer

What does this warning light on the instrument panel mean?

- ■ Low oil pressure
- ■ Battery discharge
- ■ Braking system fault
- ■ Door open

Answer

- ☑ **Braking system fault**

You should be familiar with all warning lights and buzzers fitted to your vehicle. If you're driving the vehicle for the first time ensure that you know the function of each. If the brake warning light indicates a fault in the system, stop as soon as it's safe to do so. Report the fault, and don't continue until it has been corrected.

questions

Q. 8.15

Mark one answer

You are driving along a motorway. The brake low-pressure warning device starts to operate. What should you do?

- Stop immediately in the lane you are in
- Continue slowly to the next service area
- Pull up on the hard shoulder as soon as possible
- Leave the motorway at the next exit

Q. 8.16

Mark one answer

Your vehicle has broken down at night on a two-way road. You should try to park your vehicle

- on the left of the road
- partly on the pavement
- on a grass verge
- on the right of the road

Q. 8.17

Mark one answer

Whilst driving, your power-assisted steering suddenly fails. What should you do?

- Continue driving to the nearest repair centre
- Return to the depot
- Continue your journey at a slower speed
- Park and seek assistance

answers

Answer

☑ **Pull up on the hard shoulder as soon as possible**

You should never take chances with the braking system. Pull up well to the left on the hard shoulder. Don't even attempt minor repairs on the motorway. Put on the hazard warning lights. Contact the police using the nearest emergency telephone. They will contact a recovery contractor for you.

Answer

☑ **on the left of the road**

You must ensure that your vehicle can be seen by other road users. Your reflectors should show red to the rear.

Answer

☑ **Park and seek assistance**

Faulty power steering will make your steering wheel very difficult or almost impossible to turn. To continue driving could cause danger to you and other road users. You should park safely and get assistance.

questions   answers

Q. 8.18

Mark two answers

Whilst driving your steering suddenly becomes heavy to turn. What could this indicate?

■ A puncture in a front tyre

■ Loss of air brake pressure

■ A faulty parking brake

■ A failure of power-assisted steering

Answers

☑ **A puncture in a front tyre**

☑ **A failure of power-assisted steering**

The power-assisted steering may have failed if the steering becomes heavy. It is also possible that your vehicle has a puncture or the load might have shifted. In any case you should stop safely, investigate the cause, then seek assistance.

Q. 8.19

Mark one answer

What should you do if the brake pedal becomes 'hard'?

■ Continue to drive and report it at the end of the day

■ Pump the brake pedal continuously

■ Drain the air tanks and then continue

■ Park and telephone for assistance

Answer

☑ **Park and telephone for assistance**

Don't take risks. As soon as you detect a fault on your vehicle you must take action. Where the brakes are concerned, always park and get assistance. Always report minor faults as soon as you detect them. Minor faults can become major ones if they aren't repaired quickly.

Q. 8.20

Mark one answer

Air tanks on brake systems require draining because

■ excess coolant may collect in them

■ rain water can often seep in

■ any engine leakages are directed here

■ of moisture drawn in from the atmosphere

Answer

☑ **of moisture drawn in from the atmosphere**

This moisture condenses in the air and can be transmitted around a vehicle's braking system. This is especially dangerous in cold weather, as it can lead to ice building up in the valves and pipes.

questions · answers

Q. 8.21

Mark one answer

Whilst checking your vehicle you discover an air leak in the braking system. What should you do?

- Drive slowly to the nearest garage
- Check the leak from time to time on your journey
- Leave it parked and report it immediately
- Start your journey and report it on your return

Answer

✓ **Leave it parked and report it immediately**

Under no circumstances should you attempt to move or drive a vehicle with an air leak in the braking system. Report the fault immediately, or arrange to have it repaired. Place a warning sign in a prominent position in the cab informing other drivers to prevent them unwittingly moving the vehicle.

Q. 8.22

Mark one answer

You are driving a large vehicle. A loud buzzer sounds in the cab. This is most likely to indicate low

- oil pressure
- air pressure
- tyre pressure
- fuel level

Answer

✓ **air pressure**

Warning buzzers are linked to many systems on modern vehicles. A warning light on the dashboard may help you identify the system that has caused the problem. Under no circumstances should you continue driving until the fault has been identified and rectified. Seek professional assistance if necessary.

Q. 8.23

Mark one answer

How much of the width of a tyre must have the legal limit of tread depth?

- One-quarter
- One-half
- Five-eighths
- Three-quarters

Answer

✓ **Three-quarters**

The condition of the tyres on your vehicle will contribute to its overall stability. Don't leave your tyres until their tread is at the minimum depth. Renew them before they get into that state. Ensuring that the tread is always deep enough will maintain your tyres' grip on the road.

questions

Q. 8.24

Mark two answers

As a professional driver of large vehicles, why should you carry spare bulbs?

- To fix any fault for the safety of yourself
- Because bulbs are more likely to blow when your vehicle is loaded
- To repair the lights for the sake of other road users
- Because bulbs are more likely to blow when your vehicle is empty

Answers

- ✓ **To fix any fault for the safety of yourself**
- ✓ **To repair the lights for the sake of other road users**

Keep a stock of all the various bulbs used on your vehicle. This could save you wasting time trying to locate a spare bulb.

Q. 8.25

Mark one answer

NI EXEMPT

The Vehicle Inspectorate and Police carry out spot checks of vehicle condition. If serious defects are found the vehicle is

- impounded until a new driver is found
- restricted to 30 mph for the remainder of the journey
- prohibited from further use until the defects are rectified
- ordered back to the depot to unload goods or passengers

Answer

- ✓ **prohibited from further use until the defects are rectified**

The Vehicle Inspectorate or police can order an immediate prohibition. Details are always notified to the traffic commissioners. Drivers must NOT use vehicles which they know to be faulty.

questions answers

Q. 8.26

Mark one answer

NI EXEMPT

A vehicle is found to have serious defects at a Vehicle Inspectorate spot-check. It is prohibited from further use. Who will be notified of the details?

- The Driver and Vehicle Licencing Agency
- The Traffic Commissioner
- The Road Transport Industry Training Body
- The Bus, Coach and Commercial Vehicle Council

Answer

☑ **The Traffic Commissioner**

The Vehicle Inspectorate and police carry out frequent spot checks of vehicle condition. Where serious defects are found the vehicle is prohibited from further use until the defects are rectified, and details of the prohibition are notified to the Traffic Commissioner.

Q. 8.27

Mark one answer

At very low temperatures diesel fuel will become less effective unless

- anti-freeze is added
- anti-waxing additives are added
- petrol is added
- paraffin is added

Answer

☑ **anti-waxing additives are added**

In extremely cold weather, you will have to use diesel fuel with anti-waxing additives to stop fuel lines freezing up. During the winter months this is usually put in by the fuel companies.

Q. 8.28

Mark one answer

You are about to start a long journey midway through the day. You find that your headlights are not working but you still have sidelights. What should you do?

- Don't drive until they are mended
- Drive only until light begins to fade
- Avoid driving on motorways after dark
- Drive only if the weather is good

Answer

☑ **Don't drive until they are mended**

To comply with the law, all lights must be in good working order, even in daylight when they are not being used. Check and make sure that everything is working before you set off. You may need to use your headlights or other lights if you are delayed or find yourself driving in conditions of reduced visibility.

questions   answers

Q. 8.29

Mark one answer

Before starting a journey you want to check your brake system warning lights. On some vehicles these are not operated by the ignition switch. What else can you do?

- Look for a 'check' switch on the dashboard
- Get someone behind to check your brake lights
- Check them at the end of your journey
- Pump the brake pedal a number of times

Answer

☑ **Look for a 'check' switch on the dashboard**

A warning lights system check is sometimes performed automatically when the ignition is switched on, but you may need to do this manually by operating a separate 'check' switch. Never start a journey without doing this. If there is a problem, have it properly checked out before you set off.

Q. 8.30

Mark one answer

On motorways you are usually driving at higher speeds for long distances. What effect can this have on your tyres?

- They may overheat and disintegrate
- They will be more liable to punctures
- They will lose air pressure more quickly
- They will become very slippery

Answer

☑ **They may overheat and disintegrate**

Driving at higher speeds and for longer periods, such as on motorways, can cause your tyres to overheat and disintegrate. You should make a point of checking them when you stop for a break.

Q. 8.31

Mark one answer

You notice one of your tyres has a bulge in the side. Why should you not drive the vehicle?

- Your tachograph reading will not be accurate
- Your speedometer will give an incorrect reading
- It will make the vehicle unsteady on corners
- At speed, the tyre could overheat and burst

Answer

☑ **At speed, the tyre could overheat and burst**

Your tyres must all be in good condition before you start any journey. Make sure that you inspect them before setting off and at regular intervals.

questions answers

Q. 8.32

Mark one answer

The purpose of a pre-heating device is to heat the

■ cab

■ gearbox

■ engine

■ seat

Answer

☑ **engine**

Most diesel engines have pre-heaters which heat the glow plugs in the cylinders to assist in starting when cold. The starter should only be operated when the indicator light goes out.

Q. 8.33

Mark one answer

A high-pressure fuel injector delivers fuel into the

■ carburettors

■ cylinders

■ camshaft

■ crankshaft

Answer

☑ **cylinders**

Most diesel engines use a high-pressure fuel injector system which will deliver pressurised fuel directly into the cylinders of the engine. This system is known as a direct injection engine.

Q. 8.34

Mark one answer

You should check your engine oil level regularly. Failure to do this could cause your engine to

■ run faster

■ breakdown

■ use less fuel

■ produce more power

Answer

☑ **breakdown**

As well as being very expensive to mend, a damaged engine could also cause sudden and unexpected loss of control. This could put you and other road users in danger. If your engine seizes while you are driving you should make every effort to pull up in a safe place.

questions answers

Q. 8.35

Mark one answer

While driving, your engine oil warning light comes on. Why could it be dangerous to continue driving?

■ The engine will get hot

■ The engine may seize

■ You will need to have the vehicle serviced

■ You will need to replace the carburettor

Answer

☑ **The engine may seize**

Apart from being very expensive, a seized engine could cause your vehicle to suffer sudden and unexpected loss of control, possibly stopping in a dangerous position and putting you and other road users in danger.

Q. 8.36

Mark one answer

Why is it most important to avoid overfilling the engine oil level?

■ It could leave an oil stain on the road

■ It will increase the amount of exhaust gases

■ It could increase oil pressure and cause damage

■ It will damage the exhaust system

Answer

☑ **It could increase oil pressure and cause damage**

Too much oil in an engine can be just as bad as too little. Overfilling an engine can create excess pressure, cause oil leakage through seals and result in expensive damage.

Q. 8.37

Mark one answer

Bus and lorry tyres have codes on the sidewall. What do these refer to?

■ Running pressure

■ Speed capability

■ Minimum temperature

■ Tread depth

Answer

☑ **Speed capability**

Codes are shown on the wall of the tyre. These refer to the maximum load and speed capability of the tyre.

questions

answers

Q. 8.38

Mark one answer

Why should you use an approved coolant solution in your engine?

◼ To prevent the engine freezing

◼ For easier starting from cold

◼ To prevent the air tank from freezing

◼ For effective cab heating

Answer

☑ **To prevent the engine freezing**

Coolant also contains a corrosion inhibitor which prolongs the life of the cooling system. Remember to check the coolant level regularly.

Q. 8.39

Mark one answer

When replacing a tubeless tyre it is good practice to

◼ fit the same valve

◼ replace the valve

◼ have the valve checked

◼ clean the valve

Answer

☑ **replace the valve**

Always get expert advice when dealing with tyres. It is good practice to have a new valve fitted when replacing a tubeless tyre. Good garages and specialist tyre services know the regulations.

Q. 8.40

Mark one answer

You should check the oil level when your engine is

◼ running

◼ cold

◼ warm

◼ hot

Answer

☑ **cold**

Oil is vital for lubrication of the engine and should be checked regularly and topped up as necessary. You should always check oil levels when the engine is cold and your vehicle is parked on the level.

Q. 8.41

Mark one answer

When should anti-freeze be used in the cooling system?

- [ ] In winter only
- [ ] All year round
- [ ] In summer only
- [ ] When starting from cold

Answer

- [x] **All year round**

Today all water cooled vehicles use a mixture of water and anti-freeze to make up the coolant. As well as helping to keep the engine at its correct operating temperature, it also acts as a corrosion inhibitor to prolong the life of the cooling system.

Q. 8.42

Mark one answer

What does this warning light on the instrument panel mean?

- [ ] Low fuel pressure
- [ ] Low oil pressure
- [ ] Low water pressure
- [ ] Low air pressure

Answer

- [x] **Low oil pressure**

You should be familiar with all warning lights fitted to your vehicle. The oil warning light indicates low oil pressure or lack of oil. If it lights up, report the fault and do not continue until it has been corrected.

Q. 8.43

Mark one answer

Energy saving tyres have

- [ ] increased tread depth
- [ ] reduced rolling resistance
- [ ] reduced tread depth
- [ ] increased rolling resistance

Answer

- [x] **reduced rolling resistance**

When changing or fitting new tyres, consider buying energy saving tyres. These have a reduced rolling resistance, are more economical and give improved efficiency.

questions   answers

Q. 8.44

Mark one answer

As you are driving the ignition warning light comes on. What does it warn of?

▨ Low oil pressure

▨ An electrical fault

▨ Low air pressure

▨ A hydraulic fault

Answer

☑ **An electrical fault**

The ignition light should go out when the engine has started. If it shows when driving, this indicates an electrical fault of some kind.

Q. 8.45

Mark one answer

Codes are shown on the side walls of bus and lorry tyres. What do these refer to?

▨ Tread pattern

▨ Minimum temperature

▨ Maximum load

▨ Running pressure

Answer

☑ **Maximum load**

Tyres have codes shown on the wall of the tyre. These refer to the maximum load and speed capability of the tyre.

Q. 8.46

Mark one answer

Regular maintenance and servicing will

▨ prevent unnecessary breakdowns

▨ increase fuel bills

▨ allow heavier loads to be carried

▨ reduce insurance premiums

Answer

☑ **prevent unnecessary breakdowns**

You can reduce the chance of a breakdown with preventive maintenance and regular checks.

Q. 8.47

Mark one answer

Before changing a wheel on your vehicle you should

■ leave the parking brake off

■ use chocks if available

■ dismantle the wheel and tyre

■ get someone to check the other tyres

Answer

☑ **use chocks if available**

Always make sure your vehicle is secure and level before changing a wheel. Apply the parking brake and use chocks if available. Remember to retighten all wheel nuts/studs afterwards to the correct torque.

Q. 8.48

Mark one answer

You have had to change a wheel on your vehicle. When should you next check the wheel nuts?

■ At the next service interval

■ When they are cold

■ When they are hot

■ Shortly afterwards

Answer

☑ **Shortly afterwards**

When refitting a wheel you should use a torque wrench to tighten the wheel nuts/studs. Recheck them after about 30 minutes if the vehicle has remained stationary, or after about 40 to 80 km (25 to 50 miles) of driving.

Q. 8.49

Mark two answers

You have replaced a tyre. What precautions should you take when tightening the wheel nuts?

■ Only use a wheel brace

■ Fully tighten each wheel nut before going on to the next

■ Use a calibrated torque wrench

■ Only use an air operated power tool

■ Fit and tighten the wheel nuts gradually and diagonally

Answers

☑ **Use a calibrated torque wrench**

☑ **Fit and tighten the wheel nuts gradually and diagonally**

After the tyre has been replaced and the wheel is being refitted you should tighten the wheel nuts/studs gradually and diagonally across the wheel using a calibrated torque wrench.

questions   answers

Q. 8.50

Mark one answer

A new engine has just been fitted to your vehicle. Why may it be necessary to bleed the fuel system?

- To increase the speed of your vehicle
- To remove any trapped air
- Because it is illegal not to do so
- Because it may cause the tank to freeze

Answer

☑ **To remove any trapped air**

This may be necessary to remove any airlocks that have become trapped in the fuel line.

Q. 8.51

Mark one answer

When may it become necessary to bleed the fuel system to remove any trapped air?

- When the engine has not been run for some time
- When you intend to carry unusually heavy loads
- When the engine keeps over heating
- When you wish to change the taxation on your vehicle

Answer

☑ **When the engine has not been run for some time**

If your vehicle has been standing for some time it may be necessary to remove any trapped air that has built up. This will prevent any airlocks in the fuel lines.

Q. 8.52

Mark one answer

Using poor quality diesel fuel may lead to

- better fuel economy
- lower exhaust emissions
- longer service intervals
- early blockage of a fuel injector

Answer

☑ **early blockage of a fuel injector**

Never use poor quality diesel fuel: not only is it likely to cause early blockage of the fuel injector, it may also lead to increased wear of the injector pump.

Q. 8.53

Mark three answers

Which of these components are generally found in an internal combustion engine?

- ■ crankshaft
- ■ propshaft
- ■ crown wheel
- ■ cylinder
- ■ differential
- ■ piston

Answers

- ☑ crankshaft
- ☑ cylinder
- ☑ piston

It can be helpful to understand how your vehicle works. Having some basic mechanical knowledge may help you to identify any faults that develop while you're driving.

Q. 8.54

Mark one answer

Using poor quality diesel fuel may lead to

- ■ better fuel economy
- ■ increased wear of the injection pump
- ■ longer service intervals
- ■ lower exhaust emissions

Answer

- ☑ increased wear of the injection pump

Never use poor quality diesel fuel, it may lead to early failure of the injection pump and could also cause blockage in a fuel injector. It could also lead to additional environmental pollution.

Q. 8.55

Mark three answers

In extremely cold conditions anti-freeze products should be added to the

- ■ battery fluid
- ■ cooling system
- ■ brake system
- ■ screenwash system
- ■ lubrication system
- ■ fuel system

Answers

- ☑ cooling system
- ☑ screenwash system
- ☑ fuel system

Do not confuse the three types of anti-freeze solutions.

In modern vehicles, cooling systems are filled with a fluid that is suitable for most weather conditions.

Sachets and bottles of all-weather screen wash are readily available.

Diesel fuel is usually supplied with anti-waxing agent already added.

questions answers

Q. 8.56

Mark three answers

Energy saving tyres work because they

- ☐ have reduced rolling resistance
- ☐ cost less to produce
- ☐ have no tread pattern
- ☐ never puncture at high speed
- ☐ increase fuel efficiency
- ☐ improve grip

Answers

- ☑ **have reduced rolling resistance**
- ☑ **increase fuel efficiency**
- ☑ **improve grip**

Energy saving tyres keep fuel costs down because they have lower rolling resistance and better grip than ordinary tyres. You should consider this when replacing your tyres.

Q. 8.57

Mark one answer

Advice about carrying out minor repairs can be obtained from

- ☐ DVLA guidance notes
- ☐ E.C and U.K. Directives
- ☐ the Health and Safety Executive
- ☐ the owners handbook

Answer

- ☑ **the owners handbook**

The handbook for your vehicle will clearly explain what work or maintenance the driver could carry out. Always refer to it and comply with the safety guidance that it contains.

Q. 8.58

Mark one answer

Where can you get advice about carrying out minor repairs?

- ☐ Workshop manuals
- ☐ DVLA guidance notes
- ☐ E.C and U.K. Directives
- ☐ The Health and Safety Executive

Answer

- ☑ **Workshop manuals**

Workshop manuals are available for detailed technical advice about the servicing, maintenance and repair of your vehicle. They are essential for anyone who intends to service or repair their own vehicle.

questions answers

Q. 8.59

Mark one answer

Breakdowns can be reduced by

- driving slowly
- regular servicing
- regular cleaning
- avoiding bad weather

Answer

 regular servicing

Being aware of components wearing out or requiring replacement will help prevent costly breakdowns. You should follow the manufacturer's guidelines for service intervals.

Q. 8.60

Mark one answer

Over filling your engine with oil could result in

- loss of power
- lower emissions
- better handling
- longer service intervals

Answer

 loss of power

If the oil level is too high, the moving parts of an engine could hit the oil, causing a loss of power or engine damage. Another problem of overfilling can be excess pressure which may damage oil seals and cause leaks.

Q. 8.61

Mark one answer

Your oil pressure warning light comes on while you are driving. What should you do?

- Wait until your next service interval and tell the mechanic
- Ignore the light, it is not the driver's responsibility
- Stop and check the oil level as soon as it is safe to do so
- Continue with your journey but have it checked on your arrival

Answer

✓ **Stop and check the oil level as soon as it is safe to do so**

The oil pressure light gives you a warning that something is wrong with the lubrication system. If it lights up there may be a serious fault which could lead to serious and expensive engine damage. Even if the oil level is correct you should still seek expert help or advice.

questions   answers

Q. 8.62

Mark one answer

What is the purpose of the oil filter?

- To prevent the engine over heating
- To give better fuel consumption
- To prevent the engine over reving
- To collect sediment from the oil

Answer

 To collect sediment from the oil

As the lubricating oil is pumped around the engine it collects tiny fragments of metal from the moving parts. The oil filter is designed to remove these fragments. Most filters are designed to be replaced at service intervals.

Q. 8.63

Mark one answer

Why should your engine oil be changed at the recommended intervals?

- To reduce friction and wear
- For better steering control
- To prevent oil leaks
- To improve clutch wear

Answer

 To reduce friction and wear

The oil and filter will get dirty in normal use. Following the service interval guidance will ensure that your engine will remain protected and properly lubricated and be less likely to break down.

Q. 8.64

Mark one answer

The oil level in your engine should normally be checked when the engine is

- hot
- reving
- cold
- idling

Answer

✓ **cold**

To get the most accurate reading, manufacturers advise that engine oil levels should be checked when cold.

questions

answers

Q. 8.65

Mark one answer

Where should you check your engine oil level?

- On sloping ground
- On a steep gradient
- On level ground
- On a downhill slope

Answer

☑ **On level ground**

It's no good checking the engine oil level when your vehicle is standing on a slope. You will not see an accurate reading on the dipstick.

Q. 8.66

Mark one answer

You overfill your engine with oil. What could this cause?

- Better handling
- Lower emissions
- Damaged gaskets
- Longer service intervals

Answer

☑ **Damaged gaskets**

If you overfill the engine with oil you could cause the engine to build up too much pressure when it is running. This could cause damage to oil seals and gaskets.

Q. 8.67

Mark one answer

When uncoupling a trailer the very FIRST thing you must do is

- lower the trailer legs to the ground
- apply the parking brake
- release the brake air lines
- uncouple the electrical lines

Answer

☑ **apply the parking brake**

Before leaving the cab it is very important to secure the vehicle by applying the vehicle parking brake. After leaving the cab apply the trailer parking brake.

questions   answers

Q. 8.68

Mark one answer

You are uncoupling a trailer. Before disconnecting any of the airlines, you MUST

- drain the air tanks
- apply the trailer parking brake
- lower the landing gear
- disconnect the electrical line

Answer

✓ **apply the trailer parking brake**

Whenever you drop or pick up a trailer you must always work through the process methodically to avoid causing danger to yourself or other people.

Q. 8.69

Mark one answer

When should you check the wheel nuts on your vehicle?

- Just before any journey
- Only before long trips
- Only every 1000 miles (1600 km)
- Just before a major service

Answer

✓ **Just before any journey**

Always have a walk round and visually check wheel nuts whenever you take a break. It's important after a wheel has been replaced to recheck the wheel nuts shortly after their initial tightening. Wheel nuts must always be tightened to the torque specified by the manufacturer.

Q. 8.70

Mark one answer

In your vehicle the oil pump is usually driven directly from the

- oil filter
- prop shaft
- piston valves
- engine

Answer

✓ **engine**

The oil pump is driven directly from the engine so that as the engine turns, oil is fed to the bearings quickly. This is important when first starting an engine to prevent damage to the bearings due to insufficient lubrication.

questions   answers

Q. 8.71

Mark four answers

You must inspect all tyres on your bus for

- ■ signs of wear
- ■ overheating
- ■ makers details
- ■ correct pressure
- ■ 'dust cap' in place
- ■ objects between twin tyres

Answers

- ☑ **signs of wear**
- ☑ **overheating**
- ☑ **correct pressure**
- ☑ **objects between twin tyres**

An unroadworthy vehicle will endanger the lives of your passengers. You should always make these essential checks as a matter of routine.

Q. 8.72

Mark one answer

You are driving a three-axle double-deck bus and using full steering lock. Why should you take extra care?

- ■ Passengers might alter the angle of tilt
- ■ The power steering might fail
- ■ You may damage the air suspension
- ■ You may scrub the rear tyres

Answer

- ☑ **You may scrub the rear tyres**

The course the wheels take on tight corners should be observed and allowed for when driving. Very low speed is advisable when the steering is on full lock.

Q. 8.73

Mark one answer

You are driving a three-axle double-deck bus and using full steering lock. To avoid rear tyre scrub you should use

- ■ the highest gear possible
- ■ a very low speed
- ■ the exhaust brake (retarder)
- ■ a steering ball

Answer

- ☑ **a very low speed**

This is advisable when negotiating tight corners.

questions answers

Q. 8.74

Mark one answer

On a double-deck bus, what is the minimum depth of tyre tread required over three-quarters of its width?

- 0.8 mm
- 1 mm
- 1.6 mm
- 2 mm

Answer

☑ **1 mm**

It's essential that the tyres on your vehicle are in good condition. You must never forget that you have passengers on board. Their safety must be your priority. At no time should the depth of the tread be less than 1 mm over three-quarters of the width of the tyre.

Q. 8.75

Mark one answer

During your journey you notice that your coach's right rear indicator is not working. You should

- continue your journey using arm signals
- get it repaired before continuing
- get it repaired on your return to the depot
- get your passengers to their destination then repair it

Answer

☑ **get it repaired before continuing**

All lights must be in working order, even in daylight. A faulty right rear indicator could cause a serious accident if another motorist attempted to overtake as you changed lanes or turned right.

Q. 8.76

Mark one answer

Before each journey you should check all warning lights. What should you do if a warning light remains lit?

- Report the fault when you return
- Have the fault checked before setting off
- Have the fault checked at the next service
- Ignore it until the fault shows up

Answer

☑ **Have the fault checked before setting off**

Many buses and coaches have a large panel of warning lights on the dashboard. A system check built into the ignition system will allow you to check that all the warning light bulbs are working before starting your journey. Familiarise yourself with the layout so you know which system is faulty if a warning light becomes illuminated during a journey. Always seek professional help and advice.

questions   answers

Q. 8.77

Mark one answer

Why should you check your tyres more frequently on a coach with three axles?

- Because punctures can be more difficult to detect
- Because air pressure is more easily lost
- The wheels will need balancing more often
- You have no room for a spare wheel

Answer

☑ **Because punctures can be more difficult to detect**

Tyre checks should be made as a matter of routine. Inspect both the inside and the outside walls and the treads for sign of wear, damage, bulges, separation and exposed cords.

Q. 8.78

Mark one answer

Some buses have different size wheels on the front and rear. When driving at high speeds on long journeys what do you need to be aware of?

- The larger wheels are more likely to overheat
- The smaller wheels are more likely to overheat
- The larger wheels are more likely to lose pressure
- The smaller wheels are more likely to lose pressure

Answer

☑ **The smaller wheels are more likely to overheat**

Because small wheels will need to rotate faster, they are more likely to overheat on long journeys at speed. Make sure you check them when you take rest stops.

Q. 8.79

Mark one answer

How frequently should a walk-round check be done?

- Daily
- Weekly
- Every 100 miles
- Every 1,000 miles

Answer

☑ **Daily**

You should carry out a daily walk-round check as a routine. The driver has a legal responsibility for taking all reasonable precautions to ensure that legal requirements are met before driving any vehicle. Checks should also be made at each driver change. Get into the habit of making a visual check before you move off after rest stops, as well as before you start your journey.

questions

answers

Q. 8.80

Mark one answer

Tyres which are over inflated will

- give better acceleration
- wear unevenly and quicker
- give much better grip
- last much longer

Answer

☑ **wear unevenly and quicker**

Your tyres must be in good condition and properly inflated to the manufacturer's recommended pressure. Surveys have shown that the tyres most likely to fail are those which have been over inflated.

Q. 8.81

Mark one answer

Your vehicle has a turbo engine. What should you do before switching it off?

- Release the air suspension valve
- Allow the engine to idle
- Select reverse gear
- Rev the engine up sharply

Answer

☑ **Allow the engine to idle**

You should always allow engines fitted with turbos to idle for about a minute before stopping the engine. This prevents the bearings from being starved of oil.

Q. 8.82

Mark one answer

One of your passengers tells you they have noticed a wheel nut is missing. How often should you check them?

- At the end of every week
- At the start of every week
- Every day before starting out
- Only at every service interval

Answer

☑ **Every day before starting out**

It's essential to make sure that all wheel nuts are tightened with a correctly calibrated torque wrench. The wheel nuts should be checked every day before starting your journey.

However, if one of your passengers tells you they have noticed a wheel nut is missing, check immediately. If there is a problem, don't move off until it has been rectified.

questions answers

Q. 8.83 🚌

Mark one answer

You are parking your vehicle. It is fitted with a turbo engine. You should

- ▪ rev the engine up then switch it off
- ▪ switch the engine off immediately
- ▪ allow the engine to idle then switch it off
- ▪ switch the engine off and on repeatedly

Answer

✓ **allow the engine to idle then switch it off**

Allowing engines fitted with turbos to idle for about a minute before stopping them prevents the turbo bearings from being starved of oil.

Q. 8.84 🚌

Mark two answers

When you are uncoupling a trailer you should

- ▪ disconnect the electrical line first
- ▪ unload at least some of the cargo
- ▪ choose a well lit location
- ▪ apply the trailer brake first
- ▪ choose a firm level surface

Answers

✓ **apply the trailer brake first**

✓ **choose a firm level surface**

Before uncoupling a trailer always make sure that you have parked on firm, level ground and apply the trailer parking brake. Think SAFETY FIRST.

Q. 8.85 🚌

Mark one answer

It is dark and you are on a very busy road. Your headlights have failed. The fuse box is on the outside of the bus on the right hand side. What should you do?

- ▪ Pull up on the left and call for assistance
- ▪ Drive on using sidelights at front and rear
- ▪ Try to fix the problem on your own
- ▪ Get a passenger to hold a torch for you

Answer

✓ **Pull up on the left and call for assistance**

Don't attempt to work on the right hand side of the vehicle at night without safety protection provided by a breakdown vehicle with flashing amber lights. Many accidents have occurred due to the close proximity of passing traffic.

questions

answers

Q. 8.86

Mark one answer

You are on a very busy road and it is dark. Your headlights fail suddenly. The fuse box is on the outside of the bus on the right hand side. What should you do?

- Ask a passenger to watch for traffic
- Drive on without lights
- Fix the problem yourself
- Wait for the breakdown services

Answer

✓ **Wait for the breakdown services**

Fast-moving traffic will be passing close by, so wait for the breakdown services to arrive. Their vehicle will provide safety protection while your vehicle is repaired or recovered.

Q. 8.87

Mark one answer

Your coach often tows a trailer. How often should you check the trailer tyres for pressure?

- at least once a week when they are cold
- at least once a month when they are hot
- at least once a week when they are hot
- at least once a month when fully laden

Answer

✓ **at least once a week when they are cold**

Just like your bus tyres, your trailer tyres must be in good condition. You may not tow a trailer on every journey you make, but when you do, check the trailer tyres while they are cold and make sure they are suitable for the load they will carry.

Section 9

Leaving the vehicle

This section looks at safety when leaving your vehicle.

The questions will ask you about

- **Passengers**

  choosing the correct place to stop to help your passengers leave the vehicle safely

- **The driver's cab**

  your own safety, and that of others, when you leave the vehicle's cab.

questions   answers

Q. 9.1

Mark one answer

When pulling up on the left in busy places you should be careful that

- [ ] there is good access to unload
- [ ] you have disconnected all air lines
- [ ] your nearside mirror does not strike the head of a pedestrian
- [ ] you change your tachograph mode

Answer

- [✓] **your nearside mirror does not strike the head of a pedestrian**

When pulling up on the left you should always be aware of pedestrians, particularly if they are close to the edge of the road. The height of your nearside mirror can vary depending on the size and type of vehicle you are driving. If in doubt, approach these situations with caution and stop if necessary.

Q. 9.2

Mark one answer

You have just parked a lorry at a roadside in very heavy traffic. Before dismounting from the cab you should be particularly careful to do which one of the following?

- [ ] Make sure the radio is turned down
- [ ] Check the rear view mirrors
- [ ] Make sure the hazard warning lights are on
- [ ] Check that all windows are closed

Answer

- [✓] **Check the rear view mirrors**

Getting out of the cab from the offside of a vehicle directly into the road can be hazardous, especially if traffic is travelling at speed. Use your mirrors to check behind and all around the vehicle. Ensure that you use all proper footholds and hand grips. Be responsible for your own health and safety.

Q. 9.3

Mark one answer

You are driving a long, rigid vehicle. Where must you NOT park?

- [ ] On a pedestrian crossing
- [ ] In a lay-by
- [ ] In a loading bay
- [ ] On a service area

Answer

- [✓] **On a pedestrian crossing**

There are many places where you should not park: it's important to make sure that you always select a place that is both safe and legal. Parking on or too close to a pedestrian crossing can be dangerous as this will restrict the view for drivers and pedestrians.

questions answers

Q. 9.4

Mark one answer

You want to park a semi-trailer and leave it unattended. Where should you NOT do this?

- ■ In a lorry park
- ■ On level ground
- ■ In a factory
- ■ In a lay-by

Answer

☑ **In a lay-by**

If you need to park the semi-trailer of your vehicle, find a safe place. Don't park it in a lay-by. Leave these available for drivers who wish to stop and rest. Find a place off the road, preferably a lorry park or somewhere safe which will decrease the risk of theft.

Q. 9.5

Mark one answer

Which ONE of the following is NOT important when getting out of a lorry cab?

- ■ Watching for approaching traffic
- ■ Using the mirrors
- ■ Applying the parking brake
- ■ Disconnecting the air lines

Answer

☑ **Disconnecting the air lines**

After getting out of your vehicle it's a good idea to walk round and check your tyres, load, lights, brake lines, electrical connections, etc. When you return to your vehicle, or take over a different vehicle, all the safety checks should be carried out.

Q. 9.6

Mark three answers

You are the driver of a tanker vehicle. When opening the tank hatches, what dangers should you be aware of?

- ■ Low air pressure
- ■ Speed limiters
- ■ Slippery walkways
- ■ Emergency air lines
- ■ Overhead cables
- ■ Overhead pipeways

Answers

☑ **Slippery walkways**

☑ **Overhead cables**

☑ **Overhead pipeways**

Take your time if you're using walkways at high levels. Fuel can make the surface slippery and therefore increase the safety risk.

questions   answers

Q. 9.7

Mark two answers

As a driver you should use your mirrors

- [ ] as you signal
- [ ] to check the blind spot
- [ ] when driving along
- [ ] before opening your door

Answers

- [x] **when driving along**
- [x] **before opening your door**

To be a safe driver, you must always be aware of where other road users are. That way you can plan your driving according to what is going on around you.

Before opening your door it's important to check the mirrors, as well as looking round for passing or approaching vehicles.

Q. 9.8

Mark one answer

Before you get out of your cab, you must

- [ ] empty the air tanks
- [ ] adjust your mirrors
- [ ] apply the parking brake
- [ ] check if the warning lights are working

Answer

- [x] **apply the parking brake**

The parking brake must always be set whenever you leave the vehicle, it is an offence not to leave it properly secured.

Q. 9.9

Mark one answer

Before you leave your vehicle you must always

- [ ] empty the air tanks
- [ ] apply the parking brake
- [ ] adjust your mirrors
- [ ] switch on your hazard warning lights

Answer

- [x] **apply the parking brake**

Whenever you leave the driving seat, you must always make sure that your vehicle is secured by applying the parking brake. Make sure the engine has stopped. It is an offence to leave your vehicle with the engine running.

questions   answers

Q. 9.10

Mark three answers

Before leaving the cab you should make sure that

- ▮ you remove your tachograph chart
- ▮ the engine has stopped
- ▮ all warning lights are operating
- ▮ the parking brake is on
- ▮ all documents are safely stowed
- ▮ you will not endanger people when opening the door

Answers

- ☑ the engine has stopped
- ☑ the parking brake is on
- ☑ you will not endanger people when opening the door

Always make a systematic check of the above before leaving your vehicle. It is your responsibility to make sure your vehicle and load are safe at all times. It is an offence to leave a vehicle with the engine running on a public road.

Q. 9.11

Mark one answer

Before opening your cab door you should be aware of

- ▮ vehicles passing close by
- ▮ the height of your cab from the ground
- ▮ loose grab rails near the door
- ▮ people crossing the road behind you

Answer

- ☑ vehicles passing close by

It can be dangerous for vehicles passing close by if you open the door carelessly. Always look properly to make sure that it's safe, using the mirror as well as checking blind spots before you get out of the cab.

Q. 9.12

Mark three answers

Before leaving your vehicle cab you should make sure that

- ▮ the engine is running smoothly
- ▮ the engine is stopped
- ▮ the parking brake is on
- ▮ you have removed your personal things
- ▮ the ignition system is switched off

Answers

- ☑ the engine is stopped
- ☑ the parking brake is on
- ☑ the ignition system is switched off

The vehicle must always be left safe and secure when you leave the cab.

questions   answers

Q. 9.13

Mark two answers

Before leaving your vehicle cab you should make sure that

- ▪ your seat is correctly adjusted
- ▪ the ignition system is switched on
- ▪ the engine is stopped
- ▪ the keys are in the starter switch
- ▪ the parking brake is on

Answers

- ☑ **the engine is stopped**
- ☑ **the parking brake is on**

The law requires that the parking brake is set and the engine switched off before leaving the cab of your vehicle.

Q. 9.14

Mark two answers

Hazard warning lights may be used in which TWO of these situations?

- ▪ To thank a driver who has let you pull in after overtaking
- ▪ As a warning to drivers that you are towing another vehicle
- ▪ To show your intention to go ahead at a junction when your position might suggest otherwise
- ▪ When driving on motorways or dual carriageways to warn following drivers of a hazard ahead
- ▪ When your vehicle is stopped to warn others of an obstruction

Answers

- ☑ **When driving on motorways or dual carriageways to warn following drivers of a hazard ahead**
- ☑ **When your vehicle is stopped to warn others of an obstruction**

Use your hazard warning lights when approaching a queue of traffic on the motorway or unrestricted dual carriageway; this will alert traffic behind, which may not be able to see the hazard due to the size of your vehicle. Don't use hazard warning lights as an excuse for illegal parking. They should only be used to warn others of an obstruction or hazard ahead.

questions

answers

Q. 9.15

Mark one answer

When should you use hazard warning lights?

- To warn other drivers that you are towing
- Approaching queuing traffic on a motorway
- When parked illegally on a busy road
- To thank a driver for giving way to you

Answer

☑ **Approaching queuing traffic on a motorway**

You may only use hazard warning lights while driving when you are on an unrestricted dual carriageway or motorway, to warn drivers behind you of a hazard or obstruction ahead. Only use them for just long enough to ensure that your warning has been observed.

Q. 9.16

Mark one answer

A horse is running loose on the motorway. You should

- use the size of your vehicle to block the lanes
- stop and try to catch the animal
- leave your vehicle to warn following traffic
- call the police from the next emergency telephone

Answer

☑ **call the police from the next emergency telephone**

In a situation like this it's vital that the police are alerted as soon as possible. They will be able to contact the best people to deal with the emergency, and will take control themselves, to keep things as safe as possible. On no account should you walk onto the carriageway yourself; this would be dangerous and against the law.

Q. 9.17

Mark one answer

You need to stop and get out of your vehicle. The parking brake should be used

- with the service brake
- only on uneven ground
- at all times when leaving the vehicle
- unless the vehicle is in gear

Answer

☑ **at all times when leaving the vehicle**

It is an offence to leave your vehicle unattended at any time without applying the parking brake.

questions   answers

Q. 9.18

Mark one answer

As a bus driver your main aim should be

- ▣ to keep strictly to the timetable
- ▣ the safety of your passengers
- ▣ service to your colleagues
- ▣ to keep accurate details of ticket sales

Answer

☑ **the safety of your passengers**

You should remember that, as a driver, you are there to provide a service. Your passengers rely on you to make sure that the journey is a safe and comfortable one.

Q. 9.19

Mark one answer

As the driver of a bus your FIRST priority is

- ▣ the safety and comfort of your passengers
- ▣ making sure that you are always on time
- ▣ making sure that your log book and tachograph are correctly completed
- ▣ making sure that your destination is clearly marked

Answer

☑ **the safety and comfort of your passengers**

As the driver of a PCV you have responsibilities beyond those of other drivers. Your passengers have paid for a service, and should arrive at their chosen destination safely. Customers are more likely to travel with you again if they receive a safe, courteous and comfortable service.

Q. 9.20

Mark one answer

You are driving a one-person-operated bus. You are at a bus stop issuing tickets. You should

- ▣ be in gear without any signal
- ▣ be in gear and signalling
- ▣ signal only when ready to move away
- ▣ be in neutral but signalling to move off

Answer

☑ **signal only when ready to move away**

Giving wrong signals causes uncertainty and confusion to other road users. Only give appropriate signals which are relevant to your intended actions.

questions

answers

Q. 9.21

Mark one answer

As the driver of a one-person-operated double-deck bus you should be constantly aware of passengers on the top deck. How should you do this?

- By counting passengers up and down the staircase
- By frequent checks upstairs while stopped at bus stops
- By listening to passengers in the upstairs gangway when approaching bus stops
- By making full use of the internal mirror system

Answer

☑ **By making full use of the internal mirror system**

If you're driving a one-person-operated double-deck bus you must ensure that you can see passengers who are about to descend the stairs. Make sure that you can see them in the internal mirrors. Always consider their safety and avoid harsh braking and steering.

Q. 9.22

Mark one answer

When driving a double-deck bus, the internal mirror system is used to

- watch for traffic on your right-hand side
- keep a look out for any overtaking vehicles
- keep a look out for passengers using the stairs
- watch for cyclists on your left-hand side

Answer

☑ **keep a look out for passengers using the stairs**

You must always be aware of anyone using the stairs. Be particularly careful to avoid any sudden movement, such as when braking or cornering, as this could cause them to stumble.

Q. 9.23

Mark one answer

The nearside mirror is used for checking

- if the driver's door is closed properly
- for any vehicles moving up on the left
- if passengers are seated
- for any vehicles parking in front of you

Answer

☑ **for any vehicles moving up on the left**

Always be aware of any vehicles on your nearside, particularly on dual carriageways or motorways where, because of the limits on your vehicle, it can take some distance to overtake safely. When you think you are far enough ahead to move back to the left safely, check again, as other vehicles may accelerate up on the nearside.

questions · answers

Q. 9.24

Mark one answer

When you intend to open your right-hand door you should check

- ■ the mirror
- ■ that all other doors are closed
- ■ the air pressure
- ■ that the interior is clear of passengers

Answer

☑ **the mirror**

When you pull in, other vehicles may be passing on your right-hand side. It's very important to check your mirror, as well as looking round to cover the blind spot, to make sure that it's safe before opening your door.

Q. 9.25

Mark one answer

You are stopping to collect passengers from a bus stop. Where should you pull up?

- ■ Close to the kerb
- ■ Away from the kerb
- ■ After the bus stop
- ■ Before the bus stop

Answer

☑ **Close to the kerb**

A bus that has pulled half-way into a bus stop lay-by with the rear sticking well out into the road is a danger to other vehicles. If passengers are not waiting at the bus stop it can be tempting to pull up to where they are. This may not be a safe place for your vehicle or for other road users. Be professional and be safe; pull up in the correct position.

Q. 9.26

Mark one answer

You should stop your bus to allow passengers to get on or off near

- ■ soft grass
- ■ guard rails
- ■ parked cars
- ■ the kerb

Answer

☑ **the kerb**

You should stop as close to the kerb as you can, so that passengers can reach the safety of the pavement without any difficulty.

questions

answers

Q. 9.27 🚌

Mark one answer

A bus stop is blocked and you cannot pull into it. Before opening the exit door what is the most important action to take?

- Try to get the bus stop cleared
- Carry on to the next bus stop
- Check for traffic on the left
- Check for traffic on the right

Answer

✓ **Check for traffic on the left**

You must take care of your passengers at all times. Ensure that you allow your passengers to get on or off the vehicle safely. If you're unable to stop close to the kerb, don't open the doors until you're sure it's safe. Always check the nearside mirror first.

Q. 9.28 🚌

Mark one answer

Several cars have parked blocking your bus stop. Before allowing passengers to get off you should

- move on to the next bus stop
- check it is clear of traffic on the left
- try and find the car owners
- check it is clear of traffic on the right

Answer

✓ **check it is clear of traffic on the left**

Always check your nearside mirror before opening the door to allow passengers to alight. When you have stopped away from the kerb, it is important to warn the passengers to look out for cyclists and to expect a long step down onto the road. Be ready to offer assistance if required.

Q. 9.29 🚌

Mark one answer

What should you do before allowing passengers off your bus?

- Collect their used tickets
- Activate an audible warning system
- Check mirrors before opening doors
- Ask if they have luggage to collect

Answer

✓ **Check mirrors before opening doors**

The safety of passengers is your main responsibility. Before you allow them to step down from the bus you should always check your mirrors to make sure that there's nothing approaching that could endanger them.

questions   answers

Q. 9.30

Mark one answer

Passengers may be in a hurry to get off the bus as you approach a bus stop. What should you do to reduce any dangers?

- Insist that passengers stay seated until the bus stops
- Pull up just before the stop and let passengers get off
- Let passengers on the bus before letting passengers off
- Not open the passenger doors until the bus stops

Answer

☑ **Not open the passenger doors until the bus stops**

Passengers may be in a hurry to get off at their stop. Don't brake harshly or open the doors until the vehicle has stopped. Passengers may have left their seats early and be standing up waiting to get off. Due to the necessary fittings on board, such as handrails, poles and luggage racks, there's a substantial risk of injury. Put your passengers' safety first.

Q. 9.31

Mark one answer

You are driving a half-cab bus and carrying passengers. You must have

- a chain or strap across the doorway
- electrically operated doors
- school children only on board
- a responsible person in charge of them

Answer

☑ **a responsible person in charge of them**

When you have no direct contact with your passengers, you must have a designated person in charge of the passenger saloon.

Q. 9.32

Mark three answers

As a driver, when getting out of your bus you must make sure that

- the parking brake is on
- the vehicle is stopped in a safe place
- the engine is switched off
- the air pressure gauges read full
- you are parked at a bus stop
- you always change the destination board

Answers

☑ **the parking brake is on**

☑ **the vehicle is stopped in a safe place**

☑ **the engine is switched off**

Don't park where you will cause obstruction or inconvenience to other road users. It's an offence to leave your bus with the engine running and/or without applying the parking brake.

LEAVING THE VEHICLE

questions   answers

Q. 9.33 🚌

Mark three answers

Many buses have a separate door on the offside for the driver. When leaving the bus by this door you should always

- ◼ jump down from the cab
- ◼ check for traffic which may be passing
- ◼ apply the parking brake
- ◼ climb down facing the bus using the footholds
- ◼ climb down facing away from the bus using the footholds

Answers

- ☑ **check for traffic which may be passing**
- ☑ **apply the parking brake**
- ☑ **climb down facing the bus using the footholds**

Having found a safe place to park your bus, make a final offside check before opening your door. Never jump down from the cab into the road. It's particularly dangerous as you risk injury from landing badly or falling into the path of passing traffic.

Q. 9.34 🚌

Mark two answers

When getting out of the driver's door on this bus you should

- ◼ look out for overtaking vehicles before opening the door
- ◼ climb down facing away from the bus
- ◼ climb down facing the bus
- ◼ signal your intentions to other traffic
- ◼ open the door to get a good view of approaching traffic

Answers

- ☑ **look out for overtaking vehicles before opening the door**
- ☑ **climb down facing the bus**

For your own safety, as well as that of others, you should make sure that it's safe by checking for other vehicles before getting out of the cab. Climbing down facing the bus means that you can make proper use of the footholds to lessen the risk of slipping.

questions answers

Q. 9.35

Mark two answers

This bus has a separate door for the driver, opening onto the offside. What should you do when getting out of such a vehicle?

■ Climb down facing away from the vehicle

■ Check for passing traffic

■ Climb down facing towards the vehicle

■ Jump down carefully, flexing the knees on landing

■ Climb down holding the steering wheel rim tightly

Answers

☑ **Check for passing traffic**

☑ **Climb down facing towards the vehicle**

If your vehicle has a separate offside driver's door, you must take the precaution of good observation before leaving the vehicle. Don't jump down out of the cab. Leave by climbing down facing towards the vehicle. Consider your own safety as well as that of others and always check for traffic passing closely by before getting out of your vehicle.

Q. 9.36

Mark two answers

You are driving a loaded school bus. Looking in your mirror you see smoke from the engine compartment at the rear. You must

■ stop as quickly and safely as possible

■ open the engine covers to investigate

■ drive to the bus station for a replacement vehicle

■ get everyone off the bus quickly

■ move the passengers to the front away from danger

Answers

☑ **stop as quickly and safely as possible**

☑ **get everyone off the bus quickly**

Smoke from the engine compartment is very serious, as fire within a vehicle can spread very quickly. Your first priority is to make sure that all passengers get off the bus as quickly and safely as possible.

LEAVING THE VEHICLE

questions   answers

Q. 9.37

Mark one answer

You can drive a bus at night without having the interior lights on if

- the passengers want to sleep
- most passengers request it
- there are no standing passengers
- there are no passengers

Answer

✓ **there are no passengers**

Whenever passengers are aboard, the interior lighting must be left on, but it may be turned off when the bus is empty.

Q. 9.38

Mark four answers

As a bus driver, on which FOUR occasions should you use your hazard warning lights?

- When you are temporarily obstructing traffic
- To thank a driver who has let you pull in
- To warn of an obstruction when driving on the motorway
- When parking in a restricted area
- When you have broken down
- When stationary and children are getting off a school bus

Answers

✓ **When you are temporarily obstructing traffic**

✓ **To warn of an obstruction when driving on the motorway**

✓ **When you have broken down**

✓ **When stationary and children are getting off a school bus**

All drivers may use hazard warning lights to warn other road users of danger on specific occasions. When you are driving a school bus you may also use them when you have stopped and children are getting on or off.

Q. 9.39

Mark one answer

You are driving a bus in hot weather. May the passenger door be left open to let fresh air in?

- Yes, this is normal practice
- No, unless all passengers are seated
- Yes, unless carrying school children
- No, this is not allowed

Answer

✓ **No, this is not allowed**

Under no circumstances should you drive with your passenger door open. Many vehicles have air-operated doors which close automatically when the clutch is released. Do not override this set-up. An open door invites people to make rash decisions to enter or leave the vehicle as you are about to move away, which can be extremely dangerous.

questions

answers

Q. 9.40

Mark one answer

When leaving the cab of your bus which of the following is NOT important?

▮ Applying the parking brake

▮ Switching off the engine

▮ Watching for approaching traffic

▮ Operating the fuel cut-off switch

Answer

☑ **Operating the fuel cut-off switch**

This is not normally necessary unless the vehicle has been involved in an accident and there is a risk of fire.

Q. 9.41

Mark one answer

When driving through a bus station you should

▮ ensure that your destination boards are correct

▮ drive only in first gear

▮ look out for people leaving the buses

▮ use your mirrors more than usual

Answer

☑ **look out for people leaving the buses**

Bus stations are busy places. If people are in a rush they may not always look properly before getting off the bus. You must always keep your speed down and be aware that danger may suddenly arise when you least expect it.

Q. 9.42 🚌

Mark two answers

Air suspension systems give

▮ increased fuel consumption

▮ uneven tyre wear

▮ increased speed

▮ even height

▮ a comfortable ride to passengers

Answers

☑ **even height**

☑ **a comfortable ride to passengers**

Air suspension can also help reduce wear on road surfaces, which is why it is also known as 'road-friendly suspension'.

questions   answers

Q. 9.43 🚌

Mark one answer

You are going to park your bus. What should you check before leaving it?

- The ticket dispenser
- Litter left under seats
- The parking brake is applied
- The intercom is working

Answer

✓ **The parking brake is applied**

It's an offence to leave any vehicle without applying the parking brake. Make sure that this is firmly applied before you leave the driving position.

Q. 9.44 🚌

Mark one answer

A disabled person is getting on your bus. They are having problems but say they can manage. What should you do?

- Be prepared to move off
- Smile and offer to help them
- Ask them politely to hurry up
- Do nothing, you can't leave your seat

Answer

✓ **Smile and offer to help them**

Disabled people like to keep their independence. However, if they are having problems be prepared to offer help.

Q. 9.45 🚌

Mark one answer

Damage can be caused when parking close to another vehicle if your coach is fitted with

- air brakes
- hydraulic suspension
- air suspension
- hydraulic brakes

Answer

✓ **air suspension**

Vehicles fitted with air suspension can sometimes move a considerable amount when first started, as the air bags are injected with gas. If you're too close to another vehicle or obstruction, this could result in collision damage.

Vehicle loading

This section looks at vehicle loading.

The questions will ask you about

- **Loading**
  loading and unloading goods and the use of loading equipment

- **Safety**
  stowing, fastening and controlling the load

- **Types of load**
  dealing with different kinds of loads.

questions

answers

Q. 10.1

Mark one answer

Why is it important to distribute the weight evenly over the axles when loading a lorry?

- [ ] To ensure easy unloading
- [ ] To make it easier to sheet up
- [ ] To ensure maximum ground clearance
- [ ] To ensure maximum stability

Answer

☑ **To ensure maximum stability**

A vehicle should be loaded so that the weight of a load is evenly distributed over the axles. This will increase the stability of the load. In addition you should brake in good time and when driving in a straight line wherever possible. Look well ahead so that you can avoid harsh braking. Always reduce your speed before you make a turn, so that you aren't braking and turning at the same time.

Q. 10.2

Mark one answer

Which of the following is most important when loading a vehicle?

- [ ] Spreading the load evenly
- [ ] Loading it towards the rear
- [ ] Loading it towards the front
- [ ] Easy access for unloading

Answer

☑ **Spreading the load evenly**

It is your responsibility as the driver to make sure that your vehicle load is spread evenly to avoid overloading individual axles. Overloading carries severe penalties for the driver and operator.

Q. 10.3

Mark one answer

You are driving a lorry with an ISO container on a trailer. You must make sure that

- [ ] the container is secured by ropes
- [ ] all locking levers are secured
- [ ] the trailer has a flat-bed platform
- [ ] the container is sealed

Answer

☑ **all locking levers are secured**

ISO (International Standards Organisation) cargo containers should only be carried on lorries or trailers with the appropriate securing points. These are designed to lock into the container body.

questions

answers

Q. 10.4

Mark one answer

You are loading a steel ISO container. Which statement is true?

- Its own weight will hold it in place
- It can be loaded onto any flat-bed lorry
- The locking levers must be secured
- The container should be roped in place

Answer

✓ **The locking levers must be secured**

Container loads use a different type of restraint to secure them to the vehicle. Make sure that you are familiar with all the different kinds of load restraint. The security of the load is your responsibility; don't take chances.

Q. 10.5

Mark one answer

A lorry is found to be overloaded. Who is liable to be prosecuted for this offence?

- The people who loaded the vehicle
- Both the driver and the operator
- The operator only
- The driver only

Answer

✓ **Both the driver and the operator**

If a roadside check reveals there may be contravention of vehicle weight limits, the police can escort the vehicle to the nearest official weighbridge.

Q. 10.6

Mark one answer

Who is responsible for making sure that a lorry's load is secure during a journey?

- The warehouse loader
- The driver's mate
- The driver
- The transport police

Answer

✓ **The driver**

Before you leave on a journey always check that your load is secure. When you stop for a break, always walk round your vehicle and check your load.

questions

Q. 10.7

Mark one answer

You are using three sheets to cover your load. Which of the following shows the correct overlap?

answers

Answer

Keep a check in your mirrors as you're driving to ensure that the sheets are secure. Air can force itself under the sheets and work them loose.

Q. 10.8

Mark one answer

You are covering a load using more than one sheet. You should start with the rearmost sheet first, then work forwards. This will

- ◼ stop you tripping over when walking on the load
- ◼ stop wind and rain getting under the sheets
- ◼ make it much easier to fold up the sheets
- ◼ make it easier to carry longer loads

Answer

 stop wind and rain getting under the sheets

If the load is sheeted incorrectly, when the wind gets underneath the sheet it will lift and flap about. This is dangerous, as it can catch unsuspecting pedestrians or cyclists and also seriously reduce the driver's view of what's happening to the rear.

Q. 10.9

Mark one answer

When roping down a load on your lorry what is the best knot to use?

- ◼ A dolly knot
- ◼ A reef knot
- ◼ A slip knot
- ◼ A bow-line knot

Answer

 A dolly knot

If a load is being secured by ropes you must ensure that they are tied securely to the body of the unit. The most effective method of tying is by 'dolly knots'. These are non-slip knots that hold firmly. You should practise tying these and use them appropriately.

questions

answers

Q. 10.10

Mark one answer

Ropes are unsuitable to tie down a load of scrap metal because they

- are hard to tie
- will loosen in rain
- are hard to untie
- wear and snap

Answer

☑ **wear and snap**

When securing a load, the driver must decide which is the most suitable type of restraint to use. A few extra minutes to make sure that the load is secure gives you peace of mind. It also reduces the risk of the load moving should an emergency situation arise.

Q. 10.11

Mark one answer

You are driving a tipper lorry carrying loose dry sand. Why should you sheet this load?

- To stop handling being affected
- To stop the load from shifting
- To stop the load from blowing away
- To aid your rearward vision

Answer

☑ **To stop the load from blowing away**

If you're carrying a load that consists of loose materials, it must be securely roped and sheeted. You must not risk the chance of losing any part of your load. This could cause damage or injury to other road users, and you would be held responsible.

Q. 10.12

Mark one answer

The load on a lorry becomes insecure on a journey. The driver should

- continue at a slower speed to ensure the load does not fall off
- attach 'hazard' boards to warn other road users
- park and re-secure the load before continuing
- inform base at the earliest opportunity

Answer

☑ **park and re-secure the load before continuing**

If you become aware that any part of your load is insecure you must stop as soon as it's safe to do so. Re-secure the load before continuing on your journey. If this isn't possible, then you must seek assistance. Don't take risks.

questions answers

Q. 10.13

Mark one answer

Baffle plates are fitted to tankers to help

▪ reduce wind resistance

▪ reduce the wave effect

▪ stop the brakes from locking

▪ make the steering lighter

Answer

☑ **reduce the wave effect**

Fluids carried in tanks can move in 'waves' as the vehicle's speed changes, particularly when braking and then easing off the pedal. This shift of weight could cause the vehicle to surge forward. Baffle plates are designed to reduce the wave effect in the liquid.

Q. 10.14

Mark one answer

Which of the following would reduce the 'wave effect' when driving tankers?

▪ Spray guards

▪ Harsh braking

▪ Baffle plates

▪ Wind deflectors

Answer

☑ **Baffle plates**

Modern tankers are fitted with baffle plates inside the tank compartment. This helps to minimise the movement of liquids and therefore reduce the 'wave effect'.

questions   answers

Q. 10.15

Mark one answer

You are driving an articulated tanker vehicle on a straight road. When braking to a stop the liquid load will tend to

- push the vehicle forward
- push the vehicle to the side
- make the trailer wheels bounce
- make the trailer wheels skid

Answer

✓ **push the vehicle forward**

When braking with a vehicle carrying a liquid load it's important to apply even pressure on the brake pedal. Do not relax the pedal pressure until the vehicle has stopped. Secure the vehicle with the parking brake before releasing the footbrake. This will minimise the risk of unintentional movement of the vehicle caused by 'surge' from the liquid load.

Q. 10.16

Mark one answer

You are driving a tanker that is half full. The inside of the tank is not divided into compartments. When braking to a stop you should

- avoid relaxing the footbrake
- relax the footbrake
- pump the footbrake rapidly
- use the footbrake and parking brake together

Answer

✓ **avoid relaxing the footbrake**

Baffle plates help prevent liquids 'surging' around, but extra care is still necessary when driving a tanker vehicle. When braking, always maintain steady pressure on the brake pedal until after the vehicle has stopped. This helps reduce the 'wave' effect which can build up as the liquid load surges back and forth when the vehicle changes speed.

Q. 10.17

Mark one answer

Which type of load would most benefit from being carried on a lorry fitted with road-friendly suspension?

- Steel
- Timber
- Glass
- Cables

Answer

✓ **Glass**

Fragile loads need extra care in loading and handling. The load must be secured using the most appropriate form of restraint. Air suspension reduces the vibration caused by the impact of the lorry wheels on road surfaces. This also reduces damage to the road, bridges and adjacent structures.

questions

Q. 10.18

Mark one answer

An attendant must accompany you when your load is wider than

- 2.6 metres (8 feet 5 inches)
- 3.0 metres (9 feet 9 inches)
- 3.3 metres (10 feet 9 inches)
- 3.5 metres (11 feet 5 inches)

Answer

✓ **3.5 metres (11 feet 5 inches)**

Wide loads are a hazard to other road users. In addition to having an attendant with you, you must also notify the police. Side markers must also be used to show other road users that your load overhangs the limits of your vehicle.

Q. 10.19

Mark one answer

Which of these vehicles will be most at risk of 'roll over' when laden?

Answer

✓

'Roll over' usually occurs as a result of the inside rear wheels of an articulated vehicle starting to lift when negotiating a curve, such as exiting a roundabout. Changes of direction can create a situation where the vehicle is unstable due to movement of the load. The problem frequently involves vehicles carrying fluids in bulk.

Q. 10.20

Mark one answer

Jack-knifing of an articulated lorry is more likely to occur when the trailer is

- loaded at the front
- loaded at the rear
- unloaded
- fully loaded

Answer

✓ **unloaded**

Severe braking can result in jack-knifing as the tractor unit is pushed by the semi-trailer pivoting around the coupling (fifth wheel). This is more likely to occur when the brakes are applied on a bend.

questions   answers

Q. 10.21

Mark one answer

After recoupling, how should you make sure that the tractor and trailer are secure?

- [ ] Try to move forward with the trailer parking brake on
- [ ] Reverse with the trailer parking brake on
- [ ] Try to move forward with the trailer parking brake off
- [ ] Reverse with the trailer parking brake off

Answer

- [x] **Try to move forward with the trailer parking brake on**

Ensure the locking mechanism is secure by selecting a low gear and attempting to move forward. Apply the parking brake before leaving the cab. Connect the 'dog-clip' to secure the kingpin release handle.

Q. 10.22

Mark one answer

When uncoupling or recoupling your trailer, what must you check first?

- [ ] The lights are working
- [ ] The tilt cab mechanism is secure
- [ ] The trailer brake is applied
- [ ] The air lines are safely stowed

Answer

- [x] **The trailer brake is applied**

If the trailer begins moving while you're working on it, you could put yourself and others in great danger. You must make sure that it's properly secured using the brake before you start work.

Q. 10.23

Mark one answer

You are uncoupling a lorry and trailer. After disconnecting the electric line you should

- [ ] stow it away safely
- [ ] drive forward slowly
- [ ] lower the landing gear
- [ ] apply the trailer brake

Answer

- [x] **stow it away safely**

It's important to stow away all your electric cables and air lines safely to avoid causing injury to others. Connectors left lying around can get damaged if run over by another vehicle. It's your responsibility as the driver to make sure that this does not happen.

questions   # answers

Q. 10.24

Mark one answer

Your lorry has a demountable body. Before demounting the body you should ensure that

- ☐ the rear doors are open
- ☐ the legs are up
- ☐ the body is unloaded and empty
- ☐ the surface is firm and level

Answer

 ☑ **the surface is firm and level**

If you demount the body on a poor or soft surface there is a danger of it sinking and becoming difficult to handle. Always think carefully before you demount the body and be sure that the site is suitable.

Q. 10.25

Mark one answer

After recoupling your trailer you should adjust your mirrors to enable you to see

- ☐ the full view of your load
- ☐ both pairs of rear wheels
- ☐ down each side of the trailer
- ☐ the road on the other side

Answer

 ☑ **down each side of the trailer**

The view you get in your mirrors may vary depending on the size of the trailer and the load it carries. Always adjust your mirrors to make sure that you have the best possible view down each side of the trailer before you drive away.

Q. 10.26

Mark one answer

Who is responsible for ensuring that a lorry's load does not move whilst in transit?

- ☐ The factory manager
- ☐ The lorry driver
- ☐ The driver's mate
- ☐ The loaders at the factory

Answer

☑ **The lorry driver**

You should check your load carefully before starting a journey. Every time you stop for a break, walk around the vehicle and check that your load is still secure. If the load causes danger to other road users you, as the driver, are responsible. Take time to check it properly.

questions answers

Q. 10.27

Mark one answer

Which one of the following vehicles is most likely to be affected by 'vehicle bounce'?

- A long wheel-base empty vehicle
- A short wheel-base laden vehicle
- A short wheel-base empty vehicle
- A long wheel-base laden vehicle

Answer

☑ **A short wheel-base empty vehicle**

A short wheel-base empty vehicle will bounce more noticeably than some long wheel-base vehicles. This can affect braking efficiency and all round control. Don't be tempted to push this type of vehicle into bends or corners simply because the vehicle appears to be easier to drive.

Q. 10.28

Mark one answer

Ropes should NOT be used to tie down a load of

- timber planks
- hay bales
- steel plates
- canvas sacks

Answer

☑ **steel plates**

Ropes are totally unsuitable for loads such as steel plates. If there is danger of sharp edges shearing ropes then chains must be used with a suitable tensioning device.

Q. 10.29

Mark one answer

Which of the following loads is most likely to move forward with some force if you brake sharply?

- Heavy material in canvas sacks
- Loose sand
- Timber secured with dolly knots
- Tubular metal

Answer

☑ **Tubular metal**

When deciding which type of restraint to use consider what may happen if you have to brake sharply. Tubular loads may move forward with some force if you have to brake sharply in an emergency. In such cases the headboard of the vehicle can be demolished with fatal results.

questions

answers

Q. 10.30

Mark one answer

When part loading a lorry with an empty ISO container you should position it

- [ ] close to the fifth wheel
- [ ] over the front axle
- [ ] close to the trailer edge
- [ ] over the rear axles

Answer

✓ **over the rear axles**

To increase stability and reduce the risk of the trailer wheels lifting when turning, it is preferable to locate part loads over the rear axle.

Q. 10.31

Mark one answer

When carrying spare sheets and ropes on your trailer you MUST make sure that they are

- [ ] laid out flat
- [ ] visible from the cab
- [ ] tied down securely
- [ ] stacked loosely

Answer

✓ **tied down securely**

All spare sheets and ropes must be tied down securely to prevent them falling into the path of following vehicles.

Q. 10.32

Mark one answer

Jack-knifing is more likely to occur when driving

- [ ] a flat-bed lorry
- [ ] a laden lorry
- [ ] a high-sided lorry
- [ ] an unladen lorry

Answer

✓ **an unladen lorry**

Jack-knifing occurs when the tractor unit is pushed by the semi-trailer pivoting around the coupling (fifth wheel). This is more likely to occur with an unladen vehicle.

questions answers

Q. 10.33

Mark one answer

Short wheel-base vehicles will bounce more noticeably than some long wheel-base vehicles particularly when

- [ ] laden
- [ ] turning
- [ ] empty
- [ ] unloading

Answer

- [x] **empty**

Short wheel-base vehicles will bounce more noticeably than some long wheel-base vehicles when empty. This can affect braking efficiency and all-round control.

Q. 10.34

Mark four answers

What are the main causes of a lorry shedding its load?

- [ ] Driving on motorways
- [ ] Sudden change of direction
- [ ] Driving over a level crossing
- [ ] Harsh use of brakes
- [ ] Driving too fast
- [ ] Sudden change of speed

Answers

- [x] **Sudden change of direction**
- [x] **Harsh use of brakes**
- [x] **Driving too fast**
- [x] **Sudden change of speed**

The main causes of shed loads are driver errors such as sudden changes of speed or direction, driving too fast for the conditions and skidding.

Q. 10.35

Mark one answer

You are unloading an end tipper lorry. Before tipping the body what should you do?

- [ ] Ensure the vehicle is on a firm level surface
- [ ] Park facing uphill to make unloading easy
- [ ] Ensure the vehicle is on a soft sloping surface
- [ ] Park downhill for easier unloading

Answer

- [x] **Ensure the vehicle is on a firm level surface**

Unless you are on firm, level ground there is a risk of your lorry overturning. Before raising the body, check that you are well clear of overhead power lines and other obstructions.

questions

answers

Q. 10.36

Mark one answer

You are driving a double-deck bodied lorry. What could happen if the top deck is loaded and the lower deck is empty?

- The lorry will become unstable under normal braking
- The brakes will be less effective
- The lorry may overturn when cornering
- You will need to change gear more often

Answer

☑ **The lorry may overturn when cornering**

Your lorry is more likely to overturn with only the top deck loaded. If you are only carrying half a load, this should be carried on the lower deck whenever possible.

Q. 10.37

Mark one answer

Your lorry has a double-deck body. The top tier is loaded and the lower deck is empty. When will this cause the most danger?

- In heavy fog
- In high winds
- In hot weather
- In heavy rain

Answer

☑ **In high winds**

A lorry loaded like this will be more likely to overturn in high winds or when cornering. If only carrying half a load you should try to put this on the lower deck.

Q. 10.38

Mark one answer

You are carrying another vehicle piggy-back on your lorry. Chocks should be used to secure the wheels. What else should you use?

- A trolley jack
- Axle stands
- Restraining straps
- A scaffolding bar

Answer

☑ **Restraining straps**

You should use a suitable restraint and chock the wheels when another vehicle is being carried piggy-back. Don't just rely on the parking brake.

questions   answers

Q. 10.39
Mark one answer

The lorry you are driving is heavily laden. Approaching a bend too fast may cause the load to

- push your lorry to the left
- pull your lorry to the right
- push your lorry straight on
- pull your lorry back

Answer

✓ **push your lorry straight on**

Forces acting on your lorry will continue to move it in a straight line as you enter a bend. The grip of your tyres will normally overcome this unless you are going too fast. There is a danger that you could lose your load or even tip over. REDUCE YOUR SPEED IN GOOD TIME.

Q. 10.40
Mark one answer

You are driving a vehicle with an unladen trailer. You change into a low gear while travelling at speed. What could happen?

- Your vehicle may suddenly accelerate
- The endurance brake will come on
- You will not be able to brake
- Your vehicle could go out of control

Answer

✓ **Your vehicle could go out of control**

Changing down at too high a speed will cause your vehicle to slow down suddenly. With no separate braking for the trailer the tractor could be pushed to the point where it turns over.

Q. 10.41
Mark one answer

Your lorry has a crane fitted. You are loading very heavy items. You feel that the ropes or straps may break. You should

- reposition the load
- use chains and tensioners
- tie two straps together
- continue loading carefully

Answer

✓ **use chains and tensioners**

If there is any danger that the load you are lifting with a crane is too great for the ropes or straps, or that sharp edges on the load may damage them, chains with compatible tensioners should be used.

questions   answers

Q. 10.42

Mark one answer

You are carrying other vehicles piggy-back.
You should use restraints and the parking
brake on each. What else should you do?

- Make sure the vehicles are sheeted
- Place chocks under the wheels
- Put the heavy vehicles at the top
- Rope the vehicles together

Answer

✓ **Place chocks under the wheels**

Vehicles being carried piggy-back must
always have some form of chocks applied to
their wheels, in addition to a restraint.
Never rely on just the parking brake.

Q. 10.43

Mark one answer

An articulated car transporter will be least
stable when

- only the lower deck is loaded
- only the top deck is loaded
- it is fully laden
- it is unladen

Answer

✓ **only the top deck is loaded**

Keeping the centre of gravity as low as
possible will improve the handling of your
lorry. Top-heavy loads are more unstable
and require more care when turning and
cornering.

Q. 10.44

Mark two answers

NI EXEMPT

The load on your trailer hits a railway bridge.
You must report it to

- The Police
- The Transport Police
- The Highways Agency
- The railway authority
- The Local Council

Answers

✓ **The Police**

✓ **The railway authority**

If your vehicle hits a bridge you must report
it to the police. If a railway bridge is
involved you must also report it to the
railway authority. The phone number is
usually shown on or near the bridge.

questions answers

Q. 10.45

Mark one answer

What do the legs on a demountable body allow you to do?

☐ Load and unload the body without stopping

☐ Stack one body on top of another

☐ Drive under and out from the body

☐ Alter the overall height of the vehicle

Answer

☑ **Drive under and out from the body**

Always make sure that the legs on the demountable body are properly secured before moving the vehicle.

Q. 10.46

Mark one answer

The legs on a demountable body allow you to

☐ load and unload the body without stopping

☐ stack one body on top of another

☐ alter the overall height of the vehicle

☐ demount the body without a crane or lift

Answer

☑ **demount the body without a crane or lift**

The legs can be lowered to allow the carrier vehicle to drive out from underneath the demountable body.

Q. 10.47

Mark one answer

What shape are hazardous cargo labels?

☐ Diamond

☐ Triangle

☐ Circle

☐ Oval

Answer

☑ **Diamond**

Hazardous substances in transit are readily identified by a diamond-shaped warning label. This label carries other information to identify the type of hazard more specifically, such as

• flammable gas

• toxic gas

• corrosive agents

• oxidising agents.

These are just some of the types of hazard encountered. Strict regulations apply to the storage and carriage of these goods. All drivers of this type of load must receive specific certificated training.

Restricted view

This section looks at the subject of restricted views when driving a large vehicle.

The questions will ask you about

● **Mirrors**

using your mirrors effectively to help spot hazards around you

● **Signals**

giving clear and well-timed signals to help other road users understand your intentions

● **Parking**

understanding that thoughtless parking or unloading might cause a hazard on the road

● **Moving off**

taking effective all-round observation to ensure safety

● **Blind spots**

understanding that parts of your vehicle might restrict your vision. Extra effort should be taken to observe all around your vehicle

● **Observation at junctions**

understanding that effective observation is essential to reduce the risk of an accident.

questions   answers

Q. 11.1

Mark two answers

Some lorries have an extra mirror angled down towards the nearside front wheel. This mirror is ESPECIALLY useful when

- ■ moving off
- ■ parking
- ■ checking your trailer
- ■ turning right
- ■ overtaking

Q. 11.2

Mark three answers

You wish to park your trailer. The site you choose should be

- ■ firm
- ■ downhill
- ■ uphill
- ■ legal
- ■ grassed
- ■ level

Q. 11.3

Mark three answers

You are driving a lorry. You are about to move off from behind a stationary car. What should you do?

- ■ Start to signal when moving
- ■ Signal before moving, if necessary
- ■ Check the blind spot before moving
- ■ Use both mirrors before moving
- ■ Use both mirrors only after moving

questions   answers

Q. 11.4

Mark one answer

You are driving this lorry. Emerging at this junction needs extra care because of the

▪ bollards in the middle of the road

▪ traffic from the right

▪ motorcycle on the left

▪ grass verge on the left

Answer

☑ **motorcycle on the left**

Make sure that you signal in good time so that the motorcyclist behind you knows your intention. You may have to position yourself wide in order to negotiate the junction. Be aware that the motorcyclist may see this as an opportunity to filter through on your nearside. Check your left-hand mirror carefully before you start to turn.

Q. 11.5

Mark two answers

You are turning right in this lorry (arrowed). The main dangers to be aware of are

▪ the pedestrian stepping out

▪ the following motorcyclist

▪ the oncoming car

▪ the give way lines

Answers

☑ **the pedestrian stepping out**

☑ **the following motorcyclist**

Make sure that you indicate in good time to ensure other road users know your intentions. Always check your mirrors and blind spots before turning. Make sure the following motorcyclist is not about to overtake you. Keep an eye on the pedestrian who may step out unexpectedly.

Q. 11.6

Mark one answer

You are driving this lorry (arrowed). An emergency vehicle is trying to emerge from the side road. You should

- ▮ brake hard to a stop and wave it out
- ▮ brake smoothly and allow it to emerge
- ▮ drive on, you are on the major road
- ▮ turn left quickly to give it a clear view

Answer

☑ **brake smoothly and allow it to emerge**

Good forward planning will allow you to deal safely with this situation. Good intentions are only 'good' if they are achieved safely. Reacting late to this situation may cause danger to other road users.

Good forward planning to deal with any situation involves having an all round awareness of other road users. You need to assess how your actions will affect these other road users. Acting on impulse can have disastrous consequences. Be professional and be safe at all times.

Q. 11.7

Mark one answer

You are unable to see clearly when reversing into a loading bay. You should

- ▮ get someone to guide you
- ▮ use an audible warning signal
- ▮ back into the bay until your bumper touches
- ▮ open your door and lean well out.

Answer

☑ **get someone to guide you**

Don't take chances when reversing in a confined space. It is too easy to crush or kill someone without knowing they are in danger. Always double-check, and if in doubt get help from a reliable person.

questions

answers

Q. 11.8

Mark one answer

You have a sleeper cab fitted to your lorry. This could make your driving more difficult because it

- [ ] increases your blind spots
- [ ] increases your view of the road ahead
- [ ] reduces your view in the right hand mirror
- [ ] reduces your view in the left hand mirror

Answer

- [✓] **increases your blind spots**

A sleeper cab can cause extra blind spots. Make sure that you are aware of all your blind spot areas. Be alert for vehicles just to the rear offside and nearside of your cab – they could soon become 'invisible', hidden in your blind spot.

Q. 11.9

Mark one answer

You are driving this lorry and turning right from this minor road. What should you be ESPECIALLY aware of?

- [ ] Motorcyclist from the right passing the parked van
- [ ] Vehicles coming from the left along the main road
- [ ] Pedestrians on the footpath on the main road
- [ ] Vehicles coming from the rear on the minor road

Answer

- [✓] **Motorcyclist from the right passing the parked van**

Parked vehicles near junctions can hide smaller road users such as cyclists and motorcyclists. Double-check before emerging with a large vehicle. If in doubt, move forward slowly into a position where you can safely have another look.

questions

answers

Q. 11.10

Mark two answers

You are waiting to turn right in this lorry (arrowed). What dangers should you be most aware of?

- The oncoming car
- The pedestrians
- The hazard line
- The motorcycle
- The car waiting to emerge
- The give way lines

Answers

- ☑ **The pedestrians**
- ☑ **The motorcycle**

Indicate your intentions in good time so that both the motorcyclist and pedestrians know your intention is to turn right. You should note all potential hazards and keep checking as you turn.

Q. 11.11

Mark one answer

You are parking your lorry at night. In which of these places must you use parking lights?

- On the road
- In a motorway service area
- In a factory entrance
- In dock authority areas

Answer

- ☑ **On the road**

If you stop in a lay-by you should always leave your lorry's side lights on. The lay-by might be away from street lighting, and other vehicles entering the lay-by must be able to see your vehicle. You must always leave your side lights on when parked on the road.

questions

answers

Q. 11.12

Mark one answer

What should you first check before moving to the LEFT?

■ The nearside mirror

■ The offside mirror

■ Behind, over your right shoulder

■ Behind, over your left shoulder

Answer

☑ **The nearside mirror**

The left side of the vehicle, as you face forwards, is often referred to as the nearside; the right side of the vehicle as the offside. Before you make a turn or a change of direction, however slight, you should always check the mirrors. If you intend to turn left, check your left-hand (nearside) mirror first, then your right-hand (offside) mirror, and then your left-hand mirror again as you turn.

Q. 11.13

Mark one answer

What should you first check before moving to the RIGHT?

■ The nearside mirror

■ Behind, over your left shoulder

■ Behind, over your right shoulder

■ The offside mirror

Answer

☑ **The offside mirror**

If you intend to turn right, check your right-hand (offside) mirror first, then your left-hand (nearside) mirror, then check your right-hand mirror again before you turn. You must ensure that all your mirrors are properly adjusted to give a clear view around and behind your vehicle. They should be free from dirt and grime and not be broken.

Q. 11.14

Mark one answer

You are about to move off. You should always

■ extend your right arm as far as you can out of the window

■ use only the offside mirror and move away quickly

■ signal right with indicator and arm together

■ use your mirrors and look behind

Answer

☑ **use your mirrors and look behind**

You must use the mirrors well before you signal your intention to make any manoeuvre. Use them before

- moving away
- changing direction
- turning left or right
- overtaking
- changing lanes
- slowing or stopping
- speeding up
- opening the cab door.

questions

Q. 11.15

Mark three answers

In which THREE of the following situations would you FIRST need to check your nearside mirror?

- Before moving out to pass a car parked on your left
- After passing cars on your left
- Before moving to the left
- After passing pedestrians standing on the nearside kerb
- Before moving out to the right

answers

Answers

- ☑ **After passing cars on your left**
- ☑ **Before moving to the left**
- ☑ **After passing pedestrians standing on the nearside kerb**

On a large vehicle the nearside mirror is very important and it's essential to use it before moving off. You must check for pedestrians and cyclists along the nearside of your vehicle. Cyclists may ride up on your nearside while you're stationary. If you're driving a bus, passengers may be running for your bus or waiting very close to the kerbside.

As you pass pedestrians or vehicles on your left you should use your nearside mirror and check that you are passing them safely. Leave a safety margin before you move back to the left.

questions

answers

Q. 11.16

Mark one answer

The MSM routine is used to negotiate a hazard. What do the initials MSM stand for?

- Mirror, signal, manoeuvre
- Manoeuvre, speed, mirror
- Mirror, speed, manoeuvre
- Manoeuvre, signal, mirror

Answer

☑ **Mirror, signal, manoeuvre**

Always use the MSM routine when you're approaching a hazard.

M – Mirror: check the position of the traffic behind you.

S – Signal: signal your intention to slow down or change course in good time.

M – Manoeuvre: a manoeuvre is any change in position, from slowing or stopping the vehicle to turning off a busy road.

Q. 11.17

Mark one answer

What does this sign mean?

- Contraflow bus and cycle lane
- With-flow bus and cycle lane
- No buses or cycles
- Priority to buses or cycles

Answer

☑ **With-flow bus and cycle lane**

In some towns there are special lanes set aside for certain types of vehicle. These lanes show a picture of, or state, the authorised road users, and there's usually a sign showing the time that the lane is in operation. Some lanes might only be in operation for a short time. Check the sign and use the lane only if it's permitted.

Q. 11.18

Mark one answer

You are driving in fast-moving traffic along a motorway. There is a stationary queue of traffic ahead. What should you do?

- Move to the hard shoulder
- Change lanes
- Switch on your rear foglights
- Switch on your hazard warning lights

Answer

☑ **Switch on your hazard warning lights**

Traffic queues on the motorway are becoming more common, whether due to the sheer volume of traffic at peak times or to accidents. Keep well back from the vehicle in front so you'll be able to see the problems ahead on the road. If you see a queue of stationary traffic ahead, switching on your hazard warning lights for a short while will warn those behind you of the hazard ahead.

questions   answers

Q. 11.19

Mark one answer

You are turning right onto a dual carriageway from a side road. Your vehicle is too long for the central gap. How should you proceed?

- ■ Move forward and wait in the middle
- ■ Wait until it is clear from both directions
- ■ Move out blocking traffic from the right
- ■ Edge out slowly so other traffic will see you

Answer

- ✓ **Wait until it is clear from both directions**

When turning right onto a dual carriageway don't stop in the middle, unless the gap is big enough for your vehicle to do so without impeding moving traffic. When it's busy consider turning left and using a roundabout further up the road. This will avoid you having to cross the central reservation.

Q. 11.20

Mark three answers

You want to turn left at a road junction. What is most important when deciding your position?

- ■ The length of the vehicle
- ■ The width of the roads
- ■ The camber of the road
- ■ The type of road surface
- ■ The angle of the corner

Answers

- ✓ **The length of the vehicle**
- ✓ **The width of the roads**
- ✓ **The angle of the corner**

Where you position your vehicle on approach to a left turn will depend on several factors. You should be considering and deciding on the best position as you approach. If you need to take up part of any other lane, be extra-cautious. Other road users might not understand your reasons for doing this. They might try to pass on the left in the gap that you need to make the turn. Always check the left-hand mirror as you approach and just before you turn. It's better to take extra road space on the road that you're leaving than to expect there to be extra room on the road that you're entering. There might not be any.

RESTRICTED VIEW

questions   answers

Q. 11.21

Mark one answer

You wish to turn left into a side road. In front of you is a cyclist. You should

- overtake the cyclist before the turning
- wait until the cyclist has passed the turning
- sound your horn, the cyclist will give way to you
- drive alongside and check for the cyclist in the mirrors

Answer

☑ **wait until the cyclist has passed the turning**

Stay back and allow the cyclist to proceed. You must not cut across in front of them. Beware of the cyclist who tries to ride into any blind spot on your nearside.

Q. 11.22

Mark one answer

You are waiting to turn left at a junction. In your mirror you can see a cyclist moving up between the kerb and nearside of your vehicle. You should

- allow them to move in front of you
- move off and make them wait for you
- steer to the left to make them dismount
- tell them to move out of your way

Answer

☑ **allow them to move in front of you**

You need to be aware of the limited vision you have around your vehicle due to its size and shape. Never move off without checking along the nearside of your vehicle. You should always be aware of the possibility of cyclists between your vehicle and the kerb.

Q. 11.23

Mark one answer

You are approaching a roundabout. You see a cyclist signal right. Why is the cyclist keeping to the left?

- It is a quicker route for the cyclist
- The cyclist is going to turn left
- The cyclist is more vulnerable
- The Highway Code does not apply to cyclists

Answer

☑ **The cyclist is more vulnerable**

The cyclist may not be able to get into a right-hand lane due to heavy traffic. Give the cyclist room. They may not be taking the exit you expect.

questions   answers

Q. 11.24

Mark one answer

You are entering a roundabout. A cyclist in front of you is signalling to turn right. What should you do?

- [ ] Overtake on the right
- [ ] Sound the horn
- [ ] Overtake on the left
- [ ] Allow plenty of room

Answer

✓ **Allow plenty of room**

Allow the cyclist plenty of room. Give them space to get into the correct lane. Always be prepared for them to change direction without looking or signalling their intentions.

Q. 11.25

Mark one answer

You are turning right at a T-junction. Your view to the right and left is blocked due to parked vehicles. You should

- [ ] lean forward to get a better view without crossing the give way lines
- [ ] edge out until you are about 1 metre (3 feet 3 inches) over the give way lines
- [ ] ease forward until you can see clearly past the vehicles
- [ ] ask a passenger to assist by waving you out when clear

Answer

✓ **ease forward until you can see clearly past the vehicles**

When emerging, if you can't see, then don't go. There could be an approaching cyclist or motorcyclist hidden by parked vehicles.

Q. 11.26

Mark one answer

As you are driving a group of horse riders comes towards you. The leading rider's horse suddenly becomes nervous of your presence. What should you do?

- [ ] Brake gently to a stop until they have passed
- [ ] Brake quickly to a stop, applying the parking brake
- [ ] Continue driving, keeping well in to the nearside
- [ ] Increase speed to pass the riders quickly

Answer

✓ **Brake gently to a stop until they have passed**

If any of the animals become unsettled, you should brake gently and come to a stop. A nervous animal is unpredictable, you should wait until the animal is settled or has passed by. Other road users behind you may have limited vision of the hazard, so good mirror work and early signalling will be required.

If you have to pass a group of riders on horseback you must give them plenty of room. Try not to startle the animals, the riders might be learners and have limited control.

343

questions · answers

Q. 11.27

Mark one answer

To have good all-round vision you should make sure that

- windows are open
- a sun visor is fitted
- your seat is properly adjusted
- all lights are clean

Answer

☑ **your seat is properly adjusted**

Large vehicles are designed for their specific function, and this often means the shape and size can impair all-round visibility for the driver. You must make sure that you adjust the seat so that you're able to reach all the controls and see in all the mirrors. You should be seated in such a way that you're able to lean out of the window and check all offside blind spots.

Q. 11.28

Mark one answer

You are emerging from a side road into a queue of traffic. Which of these vehicles are especially hard to see?

- Cycles
- Tractors
- Milk floats
- Cars

Answer

☑ **Cycles**

Cyclists are much narrower than any other vehicle. Always check carefully for cyclists when emerging as they are much more difficult to see than a larger vehicle.

Q. 11.29

Mark one answer

Motorcycle riders are more at risk from other road users. This is because they

- are easier for other road users to see
- are more likely to break down
- cannot give arm signals
- are more difficult for other road users to see

Answer

☑ **are more difficult for other road users to see**

Always look out for the more vulnerable users on our roads, such as

- motorcyclists
- cyclists
- pedestrians

All need extra consideration. Motorcyclists, in particular, can appear very quickly.

questions   answers

Q. 11.30

Mark one answer

What is the MAIN cause of motorcycle collisions?

- ■ Other drivers
- ■ Other motorcyclists
- ■ Wet roads
- ■ Icy roads

Answer

- ✓ **Other drivers**

Motorcyclists are more difficult to see, particularly when the light is poor or it's raining. A bright jacket or single headlight may help you identify an approaching motorcyclist, but you should be aware that not all motorcyclists wear bright clothing or use their headlights during the day.

Q. 11.31

Mark two answers

Motorcyclists often filter between lines of slow-moving vehicles. Which of the following will cause them particular danger?

- ■ The queuing vehicles
- ■ Vehicles changing lanes
- ■ Vehicles emerging from junctions
- ■ Traffic lights
- ■ Zebra crossings

Answers

- ✓ **Vehicles changing lanes**
- ✓ **Vehicles emerging from junctions**

In slow-moving traffic, particularly on dual carriageways or motorways, always be on the look-out for motorcyclists who approach from behind and filter through narrow gaps between vehicles.

Q. 11.32

Mark three answers

At road junctions, which of the following are most at risk?

- ■ Motorcyclists
- ■ Pedestrians
- ■ Car drivers
- ■ Cyclists
- ■ Lorry drivers

Answers

- ✓ **Motorcyclists**
- ✓ **Pedestrians**
- ✓ **Cyclists**

At busy junctions scan near, middle and far distances to identify all the hazards before emerging with a long vehicle. Be alert for other road users hidden by parked vehicles.

questions

answers

Q. 11.33

Mark one answer

Some large vehicles with restricted vision to the rear may be fitted with an audible warning device for reversing. In areas with a 30 mph restriction the device may be used

- between 7 am and 11.30 pm only
- between 11.30 pm and 7 am only
- during hours of daylight only
- at any time

Answer

✓ **between 7 am and 11.30 pm only**

Some vehicles are fitted with an audible warning device that sounds when the vehicle is being reversed. As these devices make a loud noise they shouldn't be used between 11.30 pm and 7 am.

These devices are an effective safety feature, but don't take away the need to use good, effective observation around the vehicle before and while reversing.

Q. 11.34

Mark one answer

Driving too close to the vehicle in front will

- decrease your view ahead
- increase your view ahead
- increase the view of following drivers
- decrease the view of following drivers

Answer

✓ **decrease your view ahead**

Don't get into a position where you reduce your vision unnecessarily, such as driving too close to the vehicle in front. At all times you must be aware that, as a driver of a large vehicle, you won't be able to see all around the vehicle. This is why you must have an excellent mirror routine and be constantly updating your information on what's going on around you.

Q. 11.35

Mark two answers

At junctions it is difficult to see motorcyclists because they

- are easily hidden in blind spots
- always ride in the gutter
- always wear black leathers
- are smaller than other vehicles

Answers

✓ **are easily hidden in blind spots**
✓ **are smaller than other vehicles**

When driving large vehicles, windscreen pillars and large mirrors can easily create large blind spots as you look left and right at junctions. Altering your body position slightly while taking observation can give you a much improved view of the traffic. If in doubt, look again. Reassess the situation. DON'T TAKE CHANCES.

questions   answers

Q. 11.36

Mark three answers

Drivers should be aware that motorcyclists are more vulnerable ESPECIALLY

- ◼ to emerging vehicles
- ◼ in gusting winds
- ◼ on poor road surfaces
- ◼ at traffic lights
- ◼ near zebra crossings
- ◼ when exiting motorways

Answers

- ☑ **to emerging vehicles**
- ☑ **in gusting winds**
- ☑ **on poor road surfaces**

Always be concerned for the safety of yourself and other road users. Be aware of the various factors that create situations where you will sometimes have to take action to keep more vulnerable road users safe.

Q. 11.37

Mark one answer

Just before turning right from a main road to a side road, you should check your right-hand mirror. This is because

- ◼ there may be pedestrians stepping off the kerb
- ◼ you need to check your position
- ◼ a motorcyclist may be overtaking you
- ◼ your rear view to the left is blocked

Answer

- ☑ **a motorcyclist may be overtaking you**

Looking and acting sensibly on what you see in your mirrors before you change speed or direction are essential. Driving a large vehicle will sometimes require you to position your vehicle well to the left before making a tight right turn. Inexperienced drivers or riders may not realise your intentions. Make sure you signal in good time. Make a final mirror check before committing yourself to the turn.

Q. 11.38

Mark one answer

Before turning left you should have a final look into the

- ◼ left-hand mirror
- ◼ interior mirror
- ◼ right-hand mirror
- ◼ overtaking mirror

Answer

- ☑ **left-hand mirror**

When making a left turn with a long vehicle you may have to adopt an unusual position well over to the centre of the road. Always signal your intentions in good time, and make good use of the nearside mirror. Be alert for less experienced road users putting themselves in danger by coming up along your nearside.

RESTRICTED VIEW

questions   answers

Q. 11.39

Mark two answers

You are driving a long vehicle. Before turning left onto a main road you should be ESPECIALLY careful of

- ▪ cyclists alongside you on the left
- ▪ motorcyclists alongside you on the left
- ▪ motorcyclists coming from your left
- ▪ cyclists coming from your left

Answers

- ☑ **cyclists alongside you on the left**
- ☑ **motorcyclists alongside you on the left**

You should always check your nearside mirror before any change of direction. Be alert for cyclists and motorcyclists who don't realise the potential danger involved in trying to squeeze through on your nearside when you are waiting at a junction. Always check for pedestrians and cyclists on the nearside of your vehicle before moving away.

Q. 11.40

Mark one answer

You want to turn right at a roundabout marked with two right-turn lanes. There is ample room for your vehicle in either lane. You should

- ▪ use the right-hand of the two lanes
- ▪ use the left-hand of the two lanes
- ▪ use the left-hand lane then move to the right as you enter the roundabout
- ▪ use the right-hand lane then move to the left as you enter the roundabout

Answer

- ☑ **use the left-hand of the two lanes**

By doing this it will make it easier for you when you leave the roundabout. If you use the right lane there could be traffic on your left and in your blind spot when you exit and try to move back to the left.

Q. 11.41

Mark one answer

Your vehicle is fitted with a reverse warning bleeper. When driving backwards you

- ▪ do not need to look round
- ▪ should only use the offside mirror
- ▪ still need to take all-round observation
- ▪ should only use the nearside mirror

Answer

- ☑ **still need to take all-round observation**

Get someone to guide you if you cannot see all around when reversing.

Q. 11.42

Mark one answer

Before reversing you MUST always

- remove your seatbelt
- look all around
- use an audible warning device
- change the tachograph setting

Answer

☑ **look all around**

Large or long vehicles can have many blind spots when reversing. It's very important to check all angles before starting to reverse and then make sure you keep checking all round while completing the manoeuvre.

Q. 11.43

Mark two answers

Some coaches have a mirror on their nearside angled down to show the front nearside wheel. This should be used when you are

- pulling in after overtaking
- pulling up to park at the kerb
- moving close to the left in normal driving
- changing lanes on a motorway

Answers

☑ **pulling up to park at the kerb**

☑ **moving close to the left in normal driving**

This mirror offers the most benefit when manoeuvring in confined spaces.

Q. 11.44

Mark one answer

You are driving a bus in a built up area. You should NOT

- block side road junctions
- leave a safe stopping distance
- anticipate traffic ahead
- use the MSM routine

Answer

☑ **block side road junctions**

This is inconsiderate to other road users. You should look at the flow of traffic and be aware of side junctions when you are slowing down or stopping.

questions

answers

Q. 11.45

Mark two answers

Which of the following are most likely to share a bus lane?

- Cyclists
- Lorries
- Orange badge holders
- Cars towing caravans
- Taxis

Answers

- ✓ **Cyclists**
- ✓ **Taxis**

Cyclists can be safer travelling in the bus lane. Taxis are allowed to use these lanes as they provide a clearer route and can be quicker, thereby encouraging people to use public transport and so reducing the amount of traffic congestion.

Q. 11.46

Mark one answer

In a bus with a high driving position you may have to look out for

- cyclists close in front
- cyclists close behind
- large vehicles close in front
- large vehicles close behind

Answer

- ✓ **cyclists close in front**

It's essential that you're constantly aware of other road users and pedestrians around you. A routine of effective mirror checking should be established. You must also know when it's essential to make checks in the blind spots, such as just below the nearside front of the vehicle. A cyclist in that space could be out of your normal vision. Constant awareness should ensure that you've seen any riders getting into that position.

Q. 11.47

Mark one answer

The 'turning circle' is the

- number of turns of the steering wheel between locks
- amount of space needed for the vehicle to turn
- amount by which the vehicle overhangs kerbs
- amount by which a vehicle cuts corners

Answer

- ✓ **amount of space needed for the vehicle to turn**

You should be familiar with the room that your vehicle requires to make turns or carry out a manoeuvre. You'll need to consider this as you approach junctions and road layouts. If you're driving a new or temporary vehicle, familiarise yourself with its characteristics before you drive on public roads.

questions answers

Q. 11.48

Mark one answer

TV and video equipment fitted to a coach must ONLY be used when

- ▪ the coach is moving slowly
- ▪ it cannot be seen by the driver
- ▪ on long motorway journeys
- ▪ the coach is on tour

Answer

☑ **it cannot be seen by the driver**

Make sure that you are not distracted by any TV or video equipment fitted to your vehicle. Your main responsibility at all times is the safety and comfort of your passengers.

Q. 11.49

Mark one answer

On a coach with high side windows it can be difficult to see either side. What should you do before you pull away?

- ▪ Get out of your vehicle and stop the traffic
- ▪ Ask a passenger to make sure it is safe to move off
- ▪ Indicate before checking all of your mirrors
- ▪ Open the window and look down and round to the right

Answer

☑ **Open the window and look down and round to the right**

High-sided coaches can create extra blind spots and you should be aware of where these are. You will need to make additional checks on this type of vehicle but don't forget your usual observations and mirror checks to make sure it is safe to move off.

Q. 11.50

Mark one answer

Your bus has a high seating position. Which of these may be out of sight below the windscreen line?

- ▪ Following vehicles
- ▪ Overtaking vehicles
- ▪ Cyclists and pedestrians
- ▪ Other buses

Answer

☑ **Cyclists and pedestrians**

Always take all-round observations before manoeuvring whether you're moving away, parking or reversing. Cyclists and pedestrians, especially children, can enter your blind spots. If you have been stopped for some time at a bus stop or in a bus station be aware that shoppers may be out of sight below the windscreen line of your bus.

Documents

This section looks at vehicle and transport documents.

The questions will ask you about

- **Documents**

  required for national and international carriage of goods and passengers

- **Drivers' responsibility**

  when receiving, carrying and delivering goods in accordance with the agreed
  conditions.

questions

answers

Q. 12.1

Mark one answer

The CMR Consignment Note is generally required for carrying goods overseas for hire or reward. How many copies of this Note are required?

■ Two

■ Three

■ Four

■ Five

Answer

☑ **Four**

Of the four copies required, the consignor, consignee and originator all have a copy, and the fourth one travels with the vehicle.

Q. 12.2

Mark one answer

You have been asked to drive a fully loaded petrol tanker back to the depot. It has a Maximum Authorised Mass (MAM) of 10 tonnes. What MUST you do?

■ Notify the police that you are moving a dangerous load

■ Have a fully qualified tanker driver with you for the journey

■ Carry a valid DVLA 'approved course' certificate

■ Complete the whole journey avoiding built up areas

Answer

☑ **Carry a valid DVLA 'approved course' certificate**

The certificate, valid for five years, is issued by DVLA on receipt of a proof of attending a course and passing a City and Guilds examination.

Q. 12.3

Mark one answer

As a driver of a goods vehicle it is your responsibility to ensure that

■ you are correctly paid for the goods after unloading

■ the goods arrive in the same condition as when loaded

■ the goods reach their destination ahead of schedule

■ your return load is at least as heavy as the outward load

Answer

☑ **the goods arrive in the same condition as when loaded**

As a professional driver you must not allow lack of attention to cause damage to the goods during transit, loading or unloading.

questions   answers

Q. 12.4

Mark one answer

You will be driving your vehicle in Europe. Which of these documents MUST you carry?

- [ ] The vehicle service record
- [ ] Your medical examination form
- [ ] Your national driving licence
- [ ] The vehicle workshop manual

Answer

✓ **Your national driving licence**

You also need to carry the insurance certificate and vehicle registration document. Other documentation may also be required for some countries; check this before starting your journey.

Q. 12.5

Mark one answer

You may be prevented from obtaining a lorry or bus licence if you have

- [ ] dyslexia
- [ ] partial blindness
- [ ] skin problems
- [ ] stomach problems

Answer

✓ **partial blindness**

Other factors such as heart and mental disorders can also prevent you from obtaining a lorry or bus licence. For enquiries about medical standards you should contact the Drivers Medical Branch, DVLA, Swansea.

Q. 12.6

Mark one answer

When driving in Europe you must carry

- [ ] a valid certificate of roadworthiness
- [ ] the vehicle registration document
- [ ] the vehicle workshop manual
- [ ] a valid breakdown cover certificate

Answer

✓ **the vehicle registration document**

You also need to carry your national driving licence and the insurance certificate. You may need to carry other documentation for some countries; it is your responsibility to check the requirements.

questions

answers

Q. 12.7

Mark one answer

You intend to drive in Europe. What must you carry?

- ■ A valid certificate of roadworthiness
- ■ Your vehicles workshop manual
- ■ Your national driving licence
- ■ A valid breakdown cover certificate

Answer

☑ **Your national driving licence**

It is your responsibility to ensure that you have the correct documentation for the journey. This includes driving licence, insurance certificate, vehicle registration document, plus others depending on your load and destination.

Q. 12.8

Mark one answer

NI EXEMPT

You are two and a half times over the legal alcohol limit. You are disqualified from driving. Before regaining your licence who will you have to satisfy that you do NOT have an alcohol problem?

- ■ The local hospital
- ■ Driver and Vehicle Licensing Agency's Medical Branch
- ■ Alcoholics Anonymous
- ■ The Vehicle Inspectorate

Answer

☑ **Driver and Vehicle Licensing Agency's Medical Branch**

If you are disqualified because you are two and a half times over the legal limit, you will have to satisfy the Driver and Vehicle Licensing Agency's Medical Branch that you do NOT have an alcohol problem, before your licence is returned.

Q. 12.9

Mark one answer

Which category licence do you need to drive a three axle double decker coach?

- ■ D1
- ■ D
- ■ D1+E
- ■ C

Answer

☑ **D**

A category D licence allows you to drive any size coach. If you want to tow a trailer over 750 kg you have to have category D+E.

Environmental issues

This section looks at environmental issues.

The questions will ask you about

- **Vehicle noise**
  using audible warning devices

- **Wind resistance**
  fitting a wind deflector to reduce fuel consumption

- **Fuel consumption**
  planning routes to reduce mileage

- **Refuelling**
  taking care when refuelling.

questions

answers

Q. 13.1

Mark two answers

Your lorry has been fitted with wind deflectors. When driving in windy conditions these will help to

- [ ] increase the amount of fuel you will use
- [ ] increase the wind resistance on your vehicle
- [ ] increase the pressure in the tyres
- [ ] reduce the wind resistance on your vehicle
- [ ] reduce the amount of fuel you will use

Answers

- [x] **reduce the wind resistance on your vehicle**
- [x] **reduce the amount of fuel you will use**

Wind deflectors direct the wind either around or over your vehicle. Your vehicle then requires less power to make progress against the wind. As a result your vehicle will use less fuel.

Q. 13.2

Mark one answer

Cab-mounted wind deflectors can reduce

- [ ] journey times
- [ ] load capacity
- [ ] tyre wear
- [ ] fuel consumption

Answer

- [x] **fuel consumption**

A wind deflector redirects the air flow around the vehicle. This reduces the amount of fuel required to propel the vehicle forward.

Q. 13.3

Mark two answers

Fuel consumption for lorries can be reduced by fitting

- [ ] single axles only
- [ ] a high-level exhaust pipe
- [ ] side skirts
- [ ] wind deflectors

Answers

- [x] **side skirts**
- [x] **wind deflectors**

Both of these reduce resistance to wind, which will help the vehicle to use less fuel.

questions   answers

Q. 13.4

Mark one answer

You are a driver who is certified to carry dangerous goods. The certificate is valid for

- one year
- two years
- five years
- ten years

Answer

✓ **five years**

The operator of a UK-registered vehicle engaged in the carriage of dangerous goods should ensure that the driver has a valid vocational training certificate. These certificates are valid for five years.

Q. 13.5

Mark one answer

An ADR qualification is necessary for drivers who carry

- school children
- liquids
- oversize loads
- dangerous goods

Answer

✓ **dangerous goods**

ADR regulations govern movement of hazardous goods. The driver of any vehicle engaged in the carriage of dangerous goods should carry the vocational training certificate at all times, and produce it on request to a police officer or goods vehicle examiner.

Q. 13.6

Mark three answers

Which of the following would help to reduce the impact that your lorry has on the environment?

- Driving through town centres
- Braking in good time
- Planning routes to avoid busy times
- Racing to make up time
- Anticipating well ahead

Answers

✓ **Braking in good time**

✓ **Planning routes to avoid busy times**

✓ **Anticipating well ahead**

Avoiding town centres will lessen the vibration and pollution caused by your vehicle. Good anticipation and forward planning will always benefit you and the environment, wherever you drive.

questions

Q. 13.7

Mark one answer

The purpose of a fly sheet tightly fastened over a tipper body is to reduce the

- drag effect
- steering effort
- legal load weight
- load capacity

Answer

☑ **drag effect**

The drag effect is caused by wind entering the body of the tipper. If the cavity is covered, then the drag is reduced.

Q. 13.8

Mark one answer

You may park a lorry over 7.5 tonnes on a verge for essential loading, but it must have

- a collection note
- an orange badge
- the owners permission
- an attendant

Answer

☑ **an attendant**

Goods vehicles with a maximum authorised mass of more than 7.5 tonnes (including any trailer) must not be parked on a verge except where this is essential for loading and unloading. In these cases, the vehicle must not be left unattended.

Q. 13.9

Mark one answer

You must not park any unattended lorry over 7.5 tonnes on a verge without

- police permission
- warning lights
- the owners permission
- a loading permit

Answer

☑ **police permission**

If your vehicle has to be left unattended on a verge for any reason, you must inform the police.

questions

answers

Q. 13.10

Mark two answers

How could you improve the fuel consumption of your lorry?

- Brake late as often as you can
- Fit a cab-mounted wind deflector
- Avoid sheeting any bulky loads
- Try to increase your overall speed
- Make regular checks on tyre pressures

Answers

- ✓ **Fit a cab-mounted wind deflector**
- ✓ **Make regular checks on tyre pressures**

As a professional driver you should consider fuel efficiency and the effect this has on the environment.

Wind deflectors can effectively lower wind resistance.

Correct tyre pressures and proper maintenance also play their part in fuel efficiency.

Q. 13.11

Mark one answer

Cab mounted wind deflectors are fitted to

- increase wind buffeting
- increase engine power
- reduce exhaust emissions
- reduce fuel consumption

Answer

- ✓ **reduce fuel consumption**

Cab mounted wind deflectors can effectively lower wind resistance created by large box bodies. Together with lower side panel skirts, they will help reduce fuel consumption.

Q. 13.12

Mark one answer

Red diesel is

- only used by private cars
- for authorised purposes only
- available at all garages
- very environmentally friendly

Answer

- ✓ **for authorised purposes only**

Red diesel is subject to less excise duty than standard diesel, so it is considerably cheaper. It should only be used for authorised purposes. Any driver whose vehicle is found to be using this fuel illegally faces severe penalties.

questions

answers

Q. 13.13

Mark one answer

You are driving a lorry with a loaded skip. The skip should be covered with a net to

- ▪ prevent rubbish from falling out of it
- ▪ protect the contents from the weather
- ▪ make it more visible to other traffic
- ▪ stop others from adding to the load

Answer

- ☑ **prevent rubbish from falling out of it**

If the load is not covered, rubbish can be caught by the wind and blown onto the carriageway. This will create unnecessary hazards for other road users.

Q. 13.14

Mark two answers

Which of the following would be most affected by a vehicle with faulty suspension?

- ▪ Underground pipes
- ▪ Road surfaces
- ▪ Tyre pressures
- ▪ Road tunnels
- ▪ Overhead gantries

Answers

- ☑ **Underground pipes**
- ☑ **Road surfaces**

If your suspension is damaged, all the weight of the vehicle is compressing the road and anything located below it. The vibrations travel through the ground and can also damage surrounding buildings.

Q. 13.15

Mark three answers

The pictured vehicle is 'environmentally friendly' because it

- ▪ reduces noise pollution
- ▪ uses diesel fuel
- ▪ uses electricity
- ▪ uses unleaded fuel
- ▪ reduces parking places
- ▪ reduces town traffic

Answers

- ☑ **reduces noise pollution**
- ☑ **uses electricity**
- ☑ **reduces town traffic**

This is the sign for a tram. These vehicles are powered by electricity and reduce the emissions released into the environment. As they can carry many people they can help reduce the number of other vehicles on the road.

questions answers

Q. 13.16

Mark two answers

Which of the following vehicles are MOST likely to cause severe damage to road surfaces?

- Lorries
- Cars
- Motorcycles
- Bicycles
- Buses

Answers

- ✓ **Lorries**
- ✓ **Buses**

Lorries and buses are much heavier than cars and will have a greater impact on the road surface.

Q. 13.17

Mark three answers

Air suspension can reduce damage to

- the fuel system
- the road surface
- passengers
- bridges
- the tachograph
- underground services

Answers

- ✓ **the road surface**
- ✓ **bridges**
- ✓ **underground services**

Air suspension reduces the pressure of the weight of the vehicle driving on an uneven surface. This in turn reduces the vibrations transmitted to buildings along the route.

Q. 13.18

Mark three answers

You are driving a vehicle fitted with 'road-friendly' suspension. This will mostly reduce damage caused to

- the drivers seat
- historical buildings
- the road surface
- overhead cables
- river banks
- bridges

Answers

- ✓ **historical buildings**
- ✓ **the road surface**
- ✓ **bridges**

Road-friendly suspension reduces the vibration caused by the impact of the wheels on the road surface.

questions

answers

Q. 13.19

Mark two answers

You can help to reduce the impact of road transport on the environment by

- ▪ avoiding high gears
- ▪ reducing rest periods
- ▪ braking in good time
- ▪ increasing your overall speed
- ▪ avoiding over-acceleration

Answers

- ☑ **braking in good time**
- ☑ **avoiding over-acceleration**

Good forward planning will reduce the emissions being dispersed into the air and cause less environmental pollution.

Q. 13.20

Mark one answer

As a driver you can help to protect the environment by

- ▪ driving faster to reduce travelling time
- ▪ avoiding town centres and using bypasses
- ▪ filling your fuel tank with red diesel fuel
- ▪ leaving your engine running in traffic jams

Answer

- ☑ **avoiding town centres and using bypasses**

By using bypasses you are less likely to be held up and can travel at a constant speed, thereby reducing the amount of pollution from your vehicle.

Q. 13.21

Mark one answer

As a driver you can help to ease traffic congestion by

- ▪ planning routes to avoid the busy times
- ▪ planning routes to avoid driving at quiet times
- ▪ driving on motorways for all journeys
- ▪ avoiding using motorways for all journeys

Answer

- ☑ **planning routes to avoid the busy times**

By planning your journey to avoid busy times you will avoid the build-up of traffic that can often occur.

questions

answers

Q. 13.22

Mark one answer

As a professional driver you should

- keep to maximum speeds for shorter journeys
- plan routes to avoid busy times and congestion
- avoid route-planning because of the time it takes
- drive at a faster speed through hazardous areas

Answer

 plan routes to avoid busy times and congestion

If you plan your journey to avoid busy times you can avoid congestion, and your overall journey time may be reduced.

Q. 13.23

Mark one answer

You have just refilled your fuel tank. You MUST make sure that the

- tank is completely full up to the filler neck
- filler cap is vented correctly by keeping it loose
- filler cap is properly closed and secure
- tank is nearly full and the filler cap is slightly loose

Answer

 filler cap is properly closed and secure

Because of the extremely slippery characteristics of diesel fuel, care must be taken at all times to avoid spillages.

Q. 13.24

Mark one answer

To prevent fuel spillages it is important to

- stop refuelling when half full
- use a filtered system
- close and secure all filler caps
- place the drip tray correctly

Answer

☑ **close and secure all filler caps**

Fuel spilled onto the road causes a serious danger to other road users, especially motorcyclists.

Q. 13.25

Mark one answer

You are following a lorry with a leaking fuel tank. What should you be especially aware of?

- ■ The road may be very slippery
- ■ The fuel may splash your vehicle
- ■ Your brake linings will become slippery
- ■ Your spray reducers will not be effective

Answer

☑ **The road may be very slippery**

The leaking fuel can make the road surface extremely slippery. Look out for this, particularly on roundabouts.

Q. 13.26

Mark one answer

You are parked for a short period in a town whilst you plan a route. You should

- ■ keep the engine running on tickover
- ■ rev the engine occasionally for air pressure
- ■ never turn off the engine for short periods
- ■ switch off the engine

Answer

☑ **switch off the engine**

This will be safer and emit less fumes into the environment. If diesel engines are left idling for any length of time they emit excessive smoke as you drive off. This is unpleasant for any pedestrians who are nearby at the time.

Q. 13.27

Mark one answer

The road surface is more likely to be damaged by large vehicles with

- ■ a mixture of tyre makes
- ■ a mixture of re-cut and new tyres
- ■ faulty spray-suppression equipment
- ■ faulty suspension

Answer

☑ **faulty suspension**

Suspension faults may result in road damage. Road-friendly suspension is being developed to lessen the impact on the environment, the road surface and under-road services.

questions

answers

Q. 13.28

Mark three answers

How could you save fuel when driving?

- By reducing overall speed
- By braking as late as you can
- By planning routes to avoid congestion
- By having properly inflated tyres
- By extending vehicles' service times

Answers

- ☑ **By reducing overall speed**
- ☑ **By planning routes to avoid congestion**
- ☑ **By having properly inflated tyres**

Your driving skills reflect on the environment. You should consider the impact your attitude will have on the environment every time you drive. By driving sensibly, maintaining your vehicle and planning ahead, you will deserve to be called a professional driver.

Q. 13.29

Mark three answers

Which three of the following could cause unnecessary pollution to the environment?

- Excessive exhaust fumes
- Regular servicing
- Vehicles driven poorly
- Badly maintained vehicles
- High level exhaust systems

Answers

- ☑ **Excessive exhaust fumes**
- ☑ **Vehicles driven poorly**
- ☑ **Badly maintained vehicles**

All drivers on the road should play their part in protecting the environment against pollution. Ensure the vehicle you drive is maintained properly. Immediately report any defects such as unusual exhaust smoke. Consider whether further training could improve your driving skills. CARE FOR THE ENVIRONMENT AS YOU DRIVE.

Q. 13.30

Mark one answer

Diesel fuel has been spilled on the road. This will cause particular danger to

- lorries
- motorcycles
- horses
- cars

Answer

- ☑ **motorcycles**

Spilt diesel creates a serious risk to other road users, especially motorcyclists. Take care when refuelling and ensure that all filler caps and tank hatches are properly closed and secure.

Q. 13.31

Mark one answer

Members of the public are encouraged to report any vehicle with

◼ excessive exhaust fumes

◼ an un-sheeted load

◼ different makes of tyres

◼ no contact address visible

Answer

☑ **excessive exhaust fumes**

You should ensure that maintenance schedules are strictly followed, and that filters are changed regularly, exhaust emissions meet current regulations and diesel injectors are operating efficiently.

Q. 13.32

Mark three answers

Vehicles have damaged the environment. This has resulted in

◼ air pollution

◼ reduced traffic noise

◼ building deterioration

◼ less road surface damage

◼ using up of natural resources

Answers

☑ **air pollution**

☑ **building deterioration**

☑ **using up of natural resources**

The increased number of vehicles on the roads has damaged the environment. Transport is an essential part of modern life, but we should not ignore its environmental consequences.

Q. 13.33

Mark one answer

You should only sound your horn in a built up area between 11.30 pm and 7.00 am when

◼ you are parked

◼ your vehicle is moving

◼ you are stationary

◼ another vehicle poses a danger

Answer

☑ **another vehicle poses a danger**

The horn should not be used between 11.30 pm and 7.00 am in built up areas unless another vehicle is unaware of you and poses a danger.

Q. 13.34

Mark one answer

You should take great care to avoid spilling diesel. It is very slippery and causes a serious risk on the road particularly to

- ■ motorcycles
- ■ tractors
- ■ buses
- ■ lorries

Answer

☑ **motorcycles**

Take care to secure caps and tank hatches – diesel is very slippery and if spilled on the road it is particularly dangerous to motorcyclists.

Q. 13.35

Mark one answer

In a diesel engine which of the following fuels would most improve vehicle emissions?

- ■ High sulphur diesel
- ■ Red diesel
- ■ Low sulphur diesel
- ■ Blue diesel

Answer

☑ **Low sulphur diesel**

This is widely available and has been formulated so that the sulphur content is very low. It makes a considerable improvement to vehicle emissions.

Q. 13.36

Mark one answer

Using which of the following fuels in a diesel engine would most help the environment?

- ■ Anti-waxing diesel
- ■ Low sulphur diesel
- ■ Red diesel
- ■ Anti-foaming diesel

Answer

☑ **Low sulphur diesel**

Sulphur produces acid gases. Diesel fuels with lower sulphur content have been produced to lessen damage to the environment.

questions

answers

Q. 13.37

Mark two answers

What must you do after filling your fuel tanks?

- Return the pump keys to the office
- Check your tachograph
- Clean up any fuel that has spilled
- Check that the filler caps are closed
- Complete the fuel log sheets
- Check your fuel gauge

Answers

- ☑ **Clean up any fuel that has spilled**
- ☑ **Check that the filler caps are closed**

If fuel has spilled it can be hazardous for anyone stepping onto it. Take care to make certain your filler caps are closed properly so that you don't spill fuel as you drive along the road.

Q. 13.38

Mark one answer

Your vehicle is fitted with a reverse warning bleeper. You MUST switch it off between the hours of 11.30 pm and 7.00 am on a road with a

- 30 mph speed limit
- temporary speed limit
- national speed limit
- 40 mph speed limit

Answer

- ☑ **30 mph speed limit**

Try to avoid making unnecessary noise. Your vehicle will make more noise than a car, so try to consider others who may be resting.

Q. 13.39

Mark one answer

Your vehicle is fitted with a reverse warning bleeper. You must switch the bleeper off when reversing

- after 11.30 pm at night along a 30 mph road
- after 11.30 pm at night along a 40 mph road
- near a school entrance
- near a hospital entrance

Answer

- ☑ **after 11.30 pm at night along a 30 mph road**

It is an offence to operate an audible warning system on a road subject to a 30 mph speed limit between 11.30 pm and 7 am. Always remember to reset the alarm outside these times.

questions

answers

Q. 13.40

Mark one answer

Fuel consumption could be made worse by continuous use of

■ air suspension

■ heated mirrors

■ air conditioning

■ electrical retarder

Answer

 air conditioning

Use air conditioning sparingly – running it continuously increases fuel consumption by about 15%.

Q. 13.41

Mark one answer

Vehicles are fitted with air suspension to

■ reduce wear to roads

■ reduce tyre wear

■ improve fuel consumption

■ help the driver stay awake

Answer

 reduce wear to roads

Air suspension causes less damage to the road surface than conventional suspension systems. Vehicles transporting glass and fragile loads normally use it and it is considered to be environmentally friendly.

Q. 13.42

Mark one answer

Your vehicle is fitted with a warning device, which sounds when reversing. When should you NOT use it in a built-up area?

■ Between 10.30 pm and 6.30 am

■ Between 11 pm and 6.30 am

■ Between 11.30 pm and 7 am

■ Between 12.30 am and 8 am

Answer

✓ **Between 11.30 pm and 7 am**

Some vehicles are fitted with an audible warning that sounds when the vehicle's reversing. This is an effective device to warn pedestrians and other road users of a reversing vehicle, and doesn't take away the need to use effective observation all around your vehicle before and while you're reversing. Don't use the device in built-up areas at night. Have some consideration for the residents and don't disturb them with excessive noise.

questions answers

Q. 13.43

Mark one answer

A vehicle 'reverse warning bleeper' must NOT be used

- in parking bays
- between 11.30 pm and 7.30 am in 30 mph limits
- between 11.30 pm and 7 am in 30 mph limits
- near hospitals

Answer

✓ **between 11.30 pm and 7 am in 30 mph limits**

Transport now operates 24 hours a day. If you are working the 'night shift', show consideration when others are at rest. You must not use your reverse warning bleepers between the hours of 11.30 pm and 7 am, and try to avoid making unnecessary noise.

Q. 13.44

Mark one answer

After refuelling your bus. What MUST you check before driving?

- Your filler caps are securely shut
- Your tank is full to the top
- The position of the emergency fuel cut off switch
- The low-fuel warning light is working

Answer

✓ **Your filler caps are securely shut**

It is a legal requirement that you check all filler caps are properly closed and secure before driving off.

Q. 13.45

Mark one answer

You are waiting at a terminus for some time. You will reduce pollution by

- revving your engine
- switching off your engine
- leaving your engine on tickover
- keeping your engine at high revs

Answer

✓ **switching off your engine**

If you have to wait for long periods of time you should turn your engine off, as noise and exhaust fumes can cause annoyance as well as pollution.

questions

answers

Q. 13.46

Mark three answers

You are waiting for some time in a stationary traffic queue. Why should you switch your engine off?

- To reduce noise levels
- To save on vehicle air pressure
- To reduce exhaust fumes
- To reduce television interference
- To prevent local annoyance

Answers

- ✓ **To reduce noise levels**
- ✓ **To reduce exhaust fumes**
- ✓ **To prevent local annoyance**

When you are delayed in a traffic jam or stationary by the side of a road or in a lay-by, switch off your engine to help protect the environment in which you live. By doing this you will be helping others who are not road users.

Q. 13.47

Mark one answer

You have been waiting in a traffic queue for several minutes. The road in front is blocked. What should you do?

- Keep your engine at tickover speed
- Rev your engine occasionally
- Switch off your engine
- Run the engine at a constant higher speed

Answer

- ✓ **Switch off your engine**

Switch your engine off when stationary for some time, especially when noise and exhaust fumes cause annoyance and could be harmful.

PROTECT YOUR ENVIRONMENT AND SAVE FUEL.

Q. 13.48

Mark one answer

Using air conditioning systems continuously will usually increase fuel consumption by about

- 15%
- 30%
- 50%
- 75%

Answer

- ✓ **15%**

Avoid using air conditioning systems for long periods as these can increase fuel consumption by about 15%. Try to drive with fuel economy and the environment in mind.

questions

answers

Mark one answer

Air pressure should be built up with the

- [ ] engine switched off
- [ ] service brake on
- [ ] engine ticking over
- [ ] engine revving up

Answer

- [x] **engine ticking over**

Vehicle designers and bus drivers have a duty in helping to reduce the effects of pollution on the environment. The most environmentally-friendly way to allow air pressure to build up is with the engine running at tick-over.

Q. 13.50

Mark one answer

The occupants of about how many cars can be carried by one double-deck bus?

- [ ] 20
- [ ] 30
- [ ] 40
- [ ] 50

Answer

- [x] **20**

By being able to carry as many passengers as 20 cars, the bus is helping to reduce pollution. The bus has only one engine and therefore emits less fumes.

Section 14

Other road users

This section looks at how other road users influence your driving.

The questions will ask you about

- **Vulnerable road users**
  children, pedestrians, cyclists, horse riders, the elderly and the disabled

- **Other vehicles**
  the difficulties faced by users of other vehicles and their fields of view.

questions   answers

Q. 14.1

Mark one answer

Your vehicle leaks diesel fuel on a roundabout. This will most affect

■ three-wheel vehicle drivers
■ motorcyclists
■ towed vehicles
■ car drivers

Answer

☑ **motorcyclists**

When diesel fuel makes contact with most types of road surface it becomes extremely slippery. This can cause danger for all types of vehicle, but particularly those with two wheels, because it reduces the grip between tyres and the road surface.

Q. 14.2

Mark one answer

You have lost the filler cap to your diesel tank. You should

■ get a replacement before driving
■ push a rag into the filler pipe
■ drive slowly back to your depot
■ only fill the tank half full

Answer

☑ **get a replacement before driving**

Don't drive without a fuel filler cap in place as fuel could spill out onto the carriageway when cornering or turning at roundabouts. Diesel fuel, in particular, will make the road surface extremely slippery, and any spillage should be reported so that the emergency services can make the road safe.

Q. 14.3

Mark three answers

Which THREE of these vehicles are most likely to be affected by strong winds?

■ Flat-bed lorries
■ Double-deck buses
■ Motorcycles
■ Horse boxes
■ Tractors
■ Estate cars

Answers

☑ **Double-deck buses**
☑ **Motorcycles**
☑ **Horse boxes**

Strong winds can force other vehicles into your path. You should be aware of the vehicles which are most likely to be affected. Adjust your speed so that you can stop or take avoiding action safely if necessary. Be vigilant for the more vulnerable road users in these conditions.

questions

answers

Q. 14.4

Mark one answer

The vehicle ahead is being driven by a learner. You should

- keep calm and be patient
- drive up close behind
- put your headlights on full beam
- sound your horn and overtake

Answer

☑ **keep calm and be patient**

Learners might take longer to react to traffic situations. Don't unnerve and intimidate them by driving up close behind.

Q. 14.5

Mark two answers

You are about to overtake horse riders. Which TWO of the following could scare the horses?

- Sounding your horn
- Giving arm signals
- Driving slowly
- Revving your engine

Answers

☑ **Sounding your horn**

☑ **Revving your engine**

When passing horses allow plenty of space and slow down. Animals can become frightened by sudden or loud noises so don't sound your horn or rev the engine.

Q. 14.6

Mark one answer

You are driving towards a zebra crossing. Waiting to cross is a person in a wheelchair. You should

■   continue on your way

■   wave to the person to cross

■   wave to the person to wait

■   be prepared to stop

Answer

☑   **be prepared to stop**

As you would with an able-bodied person, you should prepare to slow down and stop. Don't wave them across as other traffic may not stop.

Q. 14.7

Mark two answers

You have stopped at a pelican crossing. A disabled person is crossing slowly in front of you. The lights have now changed to green. You should

■   allow the person to cross

■   drive in front of the person

■   drive behind the person

■   sound your horn

■   be patient

■   edge forward slowly

Answers

☑   **allow the person to cross**

☑   **be patient**

At a pelican crossing the green light means you may proceed as long as the crossing is clear. If someone hasn't finished crossing be patient and wait for them.

questions   answers

Q. 14.8

Mark one answer

Which sign means that there may be people walking along the road?

Answer

Always check the road signs. They'll keep you informed of hazards ahead and help you to anticipate any problems. There are a number of different signs showing pedestrians. Learn the meaning of each one. This will help you to be aware of the particular hazard ahead.

Q. 14.9

Mark one answer

You are turning left at a junction. Pedestrians have started to cross the road. You should

- [ ] go on, giving them plenty of room
- [ ] stop and wave at them to cross
- [ ] sound your horn and proceed
- [ ] give way to them

Answer

 give way to them

If you're turning into a side road you should give way to pedestrians already crossing. They have priority. Don't wave them across the road, sound your horn or flash your lights. If a pedestrian is slow or indecisive be patient and wait. Don't hurry them across by revving the engine.

Q. 14.10

Mark one answer

You are turning left from a main road into a side road. People are already crossing the road into which you are turning. You should

- [ ] continue, as it is your right of way
- [ ] signal to them to continue crossing
- [ ] wait and allow them to cross
- [ ] sound your horn to warn them of your presence

Answer

 wait and allow them to cross

Always check the road you're turning into. Approaching at the correct speed will allow you enough time to observe and react.

Q. 14.11

Mark one answer

You are at a road junction, turning into a minor road. There are pedestrians crossing the minor road. You should

- ▮ stop and wave the pedestrians across
- ▮ sound your horn to let the pedestrians know that you are there
- ▮ give way to the pedestrians who are already crossing
- ▮ carry on, the pedestrians should give way to you

Answer

☑ **give way to the pedestrians who are already crossing**

Always look into the road you're turning into. If there are pedestrians crossing, be considerate, but don't wave or signal to them to cross. Signal your intention to turn as you approach.

Q. 14.12

Mark one answer

You intend to turn right into a side road. Just before turning you should check for motorcyclists who might be

- ▮ overtaking on your left
- ▮ following you closely
- ▮ emerging from the side road
- ▮ overtaking on your right

Answer

☑ **overtaking on your right**

Never attempt to change direction to the right without checking your right-hand mirror. A motorcyclist might not have seen your signal. This action should become a matter of routine.

Q. 14.13

Mark one answer

A toucan crossing is different from other crossings because

- ▮ moped riders can use it
- ▮ it is controlled by a traffic warden
- ▮ it is controlled by two flashing lights
- ▮ cyclists can use it

Answer

☑ **cyclists can use it**

Pedestrians and cyclists are shown the green light together. The signals are push-button operated and there is no flashing amber phase.

questions answers

Q. 14.14

Mark two answers

At toucan crossings

- there is no flashing amber light
- cyclists are not permitted
- there is a continuously flashing amber beacon
- pedestrians and cyclists may cross
- you only stop if someone is waiting to cross

Answers

☑ **there is no flashing amber light**

☑ **pedestrians and cyclists may cross**

There are some crossings where cycle routes lead the cyclists to cross at the same place as pedestrians. Always look out for cyclists, as they're likely to be approaching faster than pedestrians.

Q. 14.15

Mark one answer

How will a school crossing patrol signal you to stop?

- By pointing to children on the opposite pavement
- By displaying a red light
- By displaying a stop sign
- By giving you an arm signal

Answer

☑ **By displaying a stop sign**

If someone steps out into the road with a school crossing sign you must stop. Don't wave anyone across the road or get impatient and rev your engine.

Q. 14.16

Mark one answer

Where would you see this sign?

- In the window of a car taking children to school
- At the side of the road
- At playground areas
- On the rear of a school bus or coach

Answer

☑ **On the rear of a school bus or coach**

Vehicles that are used to carry children to and from school will be travelling at busy times of the day. Be prepared for a vehicle with this sign to make frequent stops. It might pick up or set down passengers in places other than normal bus stops.

Q. 14.17

Mark one answer

What does this sign mean?

- No route for pedestrians and cyclists
- A route for pedestrians only
- A route for cyclists only
- A route for pedestrians and cyclists

Answer

✓ **A route for pedestrians and cyclists**

This shared route is for pedestrians and cyclists only. Be aware that when it ends the cyclists will be rejoining the main road.

Q. 14.18

Mark one answer

What action would you take when elderly people are crossing the road?

- Wave them across so they know that you have seen them
- Be patient and allow them to cross in their own time
- Rev the engine to let them know that you are waiting
- Tap the horn in case they are hard of hearing

Answer

✓ **Be patient and allow them to cross in their own time**

Don't hurry elderly people across the road by getting too close to them or revving the engine. Be aware that they might take longer to cross. They might also be hard of hearing and not able to hear your approach.

Q. 14.19

Mark one answer

You see two elderly pedestrians about to cross the road ahead. You should

- expect them to wait for you to pass
- speed up to get past them quickly
- stop and wave them across the road
- be careful, they may misjudge your speed

Answer

✓ **be careful, they may misjudge your speed**

Their concentration, judgement, hearing and/or vision could be impaired. Be aware that if they proceed to cross they will take more time to do so.

questions answers

Q. 14.20

Mark one answer

You are coming up to a roundabout. A cyclist is signalling to turn right. What should you do?

▨ Overtake on the right

▨ Give a horn warning

▨ Signal the cyclist to move across

▨ Give the cyclist plenty of room

Answer

 ☑ **Give the cyclist plenty of room**

Leave plenty of room if you're following a cyclist who's signalling to turn right at a roundabout. Give them space and time to get into the correct lane.

Q. 14.21

Mark one answer

You are approaching this roundabout and see the cyclist signal right. Why is the cyclist keeping to the left?

▨ It is a quicker route for the cyclist

▨ The cyclist is going to turn left instead

▨ The cyclist thinks The Highway Code does not apply to bicycles

▨ The cyclist is slower and more vulnerable

Answer

☑ **The cyclist is slower and more vulnerable**

Cycling in today's heavy traffic can be hazardous. Some cyclists may not feel happy about crossing the path of traffic to take up a position in an outside lane. Be aware of this and understand that, although in the left-hand lane, the cyclist might be turning right.

questions answers

Q. 14.22

Mark one answer

You are waiting to come out of a side road. Why should you watch carefully for motorcycles?

- Motorcycles are usually faster than cars
- Police patrols often use motorcycles
- Motorcycles are small and hard to see
- Motorcycles have right of way

Answer

✓ **Motorcycles are small and hard to see**

Watch out for motorcyclists if you're waiting to emerge from a side road. They're smaller and more difficult to see. Be especially careful if there are parked vehicles restricting your view, there might be a motorcyclist approaching.

IF YOU CAN'T SEE, DON'T GO.

Q. 14.23

Mark one answer

In daylight, an approaching motorcyclist is using a dipped headlight. Why?

- So that the rider can be seen more easily
- To stop the battery overcharging
- To improve the rider's vision
- The rider is inviting you to proceed

Answer

✓ **So that the rider can be seen more easily**

A motorcycle can be lost out of sight behind another vehicle. The use of the headlight helps to make it more conspicuous and therefore more easily seen.

Q. 14.24

Mark one answer

Motorcyclists should wear bright clothing mainly because

- they must do so by law
- it helps keep them cool in summer
- the colours are popular
- drivers often do not see them

Answer

✓ **drivers often do not see them**

Although they're advised to wear clothing that's bright or reflective, motorcyclists often wear black. This means that they're difficult to see. Look out for them.

questions   answers

Q. 14.25

Mark one answer

There is a slow-moving motorcyclist ahead of you. You are unsure what the rider is going to do. Initially what should you do?

- [ ] Pass on the left
- [ ] Pass on the right
- [ ] Stay behind
- [ ] Move closer

Answer

- [x] **Stay behind**

Be patient. The motorcyclist might be turning right, changing direction or unsure of their destination. Stay behind until the rider has made a move or you are sure that you can pass safely.

Q. 14.26

Mark one answer

Motorcyclists will often look round over their right shoulder just before turning right. This is because

- [ ] they need to listen for following traffic
- [ ] motorcycles do not have mirrors
- [ ] looking around helps them balance as they turn
- [ ] they need to check for traffic in their blind area

Answer

- [x] **they need to check for traffic in their blind area**

Expect a motorcyclist who makes a quick glance over their shoulder to be changing direction. They should do this before turning. By observing this you'll get an early signal of their intention.

Q. 14.27

Mark three answers

At road junctions which of the following are most vulnerable?

- [ ] Cyclists
- [ ] Motorcyclists
- [ ] Pedestrians
- [ ] Car drivers
- [ ] Lorry drivers

Answers

- [x] **Cyclists**
- [x] **Motorcyclists**
- [x] **Pedestrians**

Good effective observation, coupled with appropriate action, can save lives.

Q. 14.28

Mark one answer

You notice horse riders in front. What should you do FIRST?

- ▨ Pull out to the middle of the road
- ▨ Be prepared to slow down
- ▨ Accelerate around them
- ▨ Signal right

Answer

✓ **Be prepared to slow down**

Always look well ahead and be ready to deal with hazards as they occur.

Q. 14.29

Mark two answers

You are approaching a roundabout. There are horses just ahead of you. You should

- ▨ be prepared to stop
- ▨ treat them like any other vehicle
- ▨ give them plenty of room
- ▨ accelerate past as quickly as possible
- ▨ sound your horn as a warning

Answers

✓ **be prepared to stop**

✓ **give them plenty of room**

Horse riders often keep to the outside of the roundabout even if they are turning right. Give them room in case they have to cross lanes of traffic.

questions   answers

Q. 14.30

Mark three answers

Which THREE should you do when passing sheep on a road?

- [■] Allow plenty of room
- [■] Drive very slowly
- [■] Pass quickly but quietly
- [■] Be ready to stop
- [■] Briefly sound your horn

Answers

- ☑ **Allow plenty of room**
- ☑ **Drive very slowly**
- ☑ **Be ready to stop**

Slow down and be ready to stop if you see animals in the road ahead. Animals are easily frightened by noise and vehicles passing too close to them. Stop if signalled to do so by the person in charge.

Q. 14.31

Mark one answer

At night you see a pedestrian wearing reflective clothing and carrying a bright red light. What does this mean?

- [■] You are approaching roadworks
- [■] You are approaching an organised walk
- [■] You are approaching a slow-moving vehicle
- [■] You are approaching an accident black spot

Answer

- ☑ **You are approaching an organised walk**

The people involved in the walk should be keeping to the left, but this can't be assumed. Pass slowly, ensuring that you have the time to do so safely. Be aware that the pedestrians have their backs to you and might not know that you're there.

Q. 14.32

Mark one answer

As you approach a pelican crossing the lights change to green. Elderly people are halfway across. You should

- [■] wave them to cross as quickly as they can
- [■] rev your engine to make them hurry
- [■] flash your lights in case they have not heard you
- [■] wait because they will take longer to cross

Answer

- ☑ **wait because they will take longer to cross**

Even if the lights turn to green, wait for them to clear the crossing. Allow them to cross the road in their own time.

questions

Q. 14.33

Mark one answer

There are flashing amber lights under a school warning sign. What action should you take?

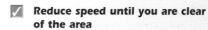

■ Reduce speed until you are clear of the area

■ Keep up your speed and sound the horn

■ Increase your speed to clear the area quickly

■ Wait at the lights until they change to green

Answer

☑ **Reduce speed until you are clear of the area**

The flashing amber lights are switched on to warn you that children may be crossing near a school.

Q. 14.34

Mark one answer

You are approaching this crossing. You should

■ prepare to slow down and stop

■ stop and wave the pedestrians across

■ speed up and pass by quickly

■ drive on unless the pedestrians step out

Answer

☑ **prepare to slow down and stop**

Be courteous and prepare to stop. Do not wave people across as this could be dangerous if another vehicle is approaching the crossing.

questions answers

Q. 14.35

Mark one answer

These road markings must be kept clear to allow

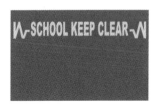

- school children to be dropped off
- for teachers to park
- school children to be picked up
- a clear view of the crossing area

Answer

✓ **a clear view of the crossing area**

Keeping the markings clear makes sure that drivers and riders passing and children crossing have a clear, unrestricted view of the crossing area.

Q. 14.36

Mark one answer

You must not stop on these road markings because you may obstruct

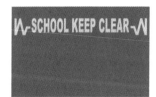

- childrens' view of the crossing area
- teachers' access to the school
- delivery vehicles' access to the school
- emergency vehicles' access to the school

Answer

✓ **childrens' view of the crossing area**

These markings are found on the road outside schools. Do NOT stop (even to set down or pick up children) or park on them. The markings are to make sure that drivers, riders and children have a clear view.

Q. 14.37

Mark one answer

Stopping on these road markings may obstruct

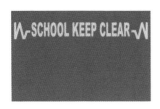

- [ ] emergency vehicles' access to the school
- [ ] drivers' view of the crossing area
- [ ] teachers' access to the school
- [ ] delivery vehicles' access to the school

Answer

☑ **drivers' view of the crossing area**

You will see these markings outside schools. They must be left clear at all times so that drivers, riders and children have a clear view.

Q. 14.38

Mark one answer

Where would you see this sign?

- [ ] Near a school crossing
- [ ] At a playground entrance
- [ ] On a school bus
- [ ] At a 'pedestrians only' area

Answer

☑ **On a school bus**

Watch out for children crossing the road from the other side of the bus.

questions   answers

Q. 14.39

Mark one answer

You are following a motorcyclist on an uneven road. You should

▪ allow less room so you can be seen in their mirrors

▪ overtake immediately

▪ allow extra room in case they swerve to avoid pot-holes

▪ allow the same room as normal because road surfaces do not affect motorcyclists

Answer

☑ **allow extra room in case they swerve to avoid pot-holes**

Pot-holes in the road can unsteady a motorcyclist. For this reason the rider might swerve to avoid an uneven road surface. Watch out at places where this is likely to occur.

Q. 14.40

Mark one answer

You are following two cyclists. They approach a roundabout in the left-hand lane. In which direction should you expect the cyclists to go?

▪ Left

▪ Right

▪ Any direction

▪ Straight ahead

Answer

☑ **Any direction**

If you're following a cyclist onto a roundabout be aware that they might not be taking the exit you anticipate. Cyclists approaching in the left-hand lane may be turning right but may not have been able to get into the correct lane due to the heavy traffic. Give them room.

Q. 14.41

Mark one answer

You are travelling behind a moped. You want to turn left just ahead. You should

▪ overtake the moped before the junction

▪ pull alongside the moped and stay level until just before the junction

▪ sound your horn as a warning and pull in front of the moped

▪ stay behind until the moped has passed the junction

Answer

☑ **stay behind until the moped has passed the junction**

Passing the moped and turning into the junction could mean that you cut across in front of the rider. This might force them to slow down, stop or even lose control.

questions

answers

Q. 14.42

Mark three answers

Which THREE of the following are hazards motorcyclists present in queues of traffic?

- [ ] Cutting in just in front of you
- [ ] Riding in single file
- [ ] Passing very close to you
- [ ] Riding with their headlight on dipped beam
- [ ] Filtering between the lanes

Answers

- [x] **Cutting in just in front of you**
- [x] **Passing very close to you**
- [x] **Filtering between the lanes**

Where there's more than one lane of queuing traffic, motorcyclists use the opportunity to make progress by riding between the lanes. Be aware that they may be passing on either side and check your mirrors before you move off, change lane, turn or make any other change of direction.

Q. 14.43

Mark one answer

You see a horse rider as you approach a roundabout. They are signalling right but keeping well to the left. You should

- [ ] proceed as normal
- [ ] keep close to them
- [ ] cut in front of them
- [ ] stay well back

Answer

- [x] **stay well back**

Allow horse riders to enter and exit the roundabout in their own time. Don't drive up close behind or alongside them, this could disturb the horses.

questions   answers

Q. 14.44

Mark one answer

How would you react to drivers who appear to be inexperienced?

- Sound your horn to warn them of your presence
- Be patient and prepare for them to react more slowly
- Flash your headlights to indicate that it is safe for them to proceed
- Overtake them as soon as possible

Answer

☑ **Be patient and prepare for them to react more slowly**

Learners might not have confidence when they first start to drive. Allow them plenty of room and don't react adversely to their hesitation. We all learn from experience, and new drivers will have had less practice in dealing with all the situations that might occur.

Q. 14.45

Mark one answer

You are following a learner driver who stalls at a junction. You should

- be patient as you expect them to make mistakes
- stay very close behind and flash your headlights
- start to rev your engine if they take too long to restart
- immediately steer around them and drive on

Answer

☑ **be patient as you expect them to make mistakes**

Learning is a process of practice and experience. Try to understand this and tolerate others who are at the beginning of this process.

Q. 14.46

Mark one answer

You are on a country road. What should you expect to see coming towards you on YOUR side of the road?

- Motorcycles
- Bicycles
- Pedestrians
- Horse riders

Answer

☑ **Pedestrians**

On a quiet country road always be aware that there may be a hazard just around the next bend, such as a slow-moving vehicle or pedestrians. There might not be a pavement and people may be walking on your side of the road.

Q. 14.47

Mark one answer

You are turning left into a side road. Pedestrians are crossing the road near the junction. You should

- ☐ wave them on
- ☐ sound your horn
- ☐ switch on your hazard lights
- ☐ wait for them to cross

Answer

☑ **wait for them to cross**

Before you turn into a junction check that it's clear. Check the pavement in each direction. If there are pedestrians crossing let them cross in their own time.

Q. 14.48

Mark one answer

You are following a car driven by an elderly driver. You should

- ☐ expect the driver to drive badly
- ☐ flash your lights and overtake
- ☐ be aware that the driver's reactions may not be as fast as yours
- ☐ stay very close behind but be careful

Answer

☑ **be aware that the driver's reactions may not be as fast as yours**

You must show consideration to other road users. Their reactions may be slower and they might need more time to deal with a situation. Be tolerant and don't lose patience or show your annoyance.

questions   answers

Q. 14.49

Mark one answer

You are following a cyclist. You wish to turn left just ahead. You should

- overtake the cyclist before the junction
- pull alongside the cyclist and stay level until after the junction
- hold back until the cyclist has passed the junction
- go around the cyclist on the junction

Answer

☑ **hold back until the cyclist has passed the junction**

Make allowances for cyclists. Allow them plenty of room, and be aware that they also have to deal with hazards. They might swerve or change direction suddenly to avoid uneven road surfaces.

Q. 14.50

Mark one answer

A horse rider is in the left-hand lane approaching a roundabout. You should expect the rider to

- go in any direction
- turn right
- turn left
- go ahead

Answer

☑ **go in any direction**

Horses and their riders will move more slowly than other road users. They might not have time to cut across busy traffic to take up positions in the offside lane. If traffic is heavy, it could also be hazardous for them to do so. Therefore a horse and rider may approach a roundabout in the left-hand lane, even though they're turning right.

questions

answers

Q. 14.51

Mark one answer

You are driving past parked cars. You notice a wheel of a bicycle sticking out between them. What should you do?

- Accelerate past quickly and sound your horn

- Slow down and wave the cyclist across

- Brake sharply and flash your headlights

- Slow down and be prepared to stop for a cyclist

Answer

✓ **Slow down and be prepared to stop for a cyclist**

Scan the road as you drive. Try to anticipate hazards by being aware of the places where they are likely to occur. You'll then be able to react in good time, if necessary.

Q. 14.52

Mark one answer

You are at the front of a queue of traffic waiting to turn right into a side road. Why is it important to check your right mirror just before turning?

- To look for pedestrians about to cross

- To check for overtaking vehicles

- To make sure the side road is clear

- To check for emerging traffic

Answer

✓ **To check for overtaking vehicles**

There could be another vehicle overtaking you. Motorcyclists often ride along the outside of traffic queues. Always check your mirror as situations behind you can change in the time you have been waiting to turn.

questions   answers

Q. 14.53

Mark one answer

You are driving past a line of parked cars. You notice a ball bouncing out into the road ahead. What should you do?

☐ Continue driving at the same speed and sound your horn

☐ Continue driving at the same speed and flash your headlights

☐ Slow down and be prepared to stop for children

☐ Stop and wave the children across to fetch their ball

Answer

☑ **Slow down and be prepared to stop for children**

Beware of children playing in the street and running out into the road. If a ball bounces out from the pavement slow down and stop. Don't encourage anyone to retrieve it. Other road users may not see your signal and you might lead a child into a dangerous situation.

Q. 14.54

Mark one answer

You want to turn right from a main road into a side road. Just before turning you should

☐ cancel your right-turn signal

☐ select first gear

☐ check for traffic overtaking on your right

☐ stop and set the handbrake

Answer

☑ **check for traffic overtaking on your right**

Motorcyclists often overtake queues of vehicles. Always make that last check in the mirror to avoid turning across their path.

questions   answers

Q. 14.55

Mark one answer

You are driving in town. There is a bus at the bus stop on the other side of the road. Why should you be careful?

- ☐ The bus may have broken down
- ☐ Pedestrians may come from behind the bus
- ☐ The bus may move off suddenly
- ☐ The bus may remain stationary

Answer

☑ **Pedestrians may come from behind the bus**

Watch out for pedestrians if you see a bus ahead. They may not be able to see you if they're crossing behind the bus.

Q. 14.56

Mark one answer

How should you overtake horse riders?

- ☐ Drive up close and overtake as soon as possible
- ☐ Speed is not important but allow plenty of room
- ☐ Use your horn just once to warn them
- ☐ Drive slowly and leave plenty of room

Answer

☑ **Drive slowly and leave plenty of room**

Take extra care if you're driving on a country road. Be ready for farm animals, horses, pedestrians and farm vehicles. Always be prepared to slow down or stop.

Q. 14.57

Mark one answer

Yellow zig zag lines on the road outside schools mean

W-SCHOOL KEEP CLEAR-W

- ☐ sound your horn to alert other road users
- ☐ stop to allow children to cross
- ☐ you must not wait or park on these lines
- ☐ you must not drive over these lines

Answer

☑ **you must not wait or park on these lines**

Parking here will block the view of the crossing area. This will endanger the lives of children on their way to and from school.

questions answers

Q. 14.58

Mark one answer

You are driving on a main road. You intend to turn right into a side road. Just before turning you should

- adjust your interior mirror
- flash your headlamps
- steer over to the left
- check for traffic overtaking on your right

Answer

☑ **check for traffic overtaking on your right**

A last check in the offside mirror will allow you sight of any cyclist or motorcyclist passing on your offside.

Q. 14.59

Mark one answer

Where in particular should you look out for motorcyclists?

- In a filling station
- At a road junction
- Near a service area
- When entering a car park

Answer

☑ **At a road junction**

Always look out for motorcyclists and cyclists, particularly at junctions. They are smaller and usually more difficult to see than other vehicles.

Q. 14.60

Mark one answer

Where should you take particular care to look out for motorcyclists and cyclists?

- On dual carriageways
- At junctions
- At zebra crossings
- On one-way streets

Answer

☑ **At junctions**

Motorcyclists and cyclists may be more difficult to see on the road. This is especially the case at junctions. You may not be able to see a motorcyclist approaching a junction if your view is blocked by other traffic. A motorcycle may be travelling as fast as a car, or faster. Make sure that you judge speeds correctly before you emerge.

Q. 14.61

Mark one answer

Powered vehicles used by disabled people are small and hard to see. How do they give early warning when on a dual carriageway?

- They will have a flashing red light
- They will have a flashing green light
- They will have a flashing blue light
- They will have a flashing amber light.

Answer

☑ **They will have a flashing amber light.**

Powered vehicles used by disabled people are small, low, hard to see and travel at very slow speeds. On a dual carriageway they will have a flashing amber light to make them more visible.

Traffic signs

This section looks at road traffic signs.

The questions will ask you about

- **Road signs**
  these tell you about the road ahead

- **Speed limits**
  signs showing speed limits

- **Regulations**
  these can be shown by means of a road sign.

questions

answers

Q. 15.1

Mark one answer

You are driving a 38 tonnes lorry on a single carriageway road. You see this sign. You may drive at up to

■	40 mph
■	50 mph
■	60 mph
■	70 mph

Answer

☑ **40 mph**

The national speed limit for a goods vehicle exceeding 7.5 tonnes on a single carriageway road is 40 mph. A speed limit does not mean it is safe to drive at that speed. Drive according to the road conditions.

Q. 15.2

Mark one answer

You are driving a 38 tonnes lorry and trailer on a dual carriageway. This sign means you may drive at up to

■	40 mph
■	50 mph
■	60 mph
■	70 mph

Answer

☑ **50 mph**

This may be the legal limit but it does not mean that it is safe to drive at that speed in all conditions. You should always take into account the road and weather conditions and drive accordingly.

questions answers

Q. 15.3

Mark one answer

As a lorry driver, when MUST you use these two signs?

☐ When the load overhangs the front or rear of the vehicle by more than one metre (3 feet 3 inches)

☐ Everytime your vehicle is being towed

☐ Everytime a police escort is required

☐ When the load overhangs the front or rear of the vehicle by more than two metres (6 feet 6 inches)

Answer

☑ **When the load overhangs the front or rear of the vehicle by more than two metres (6 feet 6 inches)**

The law requires you to use projection markers for long or wide loads. It is the driver's responsibility to ensure the markers are clean and secure and also that they are independently lit at night.

Q. 15.4

Mark one answer

You are driving an articulated lorry. What should you do when you see this sign ahead?

☐ Turn round and find an alternative route

☐ Park safely and arrange alternative transport for the goods

☐ Inform your vehicle operator and await further instructions

☐ Proceed as normal, the sign does not apply to you

Answer

☑ **Proceed as normal, the sign does not apply to you**

The sign prohibits buses and coaches with more than eight passenger seats.

questions

answers

Q. 15.5

Mark one answer

You are driving a 14 tonne lorry on a dual carriageway. What does this sign mean?

- ☐ Maximum speed 40 mph
- ☐ Maximum speed 50 mph
- ☐ Maximum speed 60 mph
- ☐ Maximum speed 70 mph

Answer

☑ **Maximum speed 50 mph**

Be aware of the speed limits applying to different types of vehicles on particular roads. These are the maximum speeds allowed but it may not always be safe to drive at this speed.

Q. 15.6

Mark one answer

You are driving a 14 tonne lorry on a motorway. What does this sign mean?

- ☐ Maximum Speed 40 mph
- ☐ Maximum speed 50 mph
- ☐ Maximum speed 60 mph
- ☐ Maximum speed 70 mph

Answer

☑ **Maximum speed 60 mph**

The maximum speed for lorries over 7.5 tonnes on a motorway is 60 mph. But it may not always be appropriate or possible to drive at this speed.

questions answers

Q. 15.7

Mark one answer

You are driving a 14 tonne lorry on a single carriageway road. What does this sign mean?

- ☐ Maximum speed 30 mph
- ☐ Maximum speed 40 mph
- ☐ Maximum speed 50 mph
- ☐ Maximum speed 60 mph

Answer

☑ **Maximum speed 40 mph**

The national speed limit for lorries over 7.5 tonnes on a single carriageway road is 40 mph.

Q. 15.8

Mark one answer

Which sign must you NOT drive your lorry past?

Answer

☑

This sign means no motor vehicles. Although a motorcycle and car are shown it applies to all classes of motor vehicle.

Q. 15.9

Mark one answer

You are driving a lorry 30 feet long and towing a trailer 15 feet long. You see this sign ahead. What should you do?

 Find an alternative route to your destination

 Stop and wait for a police escort

 Continue past the sign but reduce your speed

 Carry on, as the sign applies to the towing vehicle only

Answer

 Find an alternative route to your destination

The maximum permitted length of vehicle includes any trailer being towed. Ensure you know the total length of your vehicle.

Q. 15.10

Mark one answer

You are driving a lorry with a heavy load. You see this sign ahead. What should you be prepared to do?

 Brake to a lower speed

 Change up to a higher gear

 Stop to check your load

 Change down to a lower gear

Answer

 Change down to a lower gear

A heavy vehicle will lose speed when climbing a steep hill. Changing to a lower gear will help you to maintain an appropriate speed.

questions

Q. 15.11

Mark one answer

You are on a motorway. Your lorry has a maximum authorised mass of more than 7.5 tonnes. What does this sign mean to you?

GET IN LANE
M1 & M1 only
A 617 ANY
29   VEH
800 yards

■ You must not use the right-hand lane

■ You can only use the right-hand lane

■ You cannot leave the motorway at this junction

■ You can use the middle or right-hand lane

Answer

☑ **You must not use the right-hand lane**

At motorway roadworks some lanes may be narrower than normal and large vehicles may not be allowed to use those lanes. Look for weight limit signs to check for any lanes that you can't use. Move to the appropriate lane in good time.

Q. 15.12

Mark one answer

When a red route is in operation you must not

■ stop and park

■ overtake

■ change lanes

■ straddle the lines

Answer

☑ **stop and park**

The hours of operation of red routes vary from one area to another. As a rule you must not stop in these areas, but there may be special marked boxes where loading and unloading can be carried out at certain times. Look out for signs giving information regarding the restrictions in place.

Q. 15.13

Mark one answer

Which sign means no overtaking?

Answer

☑

This sign is placed on sections of road where overtaking would be dangerous. There will often be a plate underneath this sign telling you how far the restriction extends. You must not overtake where you see this sign until you pass another sign cancelling the restriction.

Q. 15.14

Mark one answer

What does this sign mean?

- ◼ End of restricted speed area
- ◼ End of restricted parking area
- ◼ End of clearway
- ◼ End of cycle route

Answer

☑ **End of restricted parking area**

Even though there are no restrictions, make sure that you park where you won't cause an obstruction or endanger other road users.

questions

answers

Q. 15.15

Mark one answer

Which sign means 'No stopping'?

Answer

☑

Stopping where you see this sign is likely to cause congestion. Allow the traffic to flow by obeying the signs.

Q. 15.16

Mark one answer

What is the meaning of this traffic sign?

☐ End of two-way road

☐ Give priority to vehicles coming towards you

☐ You have priority over vehicles coming towards you

☐ Bus lane ahead

Answer

☑ **You have priority over vehicles coming towards you**

Before passing this sign, make sure oncoming traffic is going to give way, even though you have priority.

Q. 15.17

Mark one answer

What does this sign mean?

- [ ] No overtaking
- [ ] You are entering a one-way street
- [ ] Two-way traffic ahead
- [ ] You have priority over vehicles from the opposite direction

Answer

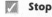 **You have priority over vehicles from the opposite direction**

You have priority, but if a vehicle approaching from the opposite direction is obviously not going to stop, slow down and give way to avoid confrontation or an accident.

Q. 15.18

Mark one answer

At a junction you see this sign partly covered by snow. What does it mean?

- [ ] Crossroads
- [ ] Give way
- [ ] Stop
- [ ] Turn right

Answer

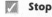 **Stop**

The 'Stop' sign is the only sign this shape. This is to give it greater prominence. You can still recognise this sign despite snow covering the wording.

questions answers

Q. 15.19

Mark one answer

What does this sign mean?

■ Service area 30 miles ahead
■ Maximum speed 30 mph
■ Minimum speed 30 mph
■ Lay-by 30 miles ahead

Answer

☑ **Minimum speed 30 mph**

This sign is shown where slow-moving vehicles would impede the flow of traffic. However, if you need to slow down to avoid a potential accident you should do so.

Q. 15.20

Mark one answer

Which of these signs means turn left ahead?

Answer

☑

This sign gives a clear instruction. You should be looking out for signs as you drive. Prepare to negotiate a left-hand turn.

Q. 15.21

Mark one answer

What does this sign mean?

■ Route for trams
■ Give way to trams
■ Route for buses
■ Give way to buses

Answer

☑ **Route for trams**

Take extra care when you first encounter trams. Look out for road markings and signs that alert you to them. Modern trams are very quiet and you may not hear them approaching.

Q. 15.22

Mark one answer

Which of these signs means that you are entering a one-way street?

Answer

☑

If the road has two lanes you can use either lane and overtake on either side. Use the lane that's more convenient for your destination unless directed by road signs or markings.

Q. 15.23

Mark one answer

What does this sign mean?

- Bus station on the right
- Contraflow bus lane
- With-flow bus lane
- Give way to buses

Answer

 Contraflow bus lane

There will also be markings on the road surface to indicate the bus lane. Don't use this lane for parking or overtaking.

Q. 15.24

Mark one answer

What does a sign with a brown background show?

- Tourist directions
- Primary roads
- Motorway routes
- Minor routes

Answer

 Tourist directions

Signs with a brown background give directions to places of interest.

Q. 15.25

Mark four answers

Which FOUR of these would be indicated by a triangular road sign?

- Road narrows
- Ahead only
- Low bridge
- Minimum speed
- Children crossing
- T-junction

Answers

 Road narrows

☑ **Low bridge**

☑ **Children crossing**

☑ **T-junction**

A triangular sign is a warning sign. Knowing this you can prepare for the hazard ahead.

Q. 15.26

Mark one answer

Which sign means that pedestrians may be walking along the road?

Answer

☑

Be cautious, especially if there is a bend in the road and you're unable to see well ahead.

If you have to pass pedestrians, leave plenty of room. Be aware that you might have to use the right-hand side of the road so look well ahead, as well as in your mirrors, before you pull out.

questions answers

Q. 15.27

Mark one answer

What does this sign mean?

- Crosswinds
- Road noise
- Airport
- Adverse camber

Answer

✓ **Crosswinds**

Where weather conditions are frequently bad, signs will give you a warning. A sign with a picture of a wind-sock will indicate there may be strong crosswinds. This sign is often found on exposed roads.

Q. 15.28

Mark one answer

What does this traffic sign mean?

- Slippery road ahead
- Tyres liable to punctures ahead
- Danger ahead
- Service area ahead

Answer

✓ **Danger ahead**

A sign showing an exclamation mark (!) will alert you to the likelihood of danger ahead. Be ready for any situation that requires you to reduce your speed.

questions   answers

Q. 15.29

Mark one answer

You are about to overtake when you see this sign. You should

- overtake the other driver as quickly as possible
- move to the right to get a better view
- switch your headlights on before overtaking
- hold back until you can see clearly ahead

Answer

☑ **hold back until you can see clearly ahead**

You won't be able to see any hazards that might be out of sight in the dip. Imagine there might be

- cyclists
- horse riders
- parked vehicles
- pedestrians.

Oncoming traffic may also present hazards that you need to deal with.

Q. 15.30

Mark one answer

What does this sign mean?

- Uneven road surface
- Bridge over the road
- Road ahead ends
- Water across the road

Answer

☑ **Water across the road**

This sign is found where a shallow stream crosses the road. Heavy rainfall could increase the flow of water. If the water looks too deep or the stream has swelled over a large distance, stop and find another route.

Q. 15.31

Mark one answer

You see this traffic light ahead. Which light(s) will come on next?

- Red alone
- Red and amber together
- Green and amber together
- Green alone

Answer

☑ **Red alone**

The amber means stop. You may only go on if the amber appears after you have crossed the stop line or you are so close that to pull up might cause an accident. This is followed by the red light.

You must remain behind the stop line until the green light shows.

Q. 15.32

Mark three answers

These flashing red lights mean STOP. In which THREE of the following places could you find them?

- Pelican crossings
- Lifting bridges
- Zebra crossings
- Level crossings
- Motorway exits
- Fire stations

Answers

☑ **Lifting bridges**
☑ **Level crossings**
☑ **Fire stations**

You must stop if the red lights are flashing. A steady amber light shows before the red lights start flashing; this means stop unless it is unsafe to do so. Don't take risks by trying to beat the amber light even if you think your way is clear.

questions answers

Q. 15.33

Mark one answer

You see this sign when driving through roadworks. What does it tell you?

- Large vehicles must go straight ahead
- Traffic is joining from the left
- All traffic must leave at the next exit
- The distance to the next exit

Answer

☑ **The distance to the next exit**

This sign gives you advance warning of a junction where the permanent sign is obscured by roadworks.

Q. 15.34

Mark one answer

What does this sign mean on a motorway?

- Right hand lane closed ahead
- One ton weight limit ahead
- Left hand lane closed ahead
- T- junction one mile ahead

Answer

☑ **Right hand lane closed ahead**

Four amber lights flash in alternate horizontal pairs to provide a warning and to draw the driver's attention to the message displayed.

Q. 15.35

Mark one answer

What does this sign mean?

- Stop only to pick up passengers
- No stopping at any time
- Stop only to set down passengers
- No stopping at peak times

Answer

☑ **No stopping at any time**

This traffic sign means no stopping on the main carriageway at any time – not even to set down passengers – unless in a lay-by.

Q. 15.36

Mark one answer

You are driving on a motorway and there is no traffic ahead. You see this sign. Where should you be driving?

- In the right-hand lane
- Along the hard shoulder
- In the left-hand lane
- Along the middle lane

Answer

☑ **In the left-hand lane**

When there is no traffic ahead of you, you should always drive in the left-hand lane.

questions

Q. 15.37

Mark one answer

What does this sign mean?

- ⬛ Accident black spot ahead
- ⬛ Ancient monument ahead
- ⬛ Humpback bridge ahead
- ⬛ Tunnel ahead

Answer

☑ **Tunnel ahead**

Check any height limits that may accompany this sign.

Q. 15.38

Mark one answer

What does this sign mean?

- ⬛ No U- turns
- ⬛ Two way traffic
- ⬛ One way system
- ⬛ End of one way system

Answer

☑ **No U- turns**

You must not make a U-turn on roads where this sign is displayed.

Q. 15.39

Mark one answer

Which of these signs shows an uphill gradient?

Answer

You will need to identify the sign in time so that you can select an appropriate gear.

Q. 15.40

Mark one answer

Which of these signs means uneven road?

Answer

Some signs can look similar to others but each one has a different meaning. You should learn the meaning of every sign.

questions
answers

Q. 15.41

Mark one answer

Some junctions are marked with advanced stop lines. What are these for?

- To allow room for pedestrians to cross the road
- To allow space for large vehicles to turn
- To allow cyclists to position in front of other traffic
- To allow you to select where to stop

Answer

☑ **To allow cyclists to position in front of other traffic**

Advanced stop lines are to allow cyclists and also buses to be positioned ahead of other traffic. When the green signal shows it allows them time and space to move off in front of the following traffic.

Q. 15.42

Mark one answer

The driver of the car in front is giving this arm signal. This means the driver

- intends to turn left
- is slowing down
- wants you to keep back
- wants you to go past

Answer

☑ **intends to turn left**

Sometimes it may be necessary to reinforce direction indicator signals and brake lights with an arm signal, for example in bright sunshine.

questions   answers

Q. 15.43

Mark one answer

This motorway sign means

- use the hard shoulder
- contraflow system ahead
- overhead bridge repairs
- all lanes ahead closed

Answer

 all lanes ahead closed

When the red lights are flashing do not go beyond this signal. This sign shows that all lanes ahead are closed and you must not enter the motorway. Motorway signals are located on the central reservation, to the left of the hard shoulder, on overhead gantries and at the entrance.

Q. 15.44

Mark one answer

This sign warns of

- a slippery road
- a double bend
- an overhead electric cable
- a series of bends

Answer

✓ **an overhead electric cable**

This sign is used to warn of overhead electric cables and is usually accompanied by a plate indicating the safe height limit.

Q. 15.45

Mark one answer

You are approaching this sign. Who has priority?

▨ Larger vehicles

▨ Oncoming traffic

▨ Smaller vehicles

▨ You have right of way

Answer

 ☑ **Oncoming traffic**

When you see this sign you must give way to traffic from the opposite direction, regardless of the size of your lorry or bus.

Q. 15.46

Mark one answer

What does this sign mean?

▨ Car lane only

▨ Single file only

▨ Queues likely

▨ Keep your distance

Answer

☑ **Queues likely**

When you see this sign beware of traffic queues ahead, check your mirrors and reduce your speed.

Exercise patience when you are delayed. Understand that annoyance and frustration lead to a poor attitude on the road and ultimately may lead to an accident.

questions answers

Q. 15.47

Mark one answer

What does this sign mean?

■ Road flooded

■ Risk of punctures

■ Loose chippings

■ Uneven surface

Answer

✓ **Loose chippings**

This is a warning sign to indicate loose chippings ahead. The sign is usually accompanied by an advisory speed limit. Vehicles travelling too fast for the conditions can throw up chippings or stones. Avoid causing damage to paintwork and windscreens by showing consideration.

Q. 15.48

Mark one answer

What does this sign mean?

■ You are allowed to carry on but only with a police escort

■ You should continue very slowly if your weight is above the limit

■ Do not cross unless the bridge is clear of other vehicles

■ Do not cross the bridge if your weight exceeds the limit

Answer

✓ **Do not cross the bridge if your weight exceeds the limit**

Vehicles over the weight advised are prohibited from using the bridge ahead. An alternative route must be found. Plan your route in advance to avoid delays and congestion. This will save time, fuel and frustration.

You must know the weight of your vehicle, including any load.

questions

Q. 15.49

Mark one answer

What does this sign mean?

- Low bridge
- Tunnel ahead
- Accident black spot
- Speed camera

Answer

 Tunnel ahead

A tunnel can present a number of dangers to large vehicles. Look out for height or width limits. Always be aware of your vehicle's size. Reduce speed; as you enter the tunnel your eyes may need to adjust to the sudden darkness. Turn on your headlights before entering the tunnel; this is compulsory in many tunnels.

Q. 15.50

Mark one answer

What does this sign mean?

- Rumble strips
- Road humps
- Uneven road
- Double humpback bridge

Answer

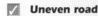 **Uneven road**

Prepare to slow down especially if carrying passengers, livestock or fragile items.

questions answers

Q. 15.51

Mark one answer

This is the first countdown marker to a

- motorway slip road
- primary road junction
- concealed level crossing
- roadside rest area

Answer

☑ **concealed level crossing**

Reduce your speed, you may well have to stop. Be sure that you can stop within the distance you can see to be clear.

Q. 15.52

Mark one answer

What do DOUBLE red lines at the edge of a road mean?

- Limited loading
- No stopping
- Bus route
- Short term parking

Answer

☑ **No stopping**

Red route signs and red road markings have replaced some yellow line restrictions.

questions   answers

Q. 15.53

Mark one answer

Where would you expect to see these road markings?

- At the entrance to a car park
- On the approach to an arched bridge
- At the start of a cycle lane
- On the approach to a lifting barrier

Answer

☑ **On the approach to an arched bridge**

High vehicles are often directed to the centre of the road to go under an arched bridge. Check that your vehicle does not exceed the height restriction indicated.

Q. 15.54

Mark one answer

You are approaching a red traffic light. What signal or signals will show next?

- red and amber, then green
- green, then amber
- amber, then green
- green and amber, then green

Answer

☑ **red and amber, then green**

If you know which light is going to show next you can plan your approach. This will help prevent excessive braking or hesitation at the junction.

questions answers

Q. 15.55

Mark two answers

The double white line along the centre of the road is continuous on your side. You may cross the line to

- ☐ overtake any slower moving vehicle
- ☐ pass a stationary vehicle
- ☐ see if it is safe to overtake
- ☐ overtake a learner driver travelling at 20 mph or less
- ☐ pass a pedal cycle travelling at 10 mph or less

Answers

- ☑ **pass a stationary vehicle**
- ☑ **pass a pedal cycle travelling at 10 mph or less**

Solid white lines are placed where it would be dangerous to overtake. If the solid line is on your side of the road you may cross it to pass a stationary vehicle, or to overtake a pedal cycle, horse or road maintenance vehicle if they are travelling at 10 mph or less. You may also cross the solid line to enter premises or a side road.

Q. 15.56

Mark one answer

Why should you NOT park on the verge where you this sign?

- ☐ Your wheels will sink into the mud
- ☐ Parking is allowed for cars only
- ☐ Parking restrictions apply
- ☐ Fuel and water tanks will leak

Answer

- ☑ **Your wheels will sink into the mud**

This sign tells you that the verge is soft, and if you park here there is a danger that your vehicle will become stuck. This can be inconvenient and could be costly if you need to be pulled out. In extreme cases your vehicle may even tip over, endangering yourself and other road users.

Q. 15.57

Mark one answer

You see this sign ahead. What should you do?

▪ Accelerate because you have priority

▪ Slow down, the road may be narrow ahead

▪ Stop and give way to oncoming traffic

▪ Maintain your speed, it's just an information sign

Answer

 Slow down, the road may be narrow ahead

Even when you have priority at a 'road narrowing', you should still slow down and approach with caution. There will be less room than normal. You should be aware that others may not obey the rules.

Q. 15.58

Mark one answer

Why should you slow down when you see this sign?

▪ Because pedestrians have right of way

▪ There is a 'road race' in progress

▪ There are pedestrian crossings ahead

▪ Because children may be crossing

Answer

 Because children may be crossing

Whenever you see this sign take extra care with these very vulnerable road users.

questions answers

Q. 15.59

Mark one answer

Why should you slow down when you see this sign?

- Your tyres may suffer a blow out
- To avoid splashing others with water
- To avoid throwing up loose chippings
- There is a road gritter ahead

Answer

☑ **To avoid throwing up loose chippings**

This sign will usually be accompanied by a reduced speed limit. When chippings fly out from your tyres they can cause a lot of damage to other vehicles, or injury to pedestrians, cyclists and motorcyclists. Slowing down will lessen the risk.

Q. 15.60

Mark one answer

What does this sign mean?

- Vehicle carrying dangerous goods in packages
- Vehicle broken down ahead
- Holiday route
- Emergency diversion route for motorway traffic

Answer

☑ **Emergency diversion route for motorway traffic**

Major roadworks often cause complicated diversions for large vehicles. Drivers may be advised to follow a special symbol until the original road is rejoined. Look for the yellow and black

- square
- triangle
- diamond
- circle

symbols combined with additional information, to help you rejoin your route.

Q. 15.61

Mark one answer

This sign means

- buses only
- bus lane
- no buses
- bus stop

Answer

☑ **no buses**

No buses with over eight passenger seats are permitted past this sign. Exceptions apply for scheduled services, school and works buses.

Q. 15.62

Mark one answer

You are driving a 12m, fully loaded coach. What should you do when you approach this sign?

- Do not proceed past the sign but find another route
- Set down all your passengers at a safe place before the sign
- Stop and check the legal lettering on the side panel
- Proceed as normal, the sign does not apply to you

Answer

☑ **Proceed as normal, the sign does not apply to you**

The sign shows the maximum authorised mass allowed for goods vehicles. This sign is used to restrict heavy lorries, for example in residential areas, but does not apply to buses and coaches.

Useful information

This part of the book gives information you may find useful. It includes

- Acceptable forms of photo ID

  which types of identity are acceptable and who can make a statement and sign a photo to confirm your identity

- Theory test centres in Great Britain and Northern Ireland

  where you can take your theory test

- Service standards

  how we judge our performance

- Complaints guide

  what to do if you have any complaints about the theory test

- Compensation code

  when you can receive compensation and what compensation you can claim.

Acceptable forms of photo ID

Forms of photographic identification acceptable at both theory and practical tests are as follows

- your passport, or document of like nature. Your passport doesn't have to be a British one, or current

- *cheque guarantee card or credit card bearing your photograph and signature

- an employer's identity or workplace pass bearing your photograph and name or signature, or both

- Trade Union Card bearing your photograph and signature

- Student Union Card with reference to either the NUS or an education establishment or a course reference number. The card must bear your photograph and name or signature, or both

- School Bus Pass bearing the name of the issuing authority and your photograph and signature

- *card issued by a Railway Authority or other authorised body for the purchase of reduced-price railway tickets (e.g. a Young Person's Railcard), bearing the name of the issuing authority and your photograph and signature

- *Gun Licence, including a Firearm or Shotgun Certificate, which bears your photograph and signature

- *Proof of Age Card issued by the Portman Group bearing your photograph and signature.

Any form of photographic identification presented must be recognisably you and, unless you can bring associated paperwork like a marriage certificate, must be in the same name as you booked your test.

If you don't have any of these you can bring a signed photograph, together with a statement like the one shown opposite that it's a true likeness of you. Both the

statement and the back of the photograph must be signed by the same person. They can be any of the following

- *Approved Driving Instructor, but not a trainee (pink licence) holder

- *DSA-certified motorcycle instructor

- Member of Parliament

- medical practitioner

- *local authority councillor

- teacher (qualified)

- Justice of the Peace

- civil servant (established)

- police officer

- bank official

- minister of religion

- barrister or solicitor

- *Commissioned Officer in Her Majesty's Forces

- *LGV Trainers on the DSA Voluntary Register of LGV Instructors.

*Not valid in Northern Ireland.

I
certify that this is a true likeness
of
been known to me for (number)
months / years in my capacity as
(name of certifier),
, who has

Signed

Dated

Daytime phone no.

LGV Trainer no.

If you have any queries about what photographic evidence we will accept, contact the enquiry line on 0870 0101 372 (0845 600 6700 in Northern Ireland).

USEFUL INFORMATION

Theory test centres in Great Britain and Northern Ireland

England

Aldershot
Barnstaple
Barrow
Basildon
Basingstoke
Bath
Berwick-upon-Tweed
Birkenhead
Birmingham
Blackpool
Bolton
Boston
Bournemouth
Bradford
Brighton
Bristol
Bury St Edmunds
Cambridge
Canterbury
Carlisle
Chelmsford
Cheltenham
Chester
Chesterfield
Colchester
Coventry
Crawley
Derby
Doncaster
Dudley
Durham
Eastbourne
Exeter
Fareham
Gillingham

Gloucester
Grantham
Grimsby
Guildford
Harlow
Harrogate
Hastings
Hereford
Huddersfield
Hull
Ipswich
Isle of Wight
Isles of Scilly
King's Lynn
Leeds
Leicester
Lincoln
Liverpool
London
– Croydon
– Ilford
– Kingston
– Palmers Green
– Southwark
– Staines
– Uxbridge
Lowestoft
Luton
Manchester
Mansfield
Middlesbrough
Milton Keynes
Morpeth
Newcastle
Northampton
Norwich

Nottingham
Oldham
Oxford
Penzance
Peterborough
Plymouth
Portsmouth
Preston
Reading
Redditch
Runcorn
Salford
Salisbury
Scarborough
Scunthorpe
Sheffield
Shrewsbury
Sidcup
Slough
Solihull
Southampton
Southend-on-Sea
Southport
St Helens
Stevenage
Stockport
Stoke-on-Trent
Stratford-upon-Avon
Sunderland
Sutton Coldfield
Swindon
Taunton
Torquay
Truro
Watford
Weymouth

Wigan
Wolverhampton
Worcester
Workington
Worthing
Yeovil
York

Scotland

Aberdeen
Ayr
Dumfries
Dundee
Dunfermline
Edinburgh
Elgin
Fort William
Gairloch
Galashiels
Glasgow Central
Glasgow North-West
Greenock
Helmsdale
Huntly
Inverness
Isle of Arran
Isle of Barra
Isle of Benbecula
Isle of Islay, Bowmore
Isle of Mull, Salen
Isle of Tiree
Kirkwall
Kyle of Lochalsh
Lerwick
Motherwell
Oban
Pitlochry

Portree
Stirling
Stornoway
Stranraer
Tarbert, Argyllshire
Tongue
Ullapool
Wick

Wales

Aberystwyth
Bangor
Builth Wells
Cardiff
Haverfordwest
Merthyr Tydfil
Newport
Rhyl
Swansea

Northern Ireland

Ballymena
Belfast
Londonderry
Newry
Omagh
Portadown

Service standards

We judge our performance against the following standards (printed in our Business Plan) which we review each year

- 90% of customers will be satisfied with the overall level of service we provide
- 95% of calls to booking offices will make contact with our automated call-handling system without receiving an engaged tone
- after a call has gone through our automated call-handling system, we will answer 90% of all incoming calls to booking offices in no more than 20 seconds
- we will give 95% of candidates an appointment at their preferred centre within two weeks of their preferred date
- we will keep 99.5% of appointments
- we will answer 97% of all letters and e-mails within 10 working days
- we will pay 95% of all refunds within 15 days of a valid claim.

Complaints guide

We aim to give our customers the best possible service. Please tell us when

- we've done well
- when you aren't satisfied.

Your comments can help us to improve the service we offer. If you have any questions about your theory test please contact us using the numbers below.

For DSA:
tel: 0870 01 01 372, fax: 0870 01 04 372.

For DVTA (in Northern Ireland):
tel: 0845 6006700, fax: 0870 01 04 372.

If you have any complaints about how your theory test was carried out, or any aspect of our customer service, please call the Customer Services section on 0870 241 0204. Alternatively you can write to the Customer Services Manager at the following address

Customer Services
Driving Theory Test
PO Box 148
Salford M5 3SY

If you're dissatisfied with the reply you can write to the Managing Director at the same address.

If you're still not satisfied, you can take up your complaint with

The Chief Executive
Driving Standards Agency
56 Stanley House
Talbot Street
Nottingham NG1 5GU

In Northern Ireland you should write to

The Chief Executive
Driver & Vehicle Testing Agency
Balmoral Road
Belfast BT12 6QL

None of this removes your right to take your complaint to your Member of Parliament, who may decide to raise your case personally with the DSA or DVTA Chief Executive, the Minister or the Parliamentary Commissioner for Administration (the Ombudsman). Please refer to our leaflet 'Service standards – putting things right.'

DSA is a Trading Fund and we are required to cover our costs from the driving test fee.

We don't have a quota for test passes or fails and if you demonstrate the standard required, you'll pass your test.

Compensation code

DSA will normally refund the test fee, or rearrange another test at no further cost to you, if

• we cancel your test

• you cancel and give us at least three clear working days' notice

• you keep the test appointment but the test doesn't take place, or isn't finished, for a reason that isn't your fault.

We'll also repay you the expenses that you had to pay on the day of the test if we cancelled your test at short notice. We'll consider reasonable claims for

• the cost of travelling to and from the test centre

• any standard pay or earnings you lost through taking unpaid holiday leave (usually for half a day), after tax and national insurance contributions.

Please write to the address below and send a receipt showing travel costs and an employer's letter, which shows what earnings you lost.

DVTA has a different compensation code. If you think you're entitled to compensation write to

Customer Services
Driving Theory Test
PO Box 148
Salford M5 3SY

This compensation code doesn't affect your existing legal rights.

Essential reading from the Driving Standards Agency

Prepare for the professional tests and a new career with the official guidance ...

Driving Goods Vehicles – the Official DSA Syllabus

This book is a useful aid for new or established drivers. It is the only official manual covering this category. It contains clear, easy to understand instructions. It has been written by the Driving Standards Agency – the people who set the tests – and set out the syllabus. Information is given on applying for a licence, medical requirements, handling techniques, driving skills, environmental impact, hazard labels and regulations.

ISBN 0 11 552543 2   £14.99

The Official Goods Vehicle Driving Video

Safe driving practice and defensive driving techniques for both new and established drivers. Covering all classes of goods vehicle above 3.5 tonnes, this video stresses how good, all round observation and sound planning can reduce accident risk. It adopts a realistic approach to meeting tight schedules whilst taking maximum care of other road users, drivers and vehicles.

ISBN 0 11 551971 8   £29.99 (INCL VAT)

Driving Buses and Coaches – the Official DSA Syllabus

A companion volume to *The Official Theory Test for Drivers of Large Vehicles*, covering every aspect of driving a passenger carrying vehicle (PCV). Definitive information on the PCV practical test: everything from initial applications and the latest legislation, through to general road safety, driving attitude, First Aid and, of course, the officially recommended syllabus.

ISBN 0 11 552544 0   £14.99

The Highway Code

The Highway Code is essential reading for everyone. It explains road traffic law and gives guidance as to best driving practice, with particular reference to vulnerable road users such as horse riders, cyclists and the elderly. The current version was prepared to reflect the changes in lifestyle and technology, giving rules for dealing with driver fatigue and recommendations about the use of mobile phones.

ISBN 0 11 552290 5   £1.49

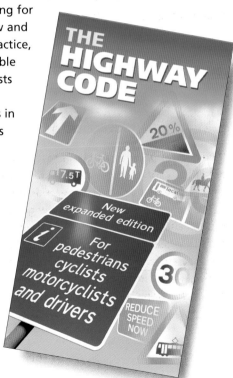

Printed in The United Kingdom for the Stationery Office 68941 02/03 C200 63789

5 easy ways to order:

- ● **Online:** Visit www.**clicktso**.com
- ○ **Tel:** Please call **0870 600 5522** *quoting ref BCH*
- ● **Fax:** Fax this form to **0870 600 5533**
- ● **Post:** **TSO, PO Box 29,**
  Norwich NR3 1GN
- ○ **TSO Bookshops:** Visit your local TSO Bookshop

Please send me the following publications:

Title	ISBN	Price	Quantity
Driving Goods Vehicles – the Official DSA Syllabus	0 11 552543 2	£14.99	....
Official Goods Vehicle Driving Video	0 11 551971 8	£29.99 (incl VAT)	....
Driving Buses and Coaches – the Official DSA Syllabus	0 11 552544 0	£14.99	....
The Highway Code	0 11 552290 5	£1.49	....

Handling charge per order: £3.00
for orders including VAT: £3.53
Total enclosed: £...............

PLEASE COMPLETE IN BLOCK CAPITALS

Name...

Address ....

....

....

.... Postcode .... [BCH]

☐ I enclose a cheque for £.................. payable to: '*TSO*'

☐ Please charge to my account with TSO, No:

....

☐ Please debit my Mastercard/Visa/Amex/Diners/Connect Card Account No.

☐☐☐☐☐☐☐☐☐☐☐☐☐☐☐☐

Signature.. Expiry date................................

☐ Please send me information about relevant products and services from TSO

We can now also send you updates on your specific area of interest by e-mail.
To register, visit **clicktso.com**